HOMER AND THE
ORAL TRADITION

HOMER AND THE ORAL TRADITION

G.S.KIRK

*Regius Professor of Greek in the
University of Cambridge*

CAMBRIDGE UNIVERSITY PRESS

CAMBRIDGE

LONDON   NEW YORK   MELBOURNE

Published by the Syndics of the Cambridge University Press
The Pitt Building, Trumpington Street, Cambridge CB2 1RP
Bentley House, 200 Euston Road, London NW1 2DB
32 East 57th Street, New York, NY 10022, USA
296 Beaconsfield Parade, Middle Park, Melbourne 3206, Australia

First published 1976

Printed in Great Britain
at the
University Printing House, Cambridge
(Harry Myers, University Printer)

Library of Congress cataloguing in publication data
Kirk, Geoffrey Stephen.
Homer and the oral tradition.
Includes index.
1. Homerus – Criticism and interpretation – Collected works.
2. Epic poetry – History and criticism – Collected works.
3. Oral tradition – Collected works.
I. Title.
PA4037.K457   883'.01   76–7806
ISBN 0 521 21309 6

CONTENTS

PREFACE

After I had given the J. H. Gray lectures in Cambridge in 1974 it occurred to me that they might most suitably be published in company with a selection of earlier work, scattered among journals for the most part, on the same broad theme. Hence the present volume. Obvious repetitions have been removed from the earlier pieces, and corrections, inter-references and references to more recent literature have been incorporated. I have not wanted to change much else. Here and there, admittedly, a point is made two or three times over in different chapters in a way that might not be desirable in a completely new book – but such points are central ones, they are needed in their individual contexts, and they differ in their detailed emphases; I therefore ask for the reader's mild indulgence. The volume as a whole ranges from technical matters of warfare and topography to those of Homeric language and style, but I think it fair to claim that it does genuinely possess a single theme – the nature and effects of the oral tradition in ancient Greece – and manifest a single point of view. That point of view was also visible in my *The Songs of Homer* (Cambridge, 1962) and in its abbreviated version *Homer and the Epic*, but it is developed here differently and in greater detail, especially by the analysis of individual passages of the *Iliad* and *Odyssey*. Clearly the present treatment is not meant to be compendious; for example I say comparatively little about the use made by singers of traditional themes, or about many detailed aspects of verbal formulas, both of them quite important and of current interest, and concentrate more on that aspect of the oral style, at the level of individual verse or phrase, that I call the cumulative technique.

Chapter 7 is a rather technical piece on enjambment and is included with a certain hesitation; but I still believe it to be useful, and have somewhat shortened and simplified the original version. In general the more specialized studies (chapters 3 and 6 as well as 7) are sandwiched between more general and easily readable discussions (especially chapters 1, 4 and 9, including the Gray lectures). Will this make the book more palatable? Perhaps not – but I hope and

Preface

believe that it does nevertheless contain a degree of both continuity and variety, as well as presenting a set of interrelated studies each of which can be read in its own right.

The core of the book is chapter 4, 'The oral and the literary epic', formed out of the three Gray lectures and composing a fifth of the whole. Of the other chapters, the introductory one was a contribution to a work that did not achieve wide circulation, the first volume of *Literature and Western Civilization*, edited by David Daiches and A. K. Thorlby (London, 1972). Chapters 2 and 6 appeared in 1961 and 1970 respectively in the *Proceedings of the Cambridge Philological Society*. Chapter 3 was a contribution to *Problèmes de la guerre en Grèce ancienne* (Mouton, Paris, 1968), edited by J.-P. Vernant. The fifth chapter appeared in *Classical Quarterly* for 1961, the seventh and eighth in *Yale Classical Studies* xx (1966) ('Homeric Studies'), edited by the late Adam Parry and myself. The closing chapter started life as an inaugural lecture at Bristol and was then printed in *Greece and Rome* for 1973. I am grateful to all these sources for permission to make new use of this material. A special word may be needed to justify re-publishing chapters 2, 5 and 6. The first, 'Dark Age and oral poet', is closely followed in a short section of my *Songs of Homer*, although it is slightly revised and simplified here; but it has an independent contribution to make and is cardinal to the theme of the present volume. Chapter 5, 'Homer and modern oral poetry: some confusions', has been fairly widely reprinted, but the commonest source in Britain, namely *The Language and Background of Homer*, edited by myself, has recently been discontinued. Chapter 6, 'Homer's *Iliad* and ours', is a reply to Adam Parry's 'Have we Homer's *Iliad*?' in the Homeric volume, cited above, of *Yale Classical Studies*; the chapter can now be read independently, although Parry's elegant arguments should be checked in their original form, by those most closely interested, in case I have not done them justice.

Less familiar Greek names are directly transliterated, more common ones keep their Latinized forms. Abbreviations should be self-evident, except perhaps for *HSCP* = *Harvard Studies in Classical Philology* and *TAPA* = *Transactions and Proceedings of the American Philological Association*. Acknowledgement of help received is made in full in the original publications, but the names of M. I. Finley, D. L. Page and Adam Parry stand out in my mind.

July 1976   G.S.K.

1

HOMER: THE MEANING OF AN
ORAL TRADITION

By about 1120 B.C. the Mycenaean Empire had sunk into final decay. The next two centuries were a period of isolation and decline; but during those years many Greeks, especially Ionians from Athens and elsewhere in Attica, joined the movements across the Aegean that led to the Hellenization of the Asia Minor coast and the foundation of the important settlements of Ionia and Aeolis. By the eighth century B.C. Greece was already through her 'Dark Age'[1] and had re-emerged as a strong and individual force in the world of the eastern and central Mediterranean; colonization proliferated north-eastward into the Black Sea and westward to Sicily and southern Italy. It was at this time that 'Homer' was active in Ionia. His is a name to which we can attach almost no plausible and meaningful biography, beyond that its bearer is held to have composed both the *Iliad* and the *Odyssey*. He was primarily, at least, an *aoidos*, a singer; the age of real literacy was still to come. Archilochus, working about 650 B.C., is the first author of whom we can be sure that he wrote his poems down, and, more important, that he composed them with the help of writing – whatever use he may have made of the old, traditional, oral techniques.[2]

From this time forward Greece became again what it had been to a slight extent in the last centuries of the Mycenaean Empire, the possessor of a literate culture. Even now the kind and degree of literacy was strictly limited. Even at the time of the greatest flowering of Greek literature, in the fifth and fourth centuries B.C., the era of Pindar, the tragedians and Plato, the ability to read and write was far from universal and the uses made of that ability, by many who possessed it, were circumscribed. Most slaves, of course, were illiterate; but so were many free-born citizens – small farmers and farm-workers and the urban proletariat. This was the case in Attica, and literacy was almost certainly less widespread in most other regions of the Greek world. A comparison with Elizabethan England

---

[1] See pp. 25ff.   [2] See pp. 197–9

might not be too misleading for the sheer scope of literacy; but it would certainly be so for its implications in depth, because for archaic Greece the age of total illiteracy, or oral poetry and word-of-mouth tradition, still lay close behind.

It lay close behind in plain chronology, but in addition the *Iliad* and *Odyssey* provided each new generation with a direct bridge into the past. It can hardly be coincidence that the greatest triumph of the oral tradition coincided so closely with the end of the oral era. Some have believed that it was precisely the availability of new writing techniques that enabled the great poems to be created out of traditional and preliterate materials. It is certainly a problem how and why the normal range of oral narrative poems (which, on the evidence of comparison with other oral cultures, as well as of the two singers described in the *Odyssey*, is unlikely to have exceeded what could be absorbed at a sitting) was so suddenly and brilliantly transcended. The concept of a monumental epic seems to imply a fully literate culture; it seems to call for a reading audience and developed book-production. Yet this cannot have been so: the production of complete and accurate texts of Homer was slow, and not for several generations was anything like an official text produced for the purposes of rhapsodic contests in the Panathenaea, the festival held every four years at Athens. There was no reading public in the full sense for a further couple of hundred years at least; the poems of Homer (or large portions of them) were learnt by heart by boys at school, and the texts owned by cultivated Athenians in the fifth century B.C. were *aide-mémoires* rather than versions to be continuously studied.

It is possible, on the other hand, that some lesser use of the new technique of writing *was* the determining factor in the ability to compose such long and complex poems out of pre-existing and much shorter oral songs. Many critics, mindful of the huge gap in quality as well as quantity that separates Homer from any other purely oral singer ever known, feel that this is so. The question is difficult, and part of the difficulty is technical. *In essence* the poems belong to an oral culture, whether or not their monumental form owes something to the main poet's ability to compose with the help of writing. And to an important extent their further transmission was oral too; these were works that continued to be known, erratically and incompletely perhaps, 'by heart'. Yet, once produced, the great poems must have had a stifling effect on their shorter and simpler, more typically oral predecessors. Their propagation throughout the Hellenic world, beyond Ionia where they were probably composed, was rapid. The memory of earlier songs seems to have been all but obliterated, and one suspects that the *Iliad* and the *Odyssey* contributed just as much as did the rise of literate forms of poetry to the obsolescence of the old narrative tradition. If this is so, then their appearance so soon before the transition from an age of illiteracy to one of partial literacy seems less strange. At the same time the aristocratic way of life reflected in the great poems, one that had to some extent supported the singers and their craft (although my own view is that the heroic epic had flourished no less strongly in informal popular gatherings),[3] was being replaced: by mercantile oligarchies in many of the settlements of Ionia during the seventh century B.C., and by more or less enlightened tyrannies in other of those settlements and in some of the most powerful cities of the mainland. Soon the *dēmos* – in Homer merely the nameless mass of dependants and upholders, in peace or war, of the great families – gained full rights of assembly and voting. This happened most notably at Athens during the course of the sixth century B.C. The *polis*, or city-state, emerged as the main focus of loyalties that had earlier been directed toward persons and families, toward feudal archetypes that still reflected some of the glow of the heroic world of Homer.

Why this emphasis on the oral nature of the *Iliad* and the *Odyssey* and on the state of literacy or illiteracy of the world into which they emerged? The answer is that orality is no mere incidental detail, an accident to be emphasized just for the sake of the unusual. It is of crucial importance for the understanding of the poems as poetry, as works of literature in the broader sense, and as vast and erratic forces in the cultural history of the ancient world. The Greeks themselves were unable to see literature as something apart. In its large-scale forms, epic or tragedy or the great histories of Herodotus or Thucydides, it was a moral and didactic endeavour as well as art. The *Iliad* and the *Odyssey*, in addition, were documents about the national past, almost the only ones that survived. It is just possible that Homer himself, and the generation for which he sang, did not see them in this light; but almost all subsequent generations certainly did so, and the modern reader who judges the *Iliad* simply as a great

---

[3] See pp. 34–7.

drama of warfare, or as a poem about the dilemma of a great hero, is missing something of the flavour it possessed for the contemporaries of Peisistratus or Pericles or Plato. Within the poems he will be liable to miss much more if he ignores the oral background out of which they grew.

The language of Homer was never spoken by any man. It is an artificial, poetical construction containing elements both of vocabulary and of phraseology that originated at different dates over a period of at least 200 and perhaps as much as 500 years. Some parts of it are highly conventional and consist of fixed or formular phrases, each designed to express a particular idea within the limits of a particular rhythmical impulse. The famous fixed epithets – goodly Odysseus, king of men Agamemnon, black ship, well-built hall, windy Troy and so on – are merely the most prominent aspect of a highly developed *system* of formular language that allowed the unlettered singer to develop a poem of a length and complexity far beyond the range of one who selects each word anew and for itself alone. Precisely how far the formular system extended, and where it merges with the symbolic and repetitive aspect of all language, remain subjects for disagreement; but the need for illiterate poetry of any length to be formular in essence is confirmed by the study both of Homer himself and of surviving oral traditions in Yugoslavia, southern Russia, Cyprus and Crete. The least complex of these traditions and the poorest in expression are also the least formular, while the best have the richest formular systems. This is important, because it confirms the suggestion that formularity increases rather than inhibits the powers of the oral singer. It thus reverses a basic rule of classical literate creation – that the repeated use of fixed or conventional language (except in special formal or hieratic circumstances) is incompatible with true originality and poetical or literary power. In this respect, as in others, the oral poet behaves quite differently from the literate one, because he accepts without question a groundwork of traditionally perfected phraseology, and indeed of traditional theme-structures, and makes his own individual contribution above and beyond that level.

In the final result the language itself, conventional though many of its elements are, acquires a special and quite original poetic quality.[4] I take as an example the first mention of Penelope in the

----

[4] See also pp. 73ff.

Odyssey, because it also describes an *aoidos* (Phemius, the regular singer in Odysseus's house in Ithaca) at work:

Τοῖσι δ' ἀοιδὸς ἄειδε περικλυτός, οἱ δὲ σιωπῇ
ἥατ' ἀκούοντες. ὁ δ' Ἀχαιῶν νόστον ἄειδε
λυγρόν, ὃν ἐκ Τροίης ἐπετείλατο Παλλὰς Ἀθήνη.
τοῦ δ' ὑπερωιόθεν φρεσὶ σύνθετο θέσπιν ἀοιδὴν
κούρη Ἰκαρίοιο, περίφρων Πηνελόπεια.
κλίμακα δ' ὑψηλὴν κατεβήσετο οἷο δόμοιο,
οὐκ οἴη, ἅμα τῇ γε καὶ ἀμφίπολοι δύ' ἕποντο.

(1, 325–31)

For them [the suitors] the famed singer was singing, and they in
silence
sat listening; and he was singing the return of the Achaeans,
the dreadful return, which Pallas Athene ordained for them from
the land of Troy.
His inspired song did she, from the upper storey, apprehend in her
heart,
the daughter of Icarius, thoughtful Penelope;
and she descended the tall stair of her house,
not alone, since with her two servants followed.

The language in this simple but touching passage is almost entirely formular, made up of phrases that occur elsewhere in the *Iliad* or the *Odyssey*, in some cases repeatedly. Thus not only the famed singer and his inspired (or divine) song, not only Pallas Athene and thoughtful Penelope and the tall stair and the two servants who followed, but also the sitting in silence, the return of the Achaeans, the apprehending in her heart, and the words for listening, singing, and descending (in those positions in the verse) are all standard in the language of Homer. So, too, are devices such as the cumulation of 'dreadful' at the beginning of the following verse upon the idea of 'return', which transforms a neutral or even friendly concept into something sinister, by an apparent afterthought; or the addition of the whole verse about Penelope's servants, an almost automatic conferment of dignity, applied in the same words elsewhere to Helen and again to Penelope herself, always as she ascends or descends these evocative stairs. The words, the phrases, the rhythms are familiar, but the style of the passage as a whole is relaxed, effortless and faintly muted rather than stale, redundant or mechanical. The familiar words and phrases and rhythmical cola, acquired from the singers of older generations and refined of needless excrescence or pointless variant, are cast up anew, sometimes in fresh combinations that are almost indistinguishable from the old simply because they are equally natural. And yet there is a quite individual poetical gain in this ability to re-create traditional language, something beyond the negative virtue of reproducing a perfected phraseology without loss. For each of these accustomed phrases, as it is dropped into the listener's consciousness, is clustered with the heroic past, ennobled rather than staled by its archaic associations, and thick with echoes of other contexts, other heroines, other actions in other islands, under the impulse of other but still familiar gods.

The diction of Homer was archaic and yet constantly renewed, and that accounts for the existence side by side of terms and linguistic forms from the Mycenaean dialect of the Achaean heroes, from the contemporary world of Homer himself and from many anonymous generations between. The importation of language from Homer's own time, or that of the generation that immediately preceded him, is quantitatively slight, and its effects are mainly superficial – or rather they cannot often be detected in the welter of language that is not identifiably formular and traditional. Yet it is significant that the language of the similes, which are especially frequent and form a conspicuous element of style in the *Iliad*, is not only often untraditional (which might be expected from their unheroic subject-matter) but is often demonstrably late within the time-range of the oral tradition. I believe that the elaboration and careful placing of many of the developed similes must be due to the monumental composer himself, and cannot either be a random procedure (or anything like it) or be derived from the older and shorter poems upon which Homer drew, and many of which he must have worked as episodes into the texture of his monumental version.

Iliad 16, 257ff., for instance, is a crucial point in the development of the poem. Patroclus is at last allowed by Achilles to fight – he leads the Myrmidons into battle and saves the Achaean ships, but at the eventual cost of his own life, which moves Achilles to avenge his death on Hector. The moment when the troops first appear is one of special emphasis. The mere sight of them and of Patroclus casts the Trojans into confusion (278ff.), and so draws Patroclus across the plain to his death. The device used to mark their appearance is a rather surprising simile; one that compares them not to lions or wild boars or other heroic beasts, but to something less obvious:

6

Homer: the meaning of an oral tradition

αὐτίκα δὲ σφήκεσσιν ἐοικότες ἐξεχέοντο
εἰνοδίοις, οὓς παῖδες ἐριδμαίνωσιν ἔθοντες,
αἰεὶ κερτομέοντες, ὁδῷ ἔπι οἰκί᾽ ἔχοντας,
νηπίαχοι. ξυνὸν δὲ κακὸν πολέεσσι τιθεῖσι.
τοὺς δ᾽ εἴ περ παρά τίς τε κιὼν ἄνθρωπος ὁδίτης
κινήσῃ ἀέκων, οἱ δ᾽ ἄλκιμον ἦτορ ἔχοντες
πρόσσω πᾶς πέτεται καὶ ἀμύνει οἷσι τέκεσσι.
τῶν τότε Μυρμιδόνες κραδίην καὶ θυμὸν ἔχοντες
ἐκ νηῶν ἐχέοντο....   (16, 259–67)

Straightway they poured forth *like wasps*
by the roadside, which boys habitually provoke,
always taunting them – wasps that have their homes by the road;
thoughtless boys; they make a common evil for many people.
Those wasps, if some traveller going by
unwittingly disturbs them, summon up all their defensive spirit
and each one of them flies forth and fights in defence of his offspring.
With heart and spirit like theirs the Myrmidons
poured then from among the ships.

The wasps make an apt, even a powerful comparison because they are wildly aggressive, insensible to danger and very frightening, especially when they swarm. They are not heroic in their ordinary associations, but the poet draws them half-humorously into the heroic context by the standard martial phrase about 'all their defensive spirit'. Their swarming, the compact and terrifying mass of them, is suggested in an oblique and rather sinister way by the vague and aphoristic language of verse 262: 'a common evil for many people'. At the same time their individuality is brought out by a strikingly anthropomorphic touch (reinforced by the 'homes' or 'houses' of 261) that establishes a counterpoint to the massed and anonymous heroes: the wasps are fighting, not for the 'heroic' ideals that are the most obvious driving force of Homeric warriors, but for their children. This artifice, only apparently naive, makes the wasps seem human at the same time as the Myrmidons are seen as partly animal; it arouses our sympathy for them as they respond so violently to trivial but powerful threats. If the image were less than piquant and pathetic in itself, it would seem absurd. As things are, it is neatly placed in a context that it illuminates more brilliantly and subtly than a more explicit and heroic image could. Moreover the simile is indispensable here, for otherwise the march-out of the Myrmidons would be inadequately stressed – particularly as Patroclus' brief address to them at 269–74 is concerned with the

7

conflict of honour between Achilles and Agamemnon rather than with the terror and magnificence of the actual moment. It is no casual afterthought, and its deliberate collocation of heroic and un-heroic suggests imperiously that it does not belong, in its present developed form at least, to the archaic tradition. It is, quite simply, Homeric.

The similes not only deal, often enough, with subjects remote from the heroic world – with wasps' nests, and small boys beating donkeys, and flies clustering around the milk-pail, and men arguing over the boundaries of their fields, and women staining ivory – but they do so in a way that reveals a quite distinct and unheroic view of life and action. Thus, if my conjecture is right and many of these similes *were* due to Homer in the eighth century B.C., then it must be accepted that the main composer of the *Iliad* (and probably that of the *Odyssey* too) was prepared on occasion to alter the whole heroic colouring of the epic tradition he had inherited. It is reasonable to expect that every generation in a long tradition of oral heroic poetry would tend to leave its own mark on the ethos of the poems; we know from the comparative study of the oral epic in Yugoslavia and elsewhere that no singer reproduces a song exactly as he has received it from his elders. Yet this special argument from the language and values of the similes goes a good way further.

The question to be asked at this point – and it is one that tends to be debated in excessively schematic terms in current Homeric scholarship – is how far the total Homeric picture of the late Achaean Age, and of the lives and thoughts of Homer's heroes of the Trojan War and its aftermath, is artificial and illusory. That it is not a completely full and accurate report of the realities of late Bronze Age Greece goes without saying; we are, after all, dealing with poems, and poems about events that lay a very long time in the past, and we must expect some degree of distortion and omission. And yet many scholars have been eager to argue – especially, curiously enough, since the decipherment of the Linear B tablets – that the Homeric poems do give, in all essentials, a more or less accurate picture of life in the Mycenaean era. There may be additions and interpolations; the description of Alcinous' mythical land of Phaeacia in the sixth and following books of the *Odyssey* may remind one of Ionian towns in the eighth century B.C. rather than of Achaean domains in the thirteenth or twelfth; but broadly speaking, according to this view, the *Iliad* and the *Odyssey* can be used as a counterpart to the tablets in the effort to reconstruct the historical realities of the Achaean Empire at the time of the historical war against Troy. Against this view other critics have argued that the social and institutional structures of the poems are really quite different from those suggested by the tablets, and indeed that the poems are permeated by ideas, values and institutions alien to those of the Mycenaean world, that were derived from the conditions of the subsequent Dark Age.[5]

The facts of the linguistic tradition and the special argument from the similes have shown that the chances of obtaining consistent and accurate Mycenaean information, with little important interference from later generations, are exceedingly remote. Admittedly the *Iliad*, because it describes a nationally organized military expedition, is easier to associate with the late Mycenaean era than with the period of disintegration that followed; its concentration on a military subject makes the preservation of a heroic standpoint more natural. With the *Odyssey*, which explores several of the facets of post-war existence, the discrepancies are more obvious, particularly because a direct comparison can be made with the glimpses of historical palace-states in the tablets from Pylos and Knossos. Little of the extraordinary cult-ridden and accountancy-dominated society of the tablets is conveyed in the relaxed and informal palace scenes of the *Odyssey*, in Ithaca, Pylos, Sparta or the imaginary world of Phaeacia. Whether or not this almost country-house atmosphere would have been possible in the last generations of a rapidly collapsing imperial system is a matter of opinion; but the absence from the *Odyssey* of elaborate divine offerings and of a highly organized scribal system for the central control of commodities (and the absence from the tablets of divination and singers) is symptomatic of the poem's historical ambiguity. Either it includes many elements and values derived from a later age, or it has distorted the original Mycenaean material through later misunderstanding, or both. Rather than embark on yet another attempt to strike a precisely formulated balance between the more concrete Mycenaean and non-Mycenaean details of the Homeric poems, I prefer to draw

[5] See also, and particularly with reference to martial matters, pp. 37-9 and 41ff. The two views are represented respectively by T. B. L. Webster, *From Homer to Mycenae* (London, 1958), *passim*, and M. I. Finley, 'Homer and Mycenae: property and tenure', *Historia* 6 (1957), 133ff.

attention to some implications of the earlier phase of the oral tradition itself – to concentrate not on such extraneous matters as shield or helmets, furniture or house-plans, or even social organization, but rather on what can loosely be called the Homeric system of values and its relation to the attitudes of the Heroic Age.

It is now more than half a century since W. P. Ker and H. M. Chadwick evolved the concept of a Heroic Age: the age of a special kind of militaristic and aristocratic society, whose leaders are bound by a rigid code of personal honour and self-esteem and by the glorification of physical prowess and personal possessions.[6] The thirteenth century B.C. in Greece (the period most clearly suggested by the Homeric poems) has consistently been treated as one of the chief exemplars of such an age, with Homer as its chief recorder. Yet the strict formulation of such a culture – its crystallization into a type free from ambiguity and confusion – has been shown to be the work not so much of the culture itself, or of its contemporary observers, as of a subsequent period of decline, conquest, migration, or drastic political and social change.

In such circumstances a kind of nostalgia ensures the simplification and exaltation of a vanished epoch of apparent glory and success. This tendency is confirmed, in the history of the epic tradition in Greece, by the diverse (and only slightly Mycenaean), characteristics of the poetical language.

Some important consequences follow. If the formulation of the Achaean heroic age were to turn out to be largely the work of a post-Mycenaean tradition, intent upon distilling, out of the partial and confused impressions of informal reminiscence, an obsolete aristocratic and militaristic ethos, then complications of that ethos, excrescences or faults in an otherwise straightforward model, are likely to be due primarily to complexities in the attitude of the original formulators of the tradition, and at a much later stage of the monumental composer, Homer. Inconsistencies in the character and attitudes of the Achaeans themselves and accidental conflations in the development of the oral tradition are likely to be additional but quite secondary causes.

Such complications in the heroic ethos are to be found in the *Odyssey* more than the *Iliad*. In a martial poem about an Achaean expeditionary force abroad, engaged in the last and greatest of all

---

[6] See further pp. 45f., and the works cited in nn. 11 and 12 there.

heroic enterprises of the Achaean world, the opportunities for non-heroic responses are relatively slight. Achilles in the ninth book rejects Agamemnon's envoys with unusually introspective passion; but when he questions the need for risking his life in day after day of bloody fighting, it is because he does not consider it worth risking *for Agamemnon*, who has engaged him in war on behalf of Helen and then arbitrarily deprived him of his own Briseis.[7] This is logic and heroic pique, not pacifism. Even the sixth book, which shows Hector momentarily tender with his wife and child, is not really unheroic; what makes him persist in fighting, even though it will mean Andromache's enslavement, is the determination not to be thought *kakos* (a coward) and to win *kleos* (glory) for himself and his father.[8] Hector is, indeed, uniquely prone to question his own motives and to think of what others will say – but this is a refinement, not an abandonment, of the heroic sense of *timē* (honour). Thus the grief that Andromache's capture would cause him is largely stimulated by the thought of what people will say about *Hector's wife* being reduced to such circumstances: his own honour is at least as important as his compassion.[9] Less understandable in terms of normal heroic standards is the gentleness of Hector toward Helen and Patroclus toward Briseis.[10] These are real idiosyncrasies, but they are easily acceptable because the relationships involved are only incidental. Achilles' temporary compassion for Priam, come to beg for the return of his son's body in book 24, is more unnerving; but then Achilles sees his own father in Priam, and in any case he rapidly suppresses the unheroic emotion and threatens a renewal of anger, the proper heroic reaction to an enemy.[11] We cannot be sure whether actual Achaean noblemen were capable of pity and tenderness even in the midst of war – presumably some of them were; but that is an academic question, because what is happening here is that the *subsequent poetical tradition* has allowed these occasional flashes of humanity to illuminate the severer architecture of the heroic soul.

With the similes, on the other hand, it is Homer himself (or at least someone at a relatively very late stage of the tradition) who has introduced a new outlook, and the same is probably true of the

[7] *Il.* 9, 321–7 and 337–43; see also the complementary discussion on pp. 51f.
[8] *Il.* 6, 441–6.   [9] *Il.* 6, 459–65.
[10] See p. 50.   [11] *Il.* 24, 507–51 and 560–70.

scenes of peaceful life wrought by Hephaestus on Achilles' new shield in book 18: the careful argument about a case of man-slaughter, the king sitting rejoicing in his fields as the harvesters cut the sheaves, the simple rustic scenes, the singing and dancing. These intrusions are morally and aesthetically permissible; they do not break the heroic mood that must predominate before Troy because they are formally enclosed in similes or in a digression about armour. From within these enclosed scenes shafts of heroic reference can be discharged (intentionally or not) without any serious disturbance of tone, and in such a way as to produce a confrontation in miniature of two separate ways of life. In the harvesting scene just mentioned the heroic attitude momentarily reasserts itself at 18, 554–60, where, as the king watches and the young men clutch their armfuls of sheaves, two separate alfresco meals are being prepared: the one a humble lunch of barley-meal, appropriately prepared by women for the workers, and the other an anomalous heroic banquet consisting of a great ox slaughtered by heralds under an oak-tree, presumably for the now ambivalent king.

In the *Odyssey* the effect is similar in quality but different in means; for this poem is set not in the typical heroic milieu of battle but against the equivocal and more varied background of a Greece to which some, but not all, of the heroes return from the ruins of Troy. That a true Achaean king, or even a true heroic king, could have travelled far and wide in search of poison for his arrows or could have had a father who dressed, behaved and lived like a peasant seems in-conceivable; yet this is what is in the poem.[12] Odysseus' wanderings on the way home to Ithaca take him beyond the known world of men (and any attempt to plot them on a map is a waste of in-genuity); yet even in these unusual circumstances of fantasy and terror, where we do not look for conventional reactions, there are certain events and attitudes that stand out as startlingly alien to the whole concept of a heroic ethos. The formal boastfulness of the Achaean warrior has become, with Odysseus and the Cyclops (for example), the braggartry of a picaresque eccentric;[13] Odysseus' account of meeting his former companions in the underworld is not so much that of a warrior as of a gentle moralist;[14] and in his deep desire to leave the goddesses Calypso and Circe for the homelier

---

[12] *Od.* 1, 260–4 and 189–93; 24, 226–31.
[13] *Od.* 9, 473–555. [14] *Od.* 11, 385–567.

mortal virtues of Penelope he is the type not of the hero (who generally sets availability above sentiment) but of the prudent antithesis to those unfortunates of Greek mythology who, like Peleus or Tithonus, suffered physical alliance with creatures who grow not old.[15] The land of the Phaeacians is a curious mixture of fairy-tale and, perhaps, the neatness of a new colony; its young men, who delight in music, ball-games, dancing and hot baths, and King Alcinous, who is ready to confess that they are quite hopeless at the rougher contests of physical prowess, belong to an age and an ideology quite apart from those of the conquerors of Troy.[16] Nausicaa, it is true, finds none of the Phaeacians attractive as **a** bridegroom and hankers after the more rugged Odysseus;[17] but merely by being put in this situation, and by the almost refined delicacy with which he wards off her admiration, Odysseus is denying the heroic mentality – or rather, and more significantly, he is showing how it *can* be adapted (although in the process it is subtly transformed) to alien circumstances. At the beginning of his acquaintance with this young girl, when he has crawled out of his thicket by the sea-shore, caked in salt, rushing among her maidens with only a branch to hide his nakedness, battered and impetuous as a mountain lion, he flatters her with soft words, likens her to a tall palm-tree he has seen on his travels and ends with a reference to her future husband and a little homily on the joys of harmonious marriage: 'For nothing is better than this, when a man and a woman dwell together in their house with their thoughts in harmony, much grief to their enemies, but joy to well-wishers; but they know it best of all.'[18] *We* find this affecting, and so no doubt did the poem's ancient audiences; but in its implied glorification of the quiet as opposed to the competitive virtues it is quite unheroic.[19] The theme of 'harm your enemies, help your friends' we may regard as typically Hellenic; but it is unique in Homer for the very good reason that such a sentiment is normally taken for granted, and does not require or allow explicit expression in a true heroic ambience. It was only when the heroic view of life had lost its power, had become permeated by other and more complex and humane attitudes, that it became necessary for poets

---

[15] *Od.* 5, 214–24; 10, 480–6; *Hy. Aphrodite* 218–40 (Tithonus).

[16] E.g. *Od.* 8, 246–9.   [17] *Od.* 6, 283f. and 244f.

[18] *Od.* 6, 127ff.; quotation, 182–5.

[19] For this distinction see A. W. H. Adkins, *Merit and Responsibility* (Oxford, 1960), pp. 34ff.

such as Theognis and Aeschylus (and Homer before them in this one exceptional statement) to reassert openly the old basis of the heroic creed against the incompatible requirements of philosophical introspection or an integrated society.

The real Achaean princes lie almost entirely beyond our reach. We can excavate their graves, measure their bones, put their metal-work in museums, even reconstruct a little of their methods of warfare, agriculture, accountancy and religious cult; but themselves we cannot recreate. Agamemnon and Achilles are not real people except in an ideal or Platonic sense; the complex human archetypes that inhabit these names are a product of the subtle embroidery of generations of epic singers, especially of Homer. The heroic attitudes had been made larger than life, and gradually they were tempered by subtleties and contradictions that in any other kind of epic tradition would not have been stated or even observed. It is largely this blend of magnificence with fallibility that makes the characters of Homer less stereotyped and ultimately much more interesting than those of the Teutonic or even the Nordic heroic epics (which embody other Heroic Ages), and renders the Greek poems more than a massive reiteration of the glories of manliness in war or the satisfactions of overcoming danger to regain hearth and home. Moreover the tempering of the heroic attitudes did not diminish their heroic effects. Paradoxically it increased them, by extending their range to situations and experiences outside the usual epic ambience. With the Teutonic epic, at least, nothing of that sort happened – largely because the distillation of the past was not so pure a process but became infected by partial literacy and, more decisively, by Christianity, a cult whose attitudes cannot be com-bined with the heroic except at the cost of sentimentality.

It is the oral nature of the Homeric poems that gives them some of their most striking qualities, both in their means of expression (the formular language) and in their social, moral and psychological tone. Moreover the societies that the poems describe, part real and part imaginary as they are, were themselves dominated by the idea of tradition, by singers and a heroic *geste* as the main form of static diversion. And even after the monumental composition of the poems, even in the seventh, sixth, fifth and fourth centuries B.C., it is on the infra-literate levels that they continued to exercise their most persistent impression – both among illiterates, that is, and among that great majority of literates for whom an author was to be recited or listened to rather than carefully read in private. These levels can only rarely be perceived beneath the surface of the new literate tradition. We can learn something of the part the *Iliad* and *Odyssey* continued to play in Greek culture by literary 'asides', and by the fact that so many of the literary papyri recovered from Hellenic settlements such as Oxyrhynchus in the Graeco-Roman Egypt of the second century A.D. were copies of Homer. Homer at that time (and not only because of his predominance as a school text) was better known than the tragedians or Demosthenes or Plato and Aristotle, or even the urbane and more contemporary figure of Menander. I only wish we could gauge with reasonable accuracy the response to Homer, generation by generation and region by region, through the climactic centuries of Greek culture; for in the process we should learn much more than is now known about the configuration of the Greek mind.

In the immediately post-oral period, and in the new forms of elegiac, iambic and lyric poetry, the heroic attitudes are often ignored as irrelevant; but often, too, they are subjected to implicit criticism or inconspicuously adapted or amended. Archilochus, who wrote his poems around the middle of the seventh century B.C., is the first major literate composer of the Hellenic tradition. Yet the epic phraseology still rings out through his verses, transposed though it often is with extreme virtuosity into different metrical patterns. His ideas as well as his language combine tradition and novelty; *his* conception of the ideal general is not a Hector or an Agamemnon but closer to an Odysseus, even with a touch of the physical abnormality of the unspeakable Thersites, 'the ugliest man who came to Troy'; for Archilochus' general is short, stocky, bandy-legged, but full of heart.[20] Appearance, aristocratic or otherwise, no longer counts for quite so much, although *aprepeia* (unseemliness) and *aidos* (the feeling of shame it arouses) are still important. Thus Tyrtaeus, writing in the martial and conservative atmosphere of Sparta soon after the time of Archilochus, adapted a well-known passage of the *Iliad* (22, 71–6) to form an impassioned appeal to young warriors to protect their elders, because for an old man to be stripped naked by enemies, to lie wounded and dying, clutching his bleeding genitals, was deeply shameful.[21] Homer had imagined such

[20] Frag. 114 (West).   [21] Frag. 10 (West).

an event only in special circumstances, as part of Priam's highly emotional vision of the approaching sack of Troy. Tyrtaeus turns it to the purpose of a more explicit profession of the responsibilities of citizenship and the beauty of youth, even in death, in contrast with the ugliness and pitifulness of old age. This suggests a fresh approach to what is important and what needs stating in life – an approach that nevertheless has to be harmonized with the persisting attitudes of the oral heroic tradition and expressed, where possible, in its language.

By the fifth century B.C. social and political conditions have changed more radically. Now Pindar calls in vain for the restoration of the world of myth and the truly aristocratic excellence that comes by nature and cannot be acquired by political or intellectual manipulation. By his standards even Homer is insufficiently austere, because by over-praising Odysseus he disguised the real responsibility for the death by suicide of the more admirable and less devious Ajax.[22] In this respect Pindar was responding, somewhat idiosyncratically, to the ambiguous epic picture of the military aristocrat. Yet his insistence was more than a personal whim, because he explicitly recognized that Homer's valuation, where it seemed misleading, was unusually dangerous; in the words of the seventh *Nemean* ode 'his fictions and soaring skill have something majestic about them; his poetic art leads us astray, beguiling us with stories'.[23]

Pindar's influence was restricted both locally and by social class. With the rise of tragedy as a great popular art the influence of poetry became universal once again, as it had been in the heyday of oral heroic song. Moreover the tragedians revived the mythical world of the old epic tradition. With them, however, the myths constitute the formal background for the exploration of predicaments that generally lay beyond the experience of the Homeric heroes. Questions of punishment and guilt, of differing loyalties and conflicting laws, of the moral status of gods, belong to a new and more introspective world. Yet even here the attitudes of the oral heroic tradition show themselves from time to time – as inadequate in some respects, exemplary in others. Sophocles in his *Ajax* develops still further the Pindaric confrontation between the inflexibility of heroic virtue in Ajax himself and the over-flexibility, amounting to

[22] *Nem.* 7, 20ff.   [23] *Nem.* 7, 22f.

devious unpredictability, of the more modern Odysseus. As a whole, however, the tragedians avoid explicit reference to Homer; and the historians Herodotus and Thucydides, too, name him mainly as an occasional source of antiquarian detail, or, as Pindar does, as the archetype of the persuasive poet. As conscious innovators they would naturally avoid excessive lip-service to a pseudo-historian they were out to supplant. Even Aristophanes, who is more conservative as well as more openly didactic, restricts himself to a few Homeric tags and glosses – except for a famous passage in the *Frogs* where he makes Aeschylus say, perhaps a little condescendingly, that Homer's glory depends on his teaching of concrete subjects such as weaponry and tactics.[24] This line of assessment continued into the next century and, through Socrates, down to Plato. Throughout these crucial generations there is more than a hint of an intellectual conspiracy – at the very least a strong unconscious wish – to downgrade Homer to the level of a purely practical and demotic instructor.

Yet in the end Plato has to treat Homer more seriously. He is, after all, regarded by the people as a great teacher; yet what he teaches is immoral, and encourages vanity or excessive emotion or disrespect for the gods. It is really for this reason that Plato proposes to crown the poets with garlands and escort them to the borders of his ideal state; from Homer downward they have represented a tradition of old-fashioned and distorted morality, all the harder to refute because it is expressed not as philosophy but as poetry. This is the true cause of what Plato termed the 'ancient quarrel between poetry and philosophy'.[25] Even Isocrates, Plato's rival and inferior, has this in common with him; for although he concedes Homer's paramount place as a teacher, he finds himself at odds with Sophists who spend their time quoting and discussing Homer and Hesiod in a quite unoriginal manner.[26] These unnamed Sophists, the aridity of whose talk one can easily imagine (although Isocrates himself would not have done much better), presumably found audiences. They are one more sign of the close grip that the poetry of Homer, conventional and outdated though it in some ways seemed to be, retained on the public imagination, especially at the level of oral and informal discussion.

[24] *Frogs*, 1035f.
[25] *Republic* III, 398A, cf. x, 606E–607A, 607B 3ff. On this whole topic see E. A. Havelock, *Preface to Plato* (Oxford, 1963), chs. 1 and 15.
[26] *Panathenaicus* 18–19.

Homer: the meaning of an oral tradition

It seems that from about 450 to about 350 B.C., at least, there was an important but largely unrecorded conflict between different systems of values. The clash was complex and untidy, not merely between an old-fashioned conservative morality and the sceptical, self-centred and pragmatic tendencies of the Sophists. The epic tradition operated ambiguously here – not only, as one might expect, on the side of the conservatives. Even apart from the Sophists, life in the developed city-state had become selfish and competitive, and certain of the more obviously 'heroic' attitudes, such as an excessive preoccupation with public esteem, were coming into their own once again. Moreover these attitudes were no longer kept in reasonable check by the fear of divine retribution – an idea nascent in the *Iliad* and overtly, if only occasionally, stated in the *Odyssey*.[27] It was thus that the Socratic and Platonic tradition, hostile to Sophists and Homer alike, sought to adduce controls based on an abstract idea of just behaviour and its relation to the human psyche. Meanwhile beneath the surface the ordinary man pursued his course, vainly trying to reconcile the traditional and oral configuration of nobility and manhood with such complex factors as the anti-aristocratic bias of democracy, the post-heroic but still archaic and respectable code of 'nothing to excess' and the atheism and scepticism of the Sophists and Euripides. Out of this conflict and these uncertainties, which are indefinite in outline but of enormous importance, the spiritual tradition of Homer, supported as ever by the sheer quality of the poems as well as by their status as national epics, emerged still vigorous if not unscathed.

[27] Especially 1, 32–43; and see Adkins, *Merit and Responsibility*, pp. 65 ff.

2

DARK AGE AND ORAL POET

Increasing acceptance that the *Iliad* and *Odyssey* are in essence oral poems, built by one or two monumental composers out of traditional elements of various dates, has altered the perspective of the problem of Homeric composition. We have become more interested in the question of which parts of the poems can be associated with which phases of the tradition; or, if this question cannot be precisely answered, in the broader problem of the general stages of development of an oral heroic tradition in Greece.

Recently there has been great emphasis on the importance of the Mycenaean period for the formation of the dactylic hexameter tradition. This emphasis has been helped by the partial understanding of the Linear B tablets, although they contain, of course, no hint of Mycenaean poetry. The tablets have confirmed, what has been suspected since their first discovery, that the organization of life in Knossos, Pylos and Mycenae was every bit as detailed and elaborate as that of other Near Eastern palace-societies, of Ugarit, Alalakh, Nuzi, Mari, and Boghaz-Keui. T. B. L. Webster argued in his *From Mycenae to Homer* (London, 1958), like L. A. Stella in *Il poema di Ulisse* (Florence, 1955), that since poetry has been found in some of these Near Eastern cultures, and since the Mycenaean system resembles them in architecture and economic organization, then the Mycenaean palaces must have had a developed poetical tradition too. This argument could be quite misleading. Yet it would be perverse to deny the probability that poetry in some form was practised in the Mycenaean palaces and even in Mycenaean villages; for it would be odd if there were no simple songs of work, death and rejoicing at least. Music there certainly was, and this implies song; witness for example the lyre-fragments in the Menidhi tomb in Attica and the Pylos fresco depicting a large bird flying away from in front of a lyre-player. It is a reasonable guess, moreover, that narrative songs were not unknown, although there can be no kind of certainty about this on the basis of the Bronze Age evidence itself.

Dark Age and oral poet

The Homeric poems do, however, provide certain special reasons for envisaging some kind of narrative tradition in the late Mycenaean period. The first point is that there is a good deal of apparently genuine and accurate information in the *Iliad* and *Odyssey* about conditions in the late Bronze Age. Body-shields, the boar's-tusk helmet and silver-studded swords represent one type of Mycenaean information, although *Realien* that can be assigned to the late Bronze Age and to no later period are otherwise extremely rare; and some of these might conceivably have survived into the early post-Mycenaean period. More significant is the detailed information in Homer about the historical expedition against Troy and its aftermath, and about the geography of Mycenaean Greece at this period. The latter information is mainly contained in the Catalogue of Ships. Many of the cities mentioned in the Catalogue were abandoned towards the end of the Mycenaean period, and knowledge of them and of their previous importance must have descended from that time. One must emphasize, however, that it need not have survived in the first instance in *poetry*; nor need the stories of the Trojan war itself. There is a strong tendency to assume that 'tradition' = 'poetry'. Admittedly there is no sign in later Greek culture of prose saga as one finds it in Norse and Celtic contexts, and I am not suggesting that the transmission of information from the end of the Mycenaean age, if it was not by means of poetry, need have been so formal as that. Yet much detailed information must have survived for two or perhaps three generations by means of more casual story-telling and reminiscing. The importance of the Achaean Catalogue is that its information is so specific, yet in many places so comparatively trivial from the point of view of that kind of unorganized tradition, that it must have been crystallized in poetry after two or three or at the most four generations if it was to survive at all. This does not mean two or three generations after the fall of Troy, however, which the Cincinnati expedition placed around 1240–1230 B.C.;[1] it means at latest two or three or four generations after the final collapse of the Mycenaean world something over a hundred years later. Until that collapse, and even for a time after it, stories of the great expedition against Troy and the disruptions that followed, and of Pylos and lesser places which had been destroyed or abandoned during the first troubles around 1200, could and would have

---

[1] See p. 53 and references there cited.

survived in informal tradition whether or not there were poems about them too. Dr F. H. Stubbings has reminded me that the conspicuous ruins of many Achaean sites would help to keep such traditions alive.

So far I have merely pointed out that the Mycenaean information in Homer need not have been incorporated in poetry in the period of the Trojan war itself, or even within the strict limits of the Mycenaean age. Much or all of it could conceivably have survived for a time in a non-poetical tradition, to be fixed in poetry later. There is no evidence for a formalized saga-tradition in Greece, but story-telling of a more fluid kind must have been common in every generation and could account for the transmission and survival of stories or motifs for considerable periods of time. In fact Homer contains many descriptions of this kind of story-telling, although these descriptions are not usually recognized simply because they themselves are in verse-form. Nestor's reminiscences in the *Iliad*, or those of Menelaus and Helen in the fourth book of the *Odyssey*, or more conspicuously Odysseus' narration of his adventures to the Phaeacians – these are examples of leisurely and extensive stories told by non-poets to a receptive audience. They are concerned with the story-teller's own experiences, but many other descriptions of figures of the past, like Tydeus, Bellerophon or Meleagros, are put into the mouths of characters in the poems and elaborated far beyond the requirements of context. The poet distinguishes this kind of story from those *sung* by Phemius and Demodocus in the *Odyssey*. On the one hand he describes an ἀοιδός singing a poem to the lyre, on the other he describes people reminiscing or telling tales in prose – although, because the *Iliad* and *Odyssey* are poems, prose here becomes poetry. It may be argued that Homer makes his characters behave artificially and tell long stories that only a singer would have handled in real life. Yet this does not explain away the whole situation; and in the fourth book of the *Odyssey* the telling of tales by a non-singer is specifically described as a means of entertainment, when Helen tells the men-folk 'Now feast on, seated in the halls, and rejoice in stories (μύθοις τέρπεσθε); for I shall tell you things suitable to the occasion' (4, 238f.). For the fixity of such stories Homer provides no evidence, but there can be little doubt that story-telling was done much more accurately in a primarily or completely illiterate society, deeply conscious of its past, than it would be in our own culture. Without reaching the degree of schematization of Norse saga it may yet have had considerable thematic and even verbal stability.

The distinction between prose tradition and poetical tradition is more important than it looks, and not only for the history of the Mycenaean period as such; for the proponents of the Mycenaean epic envisage that there was narrative poetry not merely at the very end of the Bronze Age but even at the beginning of Late Helladic III, soon after 1400, since the body-shield and silver-studded rapier seem to have become obsolete at that time.[2] Thus we are being asked to accept a *developed* and *well established* tradition of Mycenaean heroic narrative poetry, not merely the first beginnings of narrative song from the time of the Trojan war onwards.

Those who believe in developed narrative poetry have a further argument based on the survival in Homer of a small number of Mycenaean dialect-forms. This argument does not, however, dispose of the theoretical possibility that narrative poetry began (or at the very least underwent a surge of strength, scope and formalization that virtually amounted to a new beginning) after the end of the Bronze Age. Do we really imagine that Mycenaean speech-forms were abolished in a moment of time everywhere except in Arcadia and Cyprus? Let us consider a single example, which has been used as an argument for Mycenaean poetry both by T. B. L. Webster and by D. L. Page.[3] ἄναξ ἀνδρῶν 'Αγαμέμνων is obviously a very old formula, long established in the epic tradition. It describes a supreme leader such as cannot have existed after the collapse of the Mycenaean world (unless it is mere conventional grandiloquence, which is unlikely), and it does so with the Mycenaean word ϝάναξ. Webster and Page conclude that this phrase must therefore have originated in the Mycenaean period itself; but in the light of the possibility of non-poetical tradition all we are entitled to conclude is that the phrase must have been made at some period in which some Mycenaean words and speech-forms, together with a little basic Mycenaean social information, were still known. Tradition relates, and archaeology certainly does not deny, that Pelopon-

[2] H. L. Lorimer, *Homer and the Monuments* (London, 1950), pp. 152, 273; A. M. Snodgrass, *Arms and Armour of the Greeks* (London, 1967), pp. 19f., 26.

[3] T. B. L. Webster, *From Mycenae to Homer* (London, 1958), p. 107; D. L. Page, *History and the Homeric Iliad* (Berkeley, 1959), p. 188.

nesian refugees, many from Pylos, made their way to Athens as the Peloponnese was overrun by Dorians. Whatever dialect the indigenous Athenians were speaking in the first generations of the Submycenaean period – and I see no reason why they should not have used ϝάναξ and many other such words, undismayed by their duty to develop Ionic – these refugees would probably have preserved the South Mycenaean speech of their old homelands as long as possible. The same would be true in other settlements, however mean and however mixed, in which Mycenaean survivors and their children lived on. The phrase ἄναξ ἀνδρῶν 'Αγαμέμνων could in theory have been invented by men like these, or their children, or their children's children, just as well as by their ancestors in Pylos or Mycenae.

A more detailed linguistic argument has been developed by C. J. Ruijgh, to the effect that Mycenaean words in Homer are so strictly confined to certain places in the hexameter verse that they must have entered the tradition from the Mycenaean period itself in firmly fixed poetical usages.[4] But the argument against ἄναξ ἀνδρῶν applies to this contention also. More important is the fact that Mycenaean words are only rarely more strongly localized within the verse than are other words of the same metrical value; and that when there is any significant increase, as for example in the case of the particle ἰδέ, it may be because the old word is preserved to fulfil one special function for which later forms happened to be metrically unsuitable – a function that might have been determined not in the late Bronze Age but at any time when poetry was being developed and some Mycenaean forms were remembered in ordinary speech.[5]

More serious are certain arguments advanced by D. L. Page in his discussion of Homeric formulas in the fourth and sixth chapters of his *History and the Homeric Iliad*. I accept that much of the formular language of the *Iliad* and *Odyssey* is undoubtedly very old, but on the question of whether or not it goes back to Mycenaean poetry itself I take a more agnostic view than Page, encouraged by the thought that his special arguments do not preclude the possibility of early post-Mycenaean composition based on a less formalized non-poetical tradition. For example the place-names in the Achaean

---

[4] *L'Elément Achéen dans la langue épique* (Assen, 1957).
[5] See *Museum Helveticum* 17 (1960), 198ff.

Catalogue in book 2 have some very unusual (for Homer) and unusually specific epithets attached to them – like Arne of many vines, Messe of many doves. Page asks (p. 123) how these epithets could have been assigned at any period later than the late Bronze Age, when many of these places still flourished. Yet some of the epithets could have been suggested by general locality or by the place-name itself: thus Enispe might be windy because it is in mountainous Arcadia, Aigilips is rough because it means precipitous, Iton might be mother of flocks because it was at least known to be in Thessaly, Pteleos grassy for the same reason and because its very name suggests fertile lowland. Some of these descriptions, too, specific as they at first sight appear to be, applied to many or most Greek settlements.[6] In fact many of the places named survived, or their ruins survived, or their reputation survived outside Homer. Even the ones that Strabo could discover little or nothing about in the first century B.C. could have been remembered through the Submycenaean and Protogeometric period and then forgotten. Page precludes fictitious epithets, but if some of these places were being forgotten very early then fiction would be permissible. All that might be needed, then, would be the survival of a bare list, or bare regional traditions, of settlements of the late Bronze Age; the descriptions could have been added later – although not, I agree, by poets of the developed Ionian epic tradition, who evidently did not use epithets of quite this kind. There is no absolute need to go back for them into the Bronze Age itself. Conversely Page observes that some of the leaders in the Catalogue carry their normal Iliadic epithets, which he takes to imply that, since the Catalogue and the rest of the *Iliad* differ so much in other respects, these epithets at least must have originated in the common poetical source-material of the late Bronze Age. Thus Γερήνιος ἱππότα Νέστωρ, βοὴν ἀγαθὸς Διομήδης and so on are fragments of Mycenaean poetry. This is an interesting possibility, but little more. We know that the Achaean Catalogue underwent considerable later adjustment; and the main heroes, when mentioned in the Catalogue, would naturally acquire their normal formular descriptions whether these originated in the Mycenaean period or later.

One motive for excluding a post-Mycenaean origin for many of these undoubtedly old phrases is that the early post-Mycenaean

[6] A. Parry and A. Samuel, *CJ* 56 (1960), 85.

period is what is known as a Dark Age. On p. 118 of his *Iliad*-book Page quotes judgements from Gomme, Lorimer, Beazley and Dunbabin to supplement the well-known image supplied by Gilbert Murray.[7] There is no need to go outside the English language for a horrifying idea of the depths of squalor and disruption into which Greece fell at the time of the Dorian migrations. 'Disintegrated and materially degenerate', a darkness which 'far surpasses the Dark Ages which follow the fall of the Western Roman Empire', and so on – 'a horror of great darkness' is a phrase that Page himself applies. No wonder this period is regarded by so many Homeric scholars as irrelevant to the creation of the Homeric poems!

I would like to suggest as a basis for discussion that such a picture may be misleading so far as oral poetry is concerned. Even the phrase 'Dark Age' itself contains a dangerous ambiguity; for 'dark' implies both obscure or unknown, and gloomy or abject. The second meaning, however, is not an essential consequence of the first. There are periods in the history of human culture about which little is known, but which there is no reason for considering as especially decadent, unhappy or devoid of song. The Greek Dark Age is certainly an obscure one, and our evidence for it is slight. It was also without question an era that began with a serious decline of material conditions and communications consequent upon the burning and virtual abandonment of most of the main centres, leading to drastically diminished achievements in art and architecture. The Dorian invasions, so-called, are curiously inscrutable: they are guaranteed by tradition and the evidence of dialect, they coincide with the depopulation of most Mycenaean towns and palaces, but they introduce no special material characteristic beyond, possibly, the straight pin. The old idea that cremation and geometric pottery-decoration are Dorian innovations is false; here is a people whose only characteristics, apart from a new accent, seem to be the power to move and to destroy. This is what archaeology at first suggests, and it is, of course, a completely inadequate picture. It is easy to be blinded by archaeological science into accepting the material remains with which it deals as a necessarily valid criterion of human activity. It may therefore be useful to summarize the evidence for the eleventh and tenth centuries B.C., with which I am

---

[7] *The Rise of the Greek Epic*, 4th ed. (Oxford, 1934), pp. 57f.

primarily concerned, with deliberate emphasis on those factors which suggest that in spite of the undoubtedly disastrous quality of the Mycenaean collapse, communal life sufficient to have supported oral poetry went on without serious interruption in many places of previous Mycenaean influence.

The disintegration of Mycenaean culture in Greece coincides with the downfall of long-established civilizations in Asia Minor and Syria and the beginning of a long decline in Egypt. The Dorians are usually seen as a backward division of the Greek-speaking tribes that had filtered down into the Greek peninsula around 1900 B.C., and they got no further than the mountains in the north-west of central Greece. Then in the second part of the thirteenth century new barbarian movements from central Europe down toward the Mediterranean coast seem to have stimulated the Sea-People migrations in the Mediterranean itself and also prodded the Dorians further south. Simultaneously the resistance of the strongly-founded Mycenaean and Hittite cultures was on the decline; quite why we do not even now precisely know, but the economic over-organization of the clay-tablet cultures suggests how the international trade of the eastern Mediterranean could have run into its undoubted stagnation. This had in turn, no doubt, encouraged piracy, internal quarrels and wars of conquest, of which the Argonautic expedition, the destruction of Cadmeian Thebes and finally the attack on Troy were important examples. By the end of the Trojan venture the Mycenaean empire was dying on its feet, and it was thus that the Dorian tribes, aided by internal disputes, were able to finish it off in the two main thrusts that led to the destruction of Pylos around 1200 and Mycenae around 1125. The weakness of the Mycenaean world after the exhausting and ultimately fruitless war against Troy needs special emphasis, since if this is the case then the Dorians need not have been quite the numerous and well-drilled external enemy that we have sometimes been prone to imagine. And if so, then in some parts of Greece the survivors of the Mycenaean culture would have been allowed to live on more or less undisturbed, although in terribly reduced circumstances, by the Dorian insurgents.

Archaeology and tradition suggest that this happened in Amyklai, in the valley of the Eurotas close to Sparta. The peculiar Proto-geometric sherds found in the foundations of the temple of Apollo probably suggest that there was continuity of cult there from

Mycenaean times onwards,[8] and according to Strabo (VIII, 364) Ephorus gave the following account: that the Heraclid invaders of Laconia gave Amyklai to the man who had betrayed Laconia to them, and who had persuaded its previous ruler to go with the (other) Achaeans to Ionia. There is some vagueness and confusion here, but it looks as though a local tradition survived according to which the population of Amyklai remained relatively undisturbed by the Dorians. Submycenaean pottery[9] has also been found in small quantities at Asine, Tiryns and probably Mycenae itself, showing that small village settlements continued on or near the ruined citadels; although Asine may have gone more or less unscathed. At Corinth and in its neighbourhood sherds have been found that suggest some kind of settled occupation in the transitional period from Submycenaean to Protogeometric, that is, not later than around 1050. At Traghanes not far from Messenian Pylos the Mycenaean tholos-tomb continued to be reused for burials throughout the twelfth and eleventh centuries, showing that even after Pylos was abandoned a group of Achaeans went on living in the area; they had not all been murdered or driven out. This is all in the Peloponnese and in the plains, where one might have expected total disruption. Many other Achaeans must have retreated to the not-so-very remote uplands of Arcadia, where their dialect survived; others again resorted to the foothills, not the heights, of Mount Panachaikon in Achaea, where they continued to make a local late-Mycenaean pottery of which numerous examples have been found in tombs scattered over the whole area.[10] About 1050 or 1000 this last region seems to have become largely depopulated – at least there is no sign of Protogeometric pottery; though one cannot dismiss the possibility that a change in burial-custom and in the durability of graves meant that casual archaeological search has not yet brought grave-goods of this era to light. It is highly significant that there is no other sign *apart* from graves of this influx into Achaea during the period of disturbance from before 1200 onwards. These were people

---

[8] This is questioned by A. M. Snodgrass, *The Dark Age of Greece* (Edinburgh, 1971), esp. pp. 130f., although not (so far as I can see) on very strong grounds. But this book is the most important single contribution to the study of the Greek Dark Age.

[9] For the distribution of Submycenaean pottery, a convenient source is the site-index of V. R. d'A. Desborough, *Protogeometric Pottery* (Oxford, 1952), pp. 315ff. For recent finds (e.g. at Levkandi) see Snodgrass, *supra*.

[10] Emily T. Vermeule, *AJA* 64 (1960), 1ff.

who made their own pottery and went so far, as Mrs Vermeule emphasizes, as to produce one very distinctive local vase-shape. By this evidence they were by no means disorganized or utterly uncultured, yet they left no other trace of their existence. How many small Achaean communities were there, even in the Peloponnese and apart from those that we infer for Arcadia, whose grave-objects have *not* survived or been discovered, either through the nature of the terrain or because they used earth-cut graves or because of different local burial-customs or because there was no convenient tholos-tomb to reuse?

North of the Isthmus there is good evidence for continued occupation on a small scale at Thebes, where Submycenaean pottery has been found in inhumations outside the Electran gate, and probably also at Iolcus. It is possible that a sanctuary at Delphi was continuously maintained from the Bronze Age onwards, though the situation there is still obscure. The only undoubted example of post-Mycenaean *urban* survival is Athens. The Submycenaean cemetery in the Kerameikos contains many graves with relatively tolerable grave-goods, and testifies firmly to the tradition that Athens held out against Dorian pressure.[11] Organized life continued in full swing there after the collapse of the other Mycenaean centres, not only in Athens itself but also in Salamis and east Attica. Athens had not been among the first rank of palaces, although continued excavation round the slopes of the Acropolis has revealed more and more in the way of Mycenaean remains. Yet after 1100, at least, Athens became quite the most important town in Greece. Greek tradition knew that refugees from the Peloponnese, specifically from Pylos, had flowed there during the generations of Dorian infiltration. The introduction of cremation in Athens around 1050 – it had been used at Perati in Attica already in the twelfth century[12] – may have have been the result of pressure of numbers and a landless element in the population, although (as D. L. Page has pointed out to me) cremation is a costly and difficult business except in a wood-producing region. It must be remembered, too, that the Pylian refugees seem to have established themselves pretty well, for King Codrus himself was a Pylian. Athens was crowded and poor in the Submycenaean period. Emily Vermeule has declared that 'without being burned, Athens

---

[11] Kraiker and Kübler, *Kerameikos*, I (Berlin, 1939).
[12] Πρακτικά (1955), 100–8.

faded away exactly like more obviously destroyed sites; neither architecture nor art continued, only people'.[13] At this point I feel she slightly exaggerates; in general her thesis is that life was *not* utterly disrupted by the Dorians, although it sank to a low level from a combination of causes. Athens was crowded and poor in the Submycenaean period, but there is no cause for denying some degree of culture to life there, let alone to aspects of life that cannot be assessed by material remains. 'Submycenaean' never has been and never will be a term to call up images of great prosperity and beauty; yet we must be careful not to think that Submycenaean pottery necessarily indicates a crude, barbaric and utterly uncivilized way of life. The mere fact that much of the surviving pottery, and not only that major part of it that comes from Athens, was *decorated* suggests that some of the civilized arts continued, although in many cases at a reduced level. Yet not all decorated Submycenaean pottery is nasty and brutish, or even utterly tasteless (some of it is not as tasteless as some of the Mycenaean III C or even III B examples), any more than all of the Protogeometric pottery that developed out of it and its predecessors is marvellously harmonious. There is nothing whatever in the archaeological record of early Dark Age Athens to indicate that oral poetry could not have flourished there, even on the false assumption, which I shall be discussing presently, that oral poetry needs developed urban surroundings.

Dorian pressure, maintained over three or four generations, completed that disruption of close communications between the great Bronze Age palaces that had already begun by about 1300. Smaller settlements like Zygouries and Prosymna began to seem unsafe by the time that Pylos and Tiryns succumbed, and their occupants had doubtless crowded round the great surviving centres like Mycenae or were beginning like the Achaeans of Crete to move up into the hills. Then came the second phase of aggression, and Mycenae itself fell. Some were murdered, others (one supposes) fled to the mountain hamlets or drifted up through Achaea to the islands of Zacynthus, Cephallenia and Ithaca. Those who could, crossed the Isthmus to Athens and Boeotia, where the tide of migration had passed and where conditions may have regained relative stability. Others no doubt managed to reach Mycenaean outposts further east, like Delos or Miletus, Trianda in Rhodes or Enkomi in Cyprus. Yet

[13] *Archaeology* 13 (1960), 71.

even in regions like Laconia, which were to emerge as the chosen Dorian centres, there were occasional settlements like Amyklai where for one reason or another habitation had continued; and in more remote areas which the Dorians left alone there must have been many small farms and communities in which men who had survived the 1130s or 1120s lived on, procreated children, tilled fields, milked goats, and even had friends and neighbours; and in which their children did the same.

This was the worst period to live through. When the grand-children of the men of Mycenae were grown up, if not even before, a new cultural inspiration flared up in Athens, which we relate with the careful technique and fine decoration of Protogeometric pottery.[14] At about the same time the first post-Mycenaean colonies were established across the Aegean. Here the evidence is still pitifully slight, but at least we now have Smyrna. The earliest Protogeometric pottery to be found there is dated by J. M. Cook to around 1000 B.C., or at least not much later.[15] There is no doubt that the Protogeo-metric style emanated from Attica, but the early Smyrna examples are local products and unlikely to derive from the very first years of colonization. The exact date of the Aeolian and Ionian migrations is not yet determinable; but at least the evidence from Smyrna indi-cates that the main wave of eastward movement had begun by the end of the eleventh century. Athens played a major part in the organization of the Ionian stream, but people joined them from Boeotia and many other parts of Greece – even a few Dorians! This was something different from the destitute trickle that had doubtless been flowing eastwards ever since the fall of Pylos, Iolcus, Gla and Tiryns. It was something that presupposed the re-establishment of communications over many parts of the Greek mainland, and the comparative security of the sea and islands. A similar story is told by the spread of Protogeometric pottery itself; for by soon after the middle of the tenth century Athenian exports are found in all quarters of the Greek world, and local styles based on the Attic had already emerged in the Argolid, Corinthia, Phocis and Boeotia, and other areas. By 1050 possibly, 1000 probably, and 950 certainly, the true Dark Age in Greece had ended; what follows was dark in the sense of 'obscure' but not of 'utterly uncultured'.

[14] Desborough, *Protogeometric Pottery*, *passim*; Snodgrass, *Dark Age*, p. 44.
[15] *BSA* 53–4 (1958–9), 10.

Dark Age and oral poet

We have seen that even in the immediately post-Mycenaean period there were cases of presumed comparative stability where the Achaeans and their descendants lived on. Let us now look a little more closely at the implications of the Submycenaean archaeological record. Positively it reveals that certain sites continued to be inhabited without violent interruption, and that in them, and in some new sites, decorated pottery in a few of the old Mycenaean shapes and one or two new ones continued to be made. Negatively it shows that writing on tablets disappeared, that there were no stone-built city-walls or palaces or public buildings, and that the more elaborate arts like ivory-carving and gem-engraving had temporarily died out. These things represent a severe decline in culture, there is no denying it; those who write of the effects of the Dorian movement as merely political are unrealistic. At the same time we must not exaggerate these symptoms. Writing was bound to go if the palaces went; it was a cumbrous system, used so far as we can tell only for the elephantine administration of the palace-state economy. Stone-built palaces, palaces of any kind, became a thing of the past; even at Athens the Acropolis was turned into a sanctuary. Permanent public buildings, which would only have attracted Dorian looters and squatters, were in any case no longer needed, since men must have lived on the whole not in towns but in villages or hamlets. Their building-material must have been primarily mud-brick, which normally leaves no archaeological trace but was a staple material all through Greek history. Because mud-brick leaves no trace we cannot therefore refuse to accept the existence of villages or their very possibility. In such villages men could have met together in their leisure hours, either in one of the larger houses or in summer in the open air, or conceivably in some even humbler precursor of the λέσχη or club mentioned by Hesiod. Even in the mountains men could meet and drink and sing songs, as they always have in Crete and many other places. There is no need to continue: much of this is speculative, but the important point is that the evidence suggests that community life at this kind of level continued after the fall of the great palaces in many parts of Greece.

One of the bugbears of Homeric scholarship is something that Page has termed the 'remotely conceivable alternative', a thing that should not be allowed to consume too much of our time. We must now ask ourselves whether this term applies to the contention that heroic narrative poetry on the Trojan theme might either have begun, or at least first reached a stage at which substantial parts of its phraseology survived into Homer, in the centuries after 1100 rather than those before. Naturally I do not think it does apply. Those who believe that bits of Mycenaean poetry survive in Homer have to admit that, however dark they make out the Dark Age to be, at least their Mycenaean poetry *was transmitted through it*. For oral poetry to be transmitted, there have to be conditions settled enough for the singer of poems to earn at least a part of his living. To do this he must have an audience that can assemble in one place and has leisure to hear his songs. Thus the proponents of Mycenaean poetry must grant that community life and an interest in poetry *did* continue through the Dark Age.

Yet the conditions essential for the *transmission* of oral poetry are also apt for its *creation*. One must not make the mistake to which many students of the comparative oral epic are prone, of confusing the non-creative oral transmitter with the creative poet – the ῥαψῳδός with the ἀοιδός in Greek terms. The only Yugoslav bards whose procedures can be studied in detail so far, those from around Novi Pazar who are the subject of the first volume of Parry–Lord, *Serbo-Croatian Heroic Songs* (Cambridge, Mass., 1954), are reproductive and not creative. All oral poets are reproductive, of course; they learn songs from others and reproduce them for their audience. Some of them are creative too, since they add lines, themes, episodes or complete songs of their own invention, albeit with the help of the established materials and technique of a formular oral tradition. A poet who merely contaminates or conflates two or more derived songs is not creative in more than a minor sense. The monumental poets of the *Iliad* and *Odyssey*, not to speak of their predecessors, must have been creative poets; most of the seventh- and sixth-century rhapsodes essentially were not. The Novi Pazar poets are reproductive, but they are not mere reciters like the Homeric rhapsode with his staff; they are singers who use the formular technique of memory and carry out a considerable amount of selection and conflation. They think they are creative, but in the true sense they are not so. The whole question of creative, quasi-creative and merely reproductive is a complex one,[16] but for present purposes it suffices to say that non-creative phases usually seem to precede the complete decline of

[16] See pp. 137–9.

an oral tradition. This would tell against the conjecture that the early Dark Age was entirely or mainly reproductive. A stronger argument is that reproductive stages do not seem to be induced by bad conditions and bad communications; on the contrary the present non-creative stage in the Novi Pazar region of Yugoslavia has developed in conditions that must be much better than any that prevailed during the Turkish occupation, in which creative oral poetry flourished. Other extraneous factors, however, can hasten the decline of an oral tradition.[17] All that can safely be said is that if there was anything like a Mycenaean epic, which seems far from proved, then Submycenaean Greece, if it could transmit it, could also create epic poetry of its own; and on this hypothesis there are reasons for considering the Dark Age as creative rather than merely reproductive.

Critics who presuppose a Mycenaean hexameter epic tend to avoid the implications of its transmission. It is indeed a difficult problem. Page, with the oral tradition as a whole in mind, accepted that 'each generation increased the inherited stock'; but when he regarded the early post-Mycenaean period, 'the dismal night of the Dark Ages', he seemed to be appalled at what he found and inclined to discount it as a possible creative period.[18] Others, notably T. B. L. Webster and C. H. Whitman, assume that *Athens* was the only place where the epic can have advanced between 1100 and 950; Whitman placed the Ionian migration very late, on imperfect evidence, and made the Attic stage correspondingly longer and more influential. It is important to emphasize the position of Athens, but it is also important not to exaggerate it. Thus Whitman wrote as follows: 'Oral poetry requires, as a *sine qua non* of survival, a continuous tradition of bard instructing bard in the formulaic techniques, and Athens is unique in providing the necessary conditions'.[19] There is some truth in this, but I would question its detailed expression. The transmission of oral poetry does not require anything so formal as 'bard instructing bard in the formulaic techniques' – night-classes on Milman Parry as it were. The easy, informal and almost accidental way in which a gifted bard may start his career is exemplified by the case of Salih Ugljanin, a good singer from the Novi Pazar

---

[17] C. M. Bowra, *Heroic Poetry* (London, 1952), pp. 537ff.

[18] *History and the Homeric Iliad*, pp. 267 and 242.

[19] *Homer and the Heroic Tradition* (Cambridge, Mass., 1958), p. 58.

region, who told Parry that 'I began to sing once with the shepherds, and afterwards I kept on and sang at gatherings'.[20] Most of the Yugoslav singers seem to have started as boys; they liked the songs and gradually learned some of them and in doing so, more or less unconsciously, they picked up the formular tricks of oral poetry. It did not require a city for this to happen; the South-Slavic parallel suggests very strongly that the oral tradition could have flourished in some parts of the Greek countryside and away from the urban conditions of Athens itself. Webster likewise concentrates solely on Athens; he sees two inventions which 'seem to have been made in the dark period...These inventions must almost have been made in Athens' – both inventions, the nature of which I find slightly surprising, having to do with oral poetry.[21] Both these critics are so strongly drawn to Athens in part because of the evidence for material culture, but in part because they are deeply impressed by the aesthetic and structural similarities between the *Iliad* and a Geometric pot, a subject on which I shall say nothing here.

It is important but sometimes difficult to recognize that a Dark Age, especially if it is the direct aftermath of a Heroic Age, is not necessarily a bad environment for the production of oral poetry. Oral poetry is not like architecture or gem-cutting or high-class vase-making, it does not need prosperity and good material surroundings. Sometimes it flourishes best when the opposite is the case. J. A. Notopoulos has put the matter as follows: 'Parallels for the survival of folklore and oral poetry in nations which have been conquered or governed by aliens, even amid circumstances of as great destruction as is shown in the Dorian Conquest, show that cultural vacuum is by no means the necessary result of conquest'.[22] He cites the case of the Dighenes Akritas epic, which must have begun in the confused conditions round the frontiers of eighth-century Byzantium, although it is known to us in a sophisticated form of somewhat later date. A stronger parallel is provided by the Serbo-Croat tradition of Yugoslavia, which gradually enlarged on the events of the battle of Kosovo in 1389 and the anti-Turk guerrilla warfare of the centuries that followed; even though freedom, urban life, intercommunication and general security were excessively poor

---

[20] M. Parry and A. B. Lord, *Serbo-Croatian Heroic Songs*, I (Cambridge, Mass., 1954,) 60.

[21] *From Mycenae to Homer*, p. 186.

[22] *Hesperia* 29 (1960), 190.

until recently. Conditions in Russia must have been similar during the transmission and development of the heroic poetry which told of the glories of Kiev in the twelfth century; for the Mongol destruction of that city in 1240 is unlikely to have been less frightful than the Dorian movements. The truth seems to be that adverse conditions, after a period in which the heroic virtues of pride, courage and success have predominated, are often favourable to heroic poetry. However scarce are food and liquor, however harsh the invaders, songs can be sung if there is a bare minimum of shelter and village life; indeed they can be sung among refugee bands in the mountain retreats, as among the Greek Klephts; for songs about the heroic past keep alive some kind of pride and self-respect. The noblemen may have perished, the houses may be poor and the pottery ungainly, but the singer can still repeat and improvise songs; and he may do so as well against this kind of background as in the *megaron* of a royal patron. C. M. Bowra went even further:

we may surmise that the most important contribution made by this period was the formation of a belief in a heroic age. The waste and wreckage in Greece were so enormous that men must have turned back to the not-too-distant past and seen in its power and splendour something utterly alien to their own experience...From this sense of departed glory and the imaginations which it bred the Dark Age gave to the Greeks the conception of a heroic past, and to their poetry some of its most special qualities.[23]

In spite of the pioneering work of H. M. and N. K. Chadwick and its continuation by Bowra, practically no detailed attention has yet been given to the relationship between a heroic age and its aftermath. H. M. Chadwick did wonders in formulating the idea of the heroic age, but it nevertheless seems probable that much of what he meant by such an age really belongs to the centuries that follow it. Indeed our knowledge of such ages, which are usually illiterate or largely so, tends to be derived almost entirely from subsequent oral poetry. Court-poetry is undoubtedly a common phenomenon in a heroic period; but H. M. Chadwick assumed that since there are no references to court minstrels in post-heroic Teutonic and Anglo-Saxon poetry, therefore the poetry of the age of decline in the seventh century A.D. must have been non-creative.[24] This I think is a doubtful inference, especially in view of the Russian and Yugoslav

[23] *Homer and his Forerunners* (Edinburgh, 1955), p. 28.
[24] *The Heroic Age* (Cambridge, 1912), p. 89; see also p. 10 above.

material. Court-poetry is an important but not the only kind of creative oral verse. It is envisaged in the peace-time conditions of the *Odyssey*, although Phemius and Demodocus may well reflect Ionian conditions rather than those of the Bronze Age; here the invention of the early Dark Ages can be excluded. It may be significant that the Achaean princes, according to the *Iliad*, took no singers with them to Troy. In any case court-poetry, regional and panegyric as it is, may often be the *basis* of a tradition which, developing through generations of material and political decay, both defines and inflates the memory of a great king or a great campaign.

Bowra distinguished three classes of heroic oral poetry: pastoral or primitive, aristocratic, and proletarian (for which 'popular' may be a simpler substitute). The first type cannot be traced in Greece, though it is exemplified for instance by much of the Kara-Kirghiz poetry. The Greek epic is seen in aristocratic surroundings in Ithaca and Phaeacia, while the Hesiod of *Works and Days*, at least, and the poet of the *Hymn to Apollo* who sings to the Ionians at Delos, exemplify the popular singer. Many Homeric critics, however, have been obsessed with the idea that the developing Greek epic is essentially court-poetry; while others have envisaged the religious festival as the occasion most likely to produce a monumental poem. One must be careful to distinguish the circumstances in which a *monumental* epic might be sung from those of its shorter and more normal predecessors. That is why I should like to stress popular poetry of aristocratic content but un-aristocratic and informal audience, village-poetry in fact, as a possible and indeed probable component of the Greek heroic tradition in its earliest post-Mycenaean stage. There are many parallels from other cultures to show that this kind of poetry may not be inferior to the wholly aristocratic type either in skill or in complexity. This is why the exclusive emphasis on Athens in the Dark Age is misleading. In the history of a national oral tradition the audience and the social status of the singer may easily change; there is nothing to prevent aristocratic poetry becoming first popular in the most informal sense, and then more organized as festival poetry. Until the time when the singer becomes a mere reproducer or uninventive rhapsode his methods and interests remain fairly constant, whatever his background. Thus oral poetry based on the battle of Kosovo was at first sung to upper-class audiences, but later, as conditions worsened under Turkish rule, the oral narrative became a proletarian amusement. In this case its subject-matter tended to become less aristocratic, and Marko Kraljević developed as a new popular hero with many proletarian characteristics. That is not a necessary consequence, however, and conservation of aristocratic material depends on the richness and scope of that material and also on whether the post-heroic period provides a new heroic subject like guerrilla warfare.

Which elements in the Homeric poems show any special signs of poetical composition in the Dark Age? The answer to this question is bound by the nature of the evidence to be disappointing. Certain cultural characteristics obviously belong to the early centuries of the Iron Age: for example the pair of throwing-spears or the limited use of iron as a metal still rare but no longer precious. Yet neither these nor the absence of reference to writing can be necessarily assigned to the eleventh or tenth century rather than to the ninth – although the eighth at least is usually excluded by the developed formular expression of such ideas, if by nothing else. Again we may suspect certain details of military and social organization – the phratries of *Iliad*, 2, 362f.[25] and the curious position of Penelope in Ithaca – of being coloured by Dark-Age customs; but we certainly cannot prove it. The odd conception of the use of chariots that permeates the *Iliad* – where with three or four exceptions the chariot is merely a means of heroic transport to and from the point of fighting – may represent a Dark-Age perversion of a Mycenaean tradition, a tradition which cannot in any case have been a very detailed or explicit one; but again we cannot be sure that the perversion took place in the eleventh or tenth rather than the ninth century, although we may think it highly probable.

The evidence of language is equally equivocal, especially in an obviously archaistic tradition. It does not easily reveal whether a certain form, phrase, line or passage was created in the depths of the Dark Age, or at a later stage when the epic was undergoing a new phase of expansion in Asia Minor. Comparative dialect-geography makes it probable that most irresolvable contractions, including some 800 Homeric cases of -ου genitives that cannot be replaced by -οο or -οι’, together with most integral omissions of digamma, must have originated after about 1000 B.C. This shows that very many formular phrases in Homer were created or finally fixed after the

[25] A. Andrewes, *Hermes* 89 (1961), 129ff.

Mycenaean period and the early part of the Dark Age. That is no more than one would expect. It does not enable any precise estimate to be made of how many formulas were already fixed by around 1000 or 950, particularly since the conservative oral tradition preserved many old usages, although with no special consistency. This archaistic tendency restricts the evidential precision even of those few phrases to which an -oo form has to be restored, like Ἰλίοο προπάροιθε (e.g. 15, 66): although it may be said with some plausibility that -oo is post-Mycenaean and pre-contraction, and therefore Dark Age in its use *in ordinary speech*. As for the evidence of dialect, there can be little doubt that most of the predominant Ionian colouring of the poems is due to the final and most powerful stage of the epic tradition in Ionia itself, where the monumental poems were constructed and much new invention and adaptation carried out. The crucial point is the origin of the distinctively Aeolic forms. If Aeolic is a development of North-Mycenaean speech, as Ionic of South-Mycenaean, as Ernst Risch has persuasively argued, then the apparently mainland-Aeolic part of the Homeric dialect-mixture (notably ποτί and -μεν infinitives) may have established itself in the epic tradition before the Aeolic and Ionic migrations.[26] The mainland-Aeolic quality of certain important episodes and characters in the *Iliad*, notably of course Achilles, was emphasized by Bethe and cannot be ignored simply because many of Bethe's conclusions have not been accepted. It seems quite probable that oral poetry about the Trojan war flourished in Thessaly and Boeotia before the eastward migrations, and much of the Achaean Catalogue, whatever the form and degree of its Mycenaean content, was presumably a product of this poetry. Page wrote of the Old Aeolic remnants in Homer that 'it is very improbable that these first made their way into the formular language of the Epic after the diaspora which followed the Dorian occupation of Hellas'.[27] He is here thinking once more of the horror of great darkness, and he may be right: though he may not. A diaspora may be just what is needed to explain certain aspects of the dialect-mixture in Homer, and the kinds of contact between predominantly Ionic and predominantly Aeolic poetry about the Trojan war that are required to account for the *Iliad* may as well have been provided by racial contacts in Attica,

[26] *Museum Helveticum* 12 (1955), 61ff.
[27] *History and the Homeric Iliad*, p. 266.

Thessaly and Boeotia in the first part of the Dark Age as by later contacts overseas – or rather, I do not see why we should not envisage the possibility of both. At all events the absence from Homer of Doric and North-West-Greek forms does not necessarily or even probably tell against the hypothesis.

The truth is that too much still lies in darkness, although not therefore in disgrace. What I have tried to do is to rehabilitate the early post-Mycenaean period as a *possible* setting for important phases in the development of the Greek epic tradition. The possibility of Mycenaean narrative poetry cannot be rejected and should not be undervalued. The strongest argument for it is still that the dactylic hexameter appears fully-developed even in apparently obsolete formulas that must go back some considerable way in the tradition. Certainly there was a strong Mycenaean *narrative* tradition. How prominent a part was played therein by poetry is something about which it is still precarious to conjecture. At least, however, the early part of the Dark Age reveals signs that communal life was not entirely interrupted; and it is important to remain aware, against the old-fashioned assumption that all oral heroic poetry is court-poetry, that there were opportunities then for informal oral composition – which may have been particularly important in the isolation of the Trojan campaign as the heroic endeavour *par excellence* – even outside Athens.

3

WAR AND THE WARRIOR
IN THE HOMERIC POEMS

It is sometimes hard to resist the temptation of viewing the 'Homeric world' as a real one, possessing a simple historical value of its own. The truth is, of course, that the epic is to an important extent *fictitious* – more than that, it is fiction that contains contributions from different periods over a span of half a millennium or more. Yet the historian need not altogether despair. In its total complexity the world of the poems bears no exact resemblance to any historical setting in any historical period; yet many of its elements are based on fact and can be assessed in comparison with objective evidence revealed by archaeology. This applies, for example, to weapons and armour. Other and less concrete elements may be judged by the more subjective criteria of intrinsic practicality or probability or relation to known later developments. The result, inevitably, will be conjectural; but it is important to concede that it will not necessarily be equally conjectural in all its aspects, nor will the fictitious elements of the poems be equally distributed between different parts of the whole cultural background. It will be my general contention that warfare is one of the subjects on which the poems, and particularly of course the *Iliad*, are likely to be not completely misleading.[1]

There are reasons for believing that the *Iliad*, substantially as we possess it, was composed during the second half of the eighth century B.C., while the *Odyssey* (which seems for the most part to be slightly the later of the two) cannot be brought down many years, if any, below about 700 B.C.[2] As always with traditional or semi-traditional poems these chronological estimates are equivocal. We are dealing with poems which present a largely unknowable mixture of archaism and innovation, in which a legendary core of information stretching back into the late Bronze Age itself has been

---

[1] This represents a qualified adjustment of the view I expressed e.g. in *The Songs of Homer* (Cambridge, 1962), p. 39; the reasons will be given in what follows.

[2] For a recent summary of the evidence see *The Songs of Homer*, pp. 282–7.

accreted, distorted, elaborated and transformed over many generations of singers.

For the separation of historical elements in this amalgam we rely
on two objective criteria – archaeological and linguistic – and on a
quite distinct and much more personal criterion of practical
possibility, general plausibility and so on. This involves, among
other things, one's view of the whole trend of historical development from the Bronze to the Iron Age. Even the archaeological
criterion has both a narrower and a broader application. In the
former it is restricted to the assessment of individual objects – which,
it must be remembered, can be quite accurately described even in
the course of a generally unhistorical narrative. In its broader aspect
it extends to matters like the nature and distribution of fortified sites,
which are less restricted in their implications and may reflect on the
historical probability of whole sections of narrative.

The broader criteria will be used later; I consider here the
archaeological criterion in its narrower and more obvious sense. The
discovery of weapons or armour in datable contexts (mostly graves)
enables Homeric descriptions to be rated for accuracy, degree of
conflation and date of original observation – the observation, that
is, which was the ultimate source of the surviving poetical description. When Odysseus borrows from Meriones a boar's-tusk helmet
that is unique in Homer, and moreover is specified as an heirloom,[3]
we know that a piece of Achaean armour, and one that probably
passed out of use even before the time of the attack on Troy, is being
described; and that this description must be based on a very long
and in this case accurate tradition stretching back in some form into
the Bronze Age itself. The same is so with Ajax's great tower-like
shield, which is an exception and a rarity even for Homer.[4] On the
other hand when warriors are equipped, as quite often in the *Iliad*,
with a pair of javelins or throwing spears then it is probable that the
description, or at least the initial observation that gave rise to it,
belongs to the Iron rather than the Bronze Age – possibly to a period
as late as the eighth century B.C., when representations on Geometric
pots of warriors with twin spears become quite common. Yet the
poems describe thrusting-spears also (like Achilles' great Pelian

[3] *Iliad* 10, 261ff. – From now on book-numbers will refer to the *Iliad* unless the
Odyssey is specified.
[4] E.g. 7, 219ff. See works cited in n. 2 on p. 22 above.

ash-spear),[5] and preserve a tradition of Achaean armament towards the end of the Bronze Age. Indeed the monumental poet, and possibly some of his predecessors, seem insensitive to the distinction, and Paris and Menelaus are imagined in their duel as having now a thrusting-spear, now one or two throwing-spears.[6]

Objects are relatively simple. With customs, attitudes and beliefs not directly reflected in the material culture the possibilities of confusion in the tradition remain outside the scope of the archaeological criterion. Occasionally, but only occasionally, the linguistic criterion can help. Its value lies rather in the establishment of general truths about the length and complexity of the tradition than in the solving of particular problems. The poems are partly composed of standardized phrases, sorted and perfected in the course of the oral tradition and used as basic narrative tools even by the most imaginative of poets. Often these formulas were adapted to new linguistic or dialectal developments, but sometimes metre made that impossible or undesirable and the archaic language was retained. Occasionally this shows up in obscure terminology like αὐλῶπις τρυφάλεια (13, 530, of a helmet), but more often the distant origins of the poetical tradition reveal themselves in the persistence of old speech-habits like the retention of the effects of the obsolete semivowel digamma. Conversely the regular ignoring of digamma, together with the post-Bronze-Age habit of contraction and the increasing use of *v*-movable for essential rhythmical purposes, distinguish other expressions as relatively newer in the tradition.[7] Unfortunately the mixture has usually been so thorough that even when a phrase can be approximately dated, or given a fixed terminus *post* or *ante*, it cannot be held to implicate even its most immediate surroundings, let alone a whole passage or episode. Moreover these linguistic changes are very hard to date (although some linguists tend to be optimistic on this point), and their effects are erratic owing to the conservative and often archaizing nature of the oral tradition as a whole. In few cases does the linguistic criterion directly and specifically affect passages dealing with warfare, except insofar as old weapons or armour are described in recognizably old

---

[5] E.g. 16, 140ff.

[6] Cf. 3, 18f., 338f., 346–55 with 361, 379f.

[7] On contraction and digamma see P. Chantraine, *Grammaire homérique* 1 (Paris, 1953), ch. 3; *The Songs of Homer*, pp. 196–9. On *v*-movable see A. Hoekstra, *Homeric Modifications of Formulaic Prototypes* (Amsterdam, 1965), especially pp. 88ff.

language (for example φάσγανον ἀργυρόηλον, as well as the τρυφάλεια mentioned above). Conversely apparent Bronze Age objects or tactics may be described in language of which parts are relatively modern (as with the boar's-tusk helmet and Nestor's cup, or Nestor's reference to old chariot tactics).[8] These remind us that even detectably archaic elements in the cultural background of Homer have been affected by the process of transmission.

One further methodological difficulty remains. Suppose we can sort out, here and there, Homeric descriptions of martial practices and attitudes that can be connected with a particular historical period: are we entitled, even so, to use those descriptions as historical evidence? For the *Iliad* and *Odyssey*, even apart from problems of conflation and the oral tradition, are *poetry*, and into this poetry entered a great deal of quite unhistorical fantasy. The fantasy is exemplified most startlingly in the different kinds of divine intervention. Not only are nearly all the main changes of fortune in the poems determined by divine decisions reached in imaginary conclave on Ida or Olympus, but individual acts of prowess are normally the result of inspiration or actual physical regeneration by a god. Athena or Apollo lightens the limbs of Diomedes or Hector and fills him with *menos*, martial valour and sheer physical strength. The gods do more spectacular and concrete things than that: Ares kills a man in battle, Aphrodite breaks Paris's helmet-strap, Poseidon flips Aeneas through the air out of reach of Achilles, Patroclus is knocked out of his senses and stripped of his armour by an invisible Apollo to become an easy victim for Euphorbus and Hector.[9] In cases like these the gods are not mere hypostatizations of human feelings, they are independent but supernatural participants in the war. Can we take *this* kind of warfare seriously, then? Does not this element of fantasy – which infects the *Odyssey*, too, both in the folk-tale adventures of Odysseus and in his protection by Athena – imply that the historical substratum of the poems, whatever it was, has been totally and irretrievably overlaid? Fortunately, as I believe, it implies nothing so drastic. There are frequent portions of both poems, involving thousands of different incidents, in which the gods play no part and others in which they act as human beings; in which, moreover, the composer's intention is unmistakably realistic. The

---

[8] Cup, 11, 632ff.; chariots, 4, 303–9; cf. Hoekstra, *Homeric Modifications*, p. 141.
[9] 5, 841–4; 3, 374f.; 20, 325–7; 16, 787ff.

43

result is still poetry, but even poetry *can* convey historical information, and frequently does so both in oral and in literate traditions. In short, there is really no reason why the *Iliad*'s taste for divine assemblies and kindred matters (a taste that may be partly that of the monumental poet himself) should discredit the multitudinous factual passages.

The initial reservations have been set out; how far can we now proceed? It might be expected that the poems could tell us something about such diverse subjects as the attack on Troy in general, other forms of warfare practised in the period down to 700 B.C., the constitution of the Achaean army, strategy and tactics, and the details of man-to-man fighting in terms of weapons and defensive armour. More important still, the poems might be expected to reveal, for one or more historical periods, the *attitudes of men* to war and its consequences.

Some of these expectations will certainly not be fulfilled, others can only be met in terms of probabilities. One expectation can be disposed of straight away. In spite of all the detailed descriptions applied in the poems to weapons and armour, it is doubtful whether Homer can now resolve any of the questions left unanswered by archaeology. The introduction of the cut-and-thrust sword or the throwing-spear used in war; the chronology and origins of different helmet-types; the frequency of bronze armour, especially breast-plates and greaves, in the late Bronze Age; the armament of the early Iron Age; whether the war-chariot and the bow really fell virtually out of use in Greece from the end of the Bronze Age down to the eighth century – for these and other questions concerning the date, construction and viability of shields, ships or chariots the poems are of little further help. Obviously they have been useful in the past for the identification and interpretation of finds, but beyond this they are vitiated by those qualities of an oral tradition on which I have already dwelt – by conflation, distortion, misunderstanding, inaccurate archaization or undetected innovation. Thus it is clear from the LH II/IIIA tomb at Dendra that bronze breast-plates *were* known in the Achaean age[10] and that the references to them in the *Iliad* are not anachronistic (although they may still exaggerate the commonness of such armour); but more is now revealed by that one

---

[10] Cf. e.g. P. Courbin in J.-P. Vernant (ed.), *Problèmes de la guerre en Grèce ancienne* (Paris, 1968), p. 78.

discovery than can ever be worked out from the undoubtedly confused information in the poem. At the same time the inability of the poems to supply further *independent* light on armour and weapons does not mean that what they tell us of such things has to be historically discounted. Obviously not; it has to be interpreted in the light of the objective controls, and then re-evaluated as one part of the total picture of warfare presented in the oral tradition.

The late Bronze Age in Greece has been known since the last century as a Heroic Age.[11] More strictly it is the possible Bronze Age elements *in Homer* that qualify for that title. The material remains by themselves would reveal little of the society and *ethos* that W. P. Ker, H. M. Chadwick and others provisionally defined, and the administrative and economic life suggested by the Linear B tablets might be held to be directly incompatible with them. I shall have more to say on the tablets below, but in any case it is easy to be too glib with the idea of Heroic Ages, and some elements of the accepted picture are certainly wrong. In its broad lines, however, the concept is still useful. Chadwick for example believed that the ideals, way of life and material surroundings envisaged in the early Teutonic epic had much in common with Homer, and also that the Norse sagas and the Anglo-Saxon and Celtic traditions revealed surprisingly similar characteristics. He concluded that social, material and political factors could coalesce in the development of separate cultures to produce for a time aristocratic and militaristic societies of remarkable consistency. An important by-product of these societies was the oral narrative poetry (or, occasionally, formalized prose saga) through which their memory had survived. Further reflection has suggested that the poetical picture is usually developed, in something like its surviving fullness, in a subsequent period of decline.[12] Therefore certain heroic characteristics – for example superhuman strength, exaggerated sense of honour, sublime resignation to fate – may owe their prominence as much to the universal effects of nostalgic memory in an age of decay as to any precise and historical similarity of feelings in different martial epochs. Con-

[11] W. P. Ker, *Epic and Romance*, 2nd ed. (London, 1908); H. M. Chadwick, *The Heroic Age* (Cambridge, 1912). The theory is developed in H. M. and N. K. Chadwick, *The Growth of Literature* (3 vols., Cambridge, 1932–40).

[12] See e.g. C. M. Bowra, *Homer and his Forerunners* (Edinburgh, 1955), p. 28; G. S. Kirk, *The Songs of Homer*, pp. 132–8; and p.10 above.

versely, un-heroic details like the administrative system revealed by the Linear B tablets may be forgotten or suppressed. In short, the idea of a Heroic Age may be to an important extent a 'literary' crystallization rather than a direct and lifelike reflection of an actual historical period.

That is important, and must never be allowed to slip out of sight. Yet it does not mean that the historical value of the poems has to be equally depreciated in every aspect. To take a simple example, we would expect a 'heroic' poem to be inaccurate in its estimate of what size of boulder can be lifted and thrown in battle; but that does not entail that it is equally inaccurate in its description of a sword that was broken just before, or of the warlike emotions of the hero. Similarly, so it seems to me, with the Linear B tablets. Certainly I am on the side of those who hold that there was a major cultural break at the end of the Greek Bronze Age. The singers of the Homeric tradition had very little conception of the realities of life in an Achaean town or palace, in terms at least of its administration, economic structure, religious practices or social hierarchy. Moreover it seems probable that comparatively little in the way of Achaean narrative poetry survived the era of collapse, and that the memory of the late Bronze Age came down to a large extent in loose reminiscences of the survivors and their sons, to be crystallized in poetry in the so-called Dark Age.[13] In that way a great deal of the past was lost – but particularly those aspects that seemed least relevant to a present which had, as we suspect, no palaces, very few large and stratified communities and little wealth; in which a new way of life, a new economy and a new social structure were being worked out in scattered settlements among some new and uncomfortable neighbours. In *those* circumstances the over-elaborate and retrospectively tedious aspects of the world of the tablets would be totally irrelevant and soon overlooked. What was most carefully preserved, on the contrary, might naturally be what it was in comparable circumstances at other times and places – the comforting memory of successful and glorious ancestors and their last great national exploit around the walls of Troy. In short, as a guide to the sociological details of daily peace-time life in their ostensible period the *Iliad* and the *Odyssey* are in all probability lamentably deficient. As a guide to the practice of warfare and the warrior's ideology in the late Bronze

[13] See pp. 19ff.

46

Age they deserve to be taken much more seriously. With that in mind we can proceed to consider the information they offer.

Martial prowess and personal pride are the outstanding heroic qualities in the *Iliad* as in the *Nibelungenlied*. Achilles is the archetypal hero; his invincibility as a warrior is matched by his sensitivity to affront and his unwillingness to compromise his rights. Like other Achaean leaders (although Thersites provides an exception) he receives absolute loyalty and obedience from his own contingent. Between different contingents there may be tensions, but these arise from personal clashes between the leaders; and Agamemnon's special position as ἄναξ produces its own stresses. The obligation owed him and Menelaus by the other kings, βασιλῆες, is not explained. Legend rationalizes with the story of an oath of support taken by all Helen's suitors;[14] a truer clue is afforded by the formalized obligations of guests and hosts, the elaborate system of gifts and counter-gifts, which transcended the boundaries of the Achaean states and are hinted at in many incidental details in the poems.[15] Almost every Achaean centre is envisaged as sending a contingent, and a nobleman could only avoid service by paying a fine or making a personal gift to Agamemnon; although a large family might be allowed to contribute only one representative.[16] The situation is compatible both with the apparent cultural similarity and political independence of the main Achaean settlements as revealed by excavation and with the complex family connections suggested by myth. The king of Mycenae, Homer's 'Mycenae of much gold', was accepted as paramount leader, and Mycenae's physical impregnability in the thirteenth century B.C., together with its chain of presumably allied or subsidiary fortresses in the Argolid,[17] its domination of the rich plain and its control of the routes southward and over the Isthmus confirm both its exceptional power and its capability of maintaining wealth. The Homeric geography of Achaean Greece, in spite of incompatibilities between the Catalogue and the rest of the *Iliad*, has been shown by archaeological survey to

---

[14] Hesiod, frag. 204 M-W, lines 78–87; cf. *Iliad* 2, 286–8.

[15] M. I. Finley, *The World of Odysseus* (London, 1972), ch. 4.

[16] 13, 669, 23, 296f.; 24, 397–400; H. Jeanmaire, *Couroi et Courètes* (Lille and Paris, 1939), pp. 61ff.

[17] I accept the argument that the geographical proximity of Argos, Tiryns and Midea to Mycenae entails that they must have been somehow allied to Mycenae. Cf. D. L. Page, *History and the Homeric Iliad* (Berkeley, 1959), pp. 129ff.

be historical in substance. The suggested relations of kings and contingents are feasible, although they are not objectively confirmed. The nobles, the ἀριστῆες, fought because of their obligation to their king, and the kings fought because of their obligations to Agamemnon and perhaps Menelaus. Yet each demanded a return in the form of γέρα, rights or privileges, both as material (a fixed share of booty obtained or to come) and as τιμή or honour, manifested in proper respect from their equals and inferiors, by tactful invitations from Agamemnon to feast at the royal table and, for the leaders of the largest contingents or those who particularly distinguished themselves in war or debate, by membership of the βουλή or advisory council.

All these motives and relationships are mentioned in the *Iliad* and paralleled in the military and aristocratic structure of other Heroic Ages. Yet the simplifying and heroizing effects of tradition are suggested by the probable impoverishment of the Achaean palaces at the time of the attack on Troy. The real cause of any Achaean coalition at this stage was likely to be the hope of substantial gain in the form of gold, horses, women or slaves – and this practical aspect of the γέρας is likely to have been at least as important as the γέρας as τιμή. This is something the *Iliad* suppresses, as when Achilles is at pains to say that he does not need the gifts offered by Agamemnon, that his family estates in Phthia are adequate for all his needs.[18] The importance of wealth is more frankly emphasized in the *Odyssey*, where Odysseus' concern for the Phaeacian gifts and the fate of his κτήματα at home is strongly emphasized.[19]

In the *Iliad* the hero's extroverted desire for victory and honour is combined with a curious resignation to fate.

Grieve not for me too much in your heart, for no man shall hurl me down to Hades beyond my fate. But his destiny has none of men escaped, neither base man nor nobleman, when once he is born. But you go home and look after your own tasks, the loom and the shuttle, and bid the maidservants go about their work. Warfare shall be the care of men – of all men who are in Ilios, but most of all of me.[20]

These are Hector's words of comfort to Andromache, but in his heart he foresees her impending widowhood and captivity. Yet, later, heroic pride and optimism take control and persuade him to remain outside the fortress for the last and fatal encounter with Achilles.

[18] 9, 398ff.   [19] E.g. *Od.*, 13, 40–2, 215f.; 11, 178.   [20] 6, 486–93.

He resists his parents' entreaties from the walls – toys for a moment with the idea of retreat but is deterred by αἰδώς, by shame at the thought of reproach from Polydamas and the other Trojans and by a feeling of guilt about his decision to press the attack on the Achaean camp.[21] He considers, too, trying to treat with Achilles, but soon sees that this is impossible, for Achilles is ruthless. And so he stays until Achilles draws close, when he panics and runs. For even the best of fighters can panic; it is a god-sent fear, of which a hero of proved valour need not feel ashamed. Finally Hector stands his ground, deluded by a god, and his doom is sealed. Even then he tries to ensure that his body, if he is defeated, shall not be mutilated. This obsession with the return of one's corpse for proper lamentation and disposal, this horror of mutilation and neglect, admittedly runs through Greek thought down into the classical period at least; but the known Achaean tradition of elaborate royal funerals, exemplified most clearly in the shaft graves and tholos tombs of Mycenae itself, confirms that it was particularly strong in the late Bronze Age.

The actual fight is soon over:[22] Hector dodges Achilles' spear-cast, and his own fails to penetrate Achilles' shield; Hector attacks with his sword, but Achilles has retrieved his spear by divine means and pierces Hector's throat at his ease. He addresses his victim with a jeering arrogance that seems part of the heroic mentality: 'Hector, you must have said when you slew Patroclus that you would be safe, and you took no notice of me since I was far away – fool!...*you* will the dogs and birds tear shamefully apart, but to him the Achaeans will give due burial.'[23] In spite of its elements of divine intervention, this crucial encounter symbolizes a great part of the heroic character. The challenges and insults, the conflict of shame, prudence, ambition and pride, the resignation in defeat and the exultation and arrogance in victory – these may occur in other kinds of warfare in other epochs, but not in combination or nearly so starkly. My own view is that Homer is most likely to have derived them indirectly from the late Bronze Age itself, or at least from the glamourized view of that age that gained currency (as I believe) in its depressed and nostalgic successor. Admittedly the evidence is highly defective; but our knowledge of the early Iron Age, such as it is, suggests that it may have had little to offer in the way of exotic and formalized military behaviour, either in the scattered and depopulated world of Sub-

[21] 22, 99ff.   [22] 22, 273-330.   [23] 22, 331-6.

mycenaean and early Protogeometric Greece or in the following period of gradual rebuilding, colonization and constitutional change. The early Aeolic and Ionian cultures are unlikely to have polluted the tradition in this respect; and so far as we can tell it was only with the new civic and collective conception of warfare, which culminated in the development of hoplite armies, that a distinctive military *ethos*, and one of a very different kind, was reborn.

At times in the *Iliad* something close to generosity, humanity or tenderness intrudes upon the austerity of normal heroic behaviour. The epithet ἤπιος, 'gentle' or 'kind', is firmly rooted in the formular vocabulary, and the quality it represents is therefore unlikely to have been introduced for the first time by the monumental composer at the end of the tradition. Properly it applies to the attitude of a father (for example) to his children; but Hector and Patroclus are distinct from other warriors in manifesting this quality even outside the range of strictly family relationships. Hector was 'gentle' to Helen (although so, as a matter of fact, was the often short-tempered Priam, 'like a father'), and Patroclus is 'kindly', μείλιχος, to Briseis.[24] More remarkably, when Menelaus calls for helpers to save Patroclus' corpse he cries 'now let one remember the gentleness (ἐνηείης) of poor Patroclus; for when he was alive he knew how to be kindly to all men, but now death and destiny overtake him'.[25] In this extension of kindliness to two of the pivotal characters of the large-scale plot I believe we may see the influence of Homer himself, just as the chastened Achilles of the end of the poem seems to reflect a new and not strictly heroic view. This almost chivalrous approach to human relations on the battlefield derives more probably from the environment of eighth-century Ionia than from the historical realities of the late Bronze Age. It has often been suggested, and is probably true, that the oral tradition refined its material of much that was gross and barbarous. At the same time much remains to remind us of the harshness and brutality of warfare as it must have been. I am thinking not of the clinical and almost obsessive description of scores of different wounds, for that is a brilliant dramatic device that often depends as much on poetical imagination as on observation and actuality; but rather of the way in which Achilles savages the dead Hector, or of Hector's own desire to decapitate

[24] 24, 775, 770; 19, 300.
[25] 17, 670–2. See the complementary discussion of these topics on p. 11.

Patroclus and put his head on a stake.[26] Achilles, admittedly, is almost insane after Patroclus' death; but Menelaus does not demur when Agamemnon prevents him from sparing the captured Adrestus and enjoins the slaughter of all male Trojans including embryos.[27] Indeed the singer adds a significant comment, not necessarily a personal one but intended to be in tune with the heroic attitude: 'So saying the hero [sc. Agamemnon] turned his brother's mind, *fittingly dissuading him* (αἴσιμα παρειπών)'.[28]

In the *Odyssey*, likewise, the young prince Telemachus knows very well how to devise a revolting death for disloyal servants, and goes well beyond his father's recommendations.[29] The blood-stained Odysseus rouses a cackle of pure delight in the aged Eurycleia, who is probably right in thinking that Penelope herself would have enjoyed the sight.[30] Heroic mothers were accustomed to such things, and the gentle Hector prays that his son 'may bring home bloody spoils, having slain a foeman, and may his mother rejoice in her heart'.[31] Thus the expurgation, if it happened, was far from complete, and it is hard not to recognize the undertone of ruthlessness and brutality as a relic of a relatively early phase of the whole oral tradition. Moreover it is important not to mistake mere heroic practicality for post-heroic pacifism and doubt. Achilles' passionate speech of rejection to the embassy of *Iliad* 9 has often, perhaps usually, been misinterpreted in this sense. Admittedly Achilles declares that there is no pleasure in always fighting enemies and refuses to take further part in Agamemnon's war.[32] Can this really be heroic, even heroic pique? I believe it can, although no doubt Achilles' fine protest was somewhat elaborated in the course of the tradition. It is because Achilles has been robbed of his γέρας, and for this reason alone, that he questions the war. He does not dismiss warfare as such, but he dismisses it for himself in those circumstances. When he asks at 9, 337f. why the Argives must fight the Trojans, his answer is not 'for no good reason at all', but 'because of Helen', and is part of an argument to the effect that, if women matter so much to the Atreidae, then Agamemnon should have respected Achilles' right to Briseis (for whom Achilles expresses a somewhat surprising

---

[26] 22, 395ff., 18, 176f.
[27] 6, 55ff.
[28] 6, 62.
[29] *Od.* 22, 462ff., cf. 443.
[30] *Od.* 22, 408, 23, 1, 47f.
[31] 6, 480f.
[32] 9, 316ff.

fondness). Thus neither of the two great scenes in which the war and Agamemnon's leadership are questioned – for the Thersites episode must be added to Achilles' speech – is really anti-heroic, or need be envisaged as deriving from a time when the heroic attitude to war was being remodelled on more humane lines. Thersites' protest is actuated by pure malice, Achilles' by the knowledge of a serious affront to his dignity and the realization that his material rewards did not match his services.

There must always, in the nature of things, be some uncertainty about how far the Homeric picture of the Achaean warrior before Troy originated in or soon after the Bronze Age itself. About the war in more general terms, its cause and reality and tactical development, the poems are less detailed and less overtly informative – but more easily checked and supplemented by practical probabilities. Partly, too, we rely on elimination to confirm the poetical tradition in its account of a large-scale war; for on our present knowledge of Greek history in the early Iron Age warfare must have been scattered and local, unlikely to produce contaminating ideas of massed tactics or major siege warfare. If this is true (and it must be remembered how little is known of the establishing of the Greek settlements in Asia Minor, or of wars or skirmishes conducted for example by Athens and represented on its pottery of the late ninth and eighth century B.C.), then nothing resembling the events described in the *Iliad* occurred between the Trojan expedition and the earliest hoplite battles of the seventh century. That would have the advantage of inhibiting *contamination* of the martial tradition stemming from the late Bronze Age, although it would also encourage *misunderstanding* of practices already obsolete. This is indeed what seems to have happened.

In all this I have been anticipating the answer to an important question: was there a Trojan war, a Panachaean attack on Troy, at all? The question has been raised in recent years,[33] in part because of an apparent chronological difficulty. Accepting from the Cincinnati excavators that Troy VI was destroyed by earthquake shortly after 1300 B.C., and that Troy VIIa, which was burned apparently by human agency, is the settlement that qualifies to be

[33] Notably by M. I. Finley, in M. I. Finley, J. L. Caskey, G. S. Kirk and D. L. Page, 'The Trojan War', *JHS* 84 (1964), 1–20. M. I. Finley's contribution is on pp. 1–9; the other contributions express disagreement from different viewpoints.

the one captured by the Achaeans,[34] we must ask ourselves precisely when the VIIa city fell and what was happening elsewhere at the time. The date of the end of Troy VIIa is to be gauged by the latest datable pottery discovered in the ruins of the burned settlement, together with the earliest datable pottery in its VIIb 1 successor. Local Trojan wares are not reliably datable, but Mycenaean imports may be, and the matter depends on the proper assessment of some ninety Mycenaean sherds. In their full publication C. W. Blegen and his collaborators opted for *ca.* 1240–1230 B.C.;[35] but Blegen himself has subsequently moved back to 1250 or even 1260 or 1270.[36] The real question is whether the latest Mycenaean fragments from Troy VIIa are to be placed in the middle, or at the end, of the LH IIIB style. To some expert eyes they have appeared to belong to the end of the style, or even in one or two cases to LH IIIC. If so, then Troy may have been captured around 1200 B.C. In that case, of course, it fell at the very time when the Achaean palaces themselves, most dramatically Pylos, were under severe and often final attack. It has been suggested, therefore, that the burning of Troy cannot have been the work of the disintegrating Achaeans, but must have been part of the wave of destruction caused by the 'Land and Sea Raiders' who swept down through Syria into Egypt around 1190 B.C. after an initial probe a generation earlier. Certainly the whole Near East was disrupted by northern invaders and local malcontents at the turn of the thirteenth and twelfth centuries: should not the fall both of Troy and of Pylos be seen as part of this general movement? In that case, what of the Homeric tradition of an Achaean attack on Troy? It must be abandoned, or seen as a fictitious embroidery, perhaps on the basis of a few Achaean buccaneers who attached themselves to a primarily northern horde.

Such a view would gravely damage the credibility of Homer as a source for Achaean war and warfare; but it is improbable that the view is correct. It is true that there is no conclusive archaeological evidence that the enemies who sacked Troy VIIa were Achaeans. Essentially the historicity of the Trojan war, in the sense of a super-ficially successful Panachaean attack on Troy, depends on the

[34] C. W. Blegen *et al.*, *Troy III* (Princeton, 1953), p. 18 (destruction of Troy VI); *Troy IV* (Princeton, 1958), pp. 9, 12 (destruction of Troy VIIa).

[35] *Troy IV*, p. 12 (1240); cf. p. 9 (Furumark's *ca.* 1230, with leeway).

[36] E.g. C. W. Blegen, *Troy and the Trojans* (London, 1963), pp. 160, 163, 174.; for a more sceptical reaction see M. I. Finley, *Proc. Brit. Acad.* 60 (1974), 394 and 405 f.

Homeric tradition. One must ask oneself, therefore, whether this entire tradition can have been almost wholly wrong – whether the possible participation of a few Achaeans in a non-Greek force could have been blown up, in the course of centuries, into Agamemnon's army of the *Iliad*. My own view, and that of the majority, is that it could not. This view is based on the relative accuracy of many parts of the Homeric tradition, where it can be checked, and on a comparison with the type and extent of distortion that other oral traditions display.[37] As for the pottery evidence, it seems that the stylistic distinctions between the late phases of LH IIIB and the earliest IIIC cannot be pressed at all hard; so that to insist on a date of around 1200 B.C., as against around 1230, is not justifiable. At the same time the effort to put the fall of Troy well into the first half of the thirteenth century does not seem warranted. If that effort is influenced by the feeling that more than a single generation must have intervened between the expedition to Troy and the collapse of Pylos and many other Achaean palaces,[38] then the case is even weaker; for a great deal can happen in a single generation, even outside an atomic age. Admittedly, if the Trojan expedition took place only a single generation or so before disaster struck at the Achaean empire, that is significant for the whole motive of the attack and for the aims and morale of the men who engaged in it. In this case – and there are other reasons in favour of the theory – the Trojan war is to be seen as an unsuccessful attempt to restore a failing empire, to restock empty store-rooms and a declining labour force, rather than as the confident and autocratic gesture the *Iliad* implies; and its traditional length, and the stories in the *Odyssey* of the Returns of its main participants, reveal it as a costly failure in terms of real gain.

Is the idea of a Panachaean coalition feasible, if the Achaean world really was in a state of decline? Probably, in any event, the coalition was exaggerated. It is hardly conceivable that virtually every Achaean town (with notable exceptions in the central Aegean islands) should have contributed a contingent. The Catalogue of Ships, authentic as many of its geographical details may be, need

[37] See the contributions by D. L. Page and myself to the discussion cited in n. 33.

[38] As with Blegen, *Troy and the Trojans*, p. 163, and also V. R. d'A. Desborough, *The Last Mycenaeans and their Successors* (Oxford, 1964), p. 220 *ad fin.*

not be an actual list of participants in this particular operation. Just as the numbers of those involved in the fighting are vastly exaggerated, both in the Achaean totals of the Catalogue and in the total of 50,000 men given for the Trojans and their allies at the end of *Iliad* 8, so may the scope of participation on the Achaean side have been greatly expanded in the course of an essentially magnifying and heroizing tradition. This sort of thing is, in fact, just what one would expect of oral poetry. The possibility remains, I suppose, that the idea of an inter-Achaean force (rather than one composed of contingents of those directly involved, namely from Mycenae and its dependencies and Lacedaemon and its immediate allies in Laconia) is due to poetical embroidery. The coalition idea was certainly not new, whether or not it was historical; the Argonautic expedition from Iolcus and the mainly Peloponnesian Seven against Thebes existed as conceivable prototypes. It is quite probable that the idea of a vast united expedition appealed to singers for its own sake, as a means of making their subject more imposing and giving it a less regional appeal. One may nevertheless doubt whether the historical events which, however small and relatively unimportant they may have been, surely underlay even the Argonauts and the Seven, were events that only concerned a single Achaean city. The feasibility of joint operations in the Achaean world is something we cannot properly estimate, but at least there are strong indications from the Linear B tablets from Knossos, Pylos and Mycenae that the palaces had organizational links over a long period; and the homogeneity of Achaean material culture, especially in the thirteenth century, might imply a degree of political as well as cultural unity.[39] According to the tradition, too, the kings of the various centres were closely connected with each other by kinship and marriage, and so would have found it easy to co-operate (as well, on occasion, as to quarrel); the stratification of status on the basis of wealth would have made alliances comparatively easy to organize.

The gathering of a large force from several different centres must have been a problem, and the tale of the delay to the fleet at Aulis and the sacrifice of Iphigeneia may reflect more mundane difficulties which were actually encountered. There is no need for strict logic in the choice of assembly-point, but even so Aulis seems rather unsatisfactory. It was too far from the geographical centre of the

---

[39] Desborough, *ibid.*, p. 219.

Achaean world to be convenient for a preliminary assessment of forces available, while for a more advanced rendezvous it was on the wrong side of the Euripus. The Euripus has six tides a day and currents of five knots and above, and its intervals of still water are very brief and often unpredictable.[40] The passage of even so few as a hundred ships – and we can hardly imagine a total force of less – would take at least a day or two, and necessitate a new gathering place, like Halos, to the north of the narrows. But the crucial point of assembly would be close to the coastland of Troy. The Achaean ships could not arrive on the Trojan shore piece-meal, nor could they have sailed across the north Aegean in convoy. They must have met somewhere close to Troy, but safe from attack – not in Tenedos according to the *Iliad* (for that was to be sacked later by Achilles),[41] but in Lemnos, which is most clearly indicated at 8, 230. A post-Homeric tradition to the effect that the Achaeans first attacked Teuthrania by mistake may equally reflect the difficulties of a concerted landfall on distant and hostile shores.[42]

The idea of a mass landing on the Scamander plain is quite acceptable in practical terms. However, according to the *Iliad* it was only in the tenth year that the Achaeans had to build a wall and trench round their beached ships, and this motif is precipitately introduced and erratically maintained in our poem. Thucydides (1, 11) thought the ships must have been defended from their first landing, and he must be right. Stores need not have been brought in great profusion, since the rich Trojan plain itself would provide enough to live on. Sheep, goats and crops could not be completely defended by an army based inside or around the fortress of Troy. Horses, too, may have fallen into Achaean hands from the surrounding district, which by the evidence of formular Trojan epithets in the *Iliad* was famous for horse-rearing. Certainly the transport of large numbers of horses by ship across the Aegean would have been formidable; and that the Achaeans had a considerable number of chariots before Troy is suggested by the Homeric tradition itself, by the likelihood that the Trojans had chariots, by the availability of chariots on the

---

[40] So e.g. *British Admiralty Mediterranean Pilot* vol. IV (London, 1955), p. 236.

[41] 11, 625 – the implication is surely that this raid occurred once the siege was under way. According to the *Cypria*, however, the Achaeans did gather in Tenedos, and it was there that Philoctetes was bitten: Proclus, *Chrestomathia*, ed. T. W. Allen, *Homeri opera* v, Oxford Classical Texts, p. 104.

[42] Also from the *Cypria*: Proclus, *loc. cit supra*.

Achaean mainland according to the Pylos tablets and by the suit-ability of the terrain round Troy.

Why the Achaeans decided to attack Ilios will never, perhaps, be fully explained; nor will its ability to hold out for any length of time, even if for far less than the ten years of the tradition – although the primitive quality of Greek siege-techniques, even down to the time of Alexander, accounts for a great deal. I have already suggested that the attack was an act, in some respects, of desperation; but I think it may have been precipitated by two special factors (beyond the personal motive offered by the tradition, which cannot be excluded): first the decline of useful trading ties with Troy, suggested by the progressively fewer imported Achaean pots discovered in the latest phase of Troy VI and in the brief life of Troy VIIa;[43] and second, and more important, the knowledge that Troy's impregnability, founded on her massive walls completed in the later centuries of the sixth city, had been diminished by the earthquake that put an end to that long-lived and thriving settlement. That Troy VI was termin-ated by earthquake very soon after 1300 B.C. cannot be doubted. The chronological implications of the imported pottery are, this time, unambiguous; and the toppling of sections of the massive walls, the blocking of streets and the crushing of houses are beyond dispute – and beyond human agency. The walls were certainly repaired by the survivors, although in places the huge fallen blocks were allowed to lie. These survivors were the new inhabitants of Troy VIIa; from now on the fortress was to accommodate not merely the large halls of the king and his family and officials but also the small terraced dwellings of many ordinary townsmen who had previously lived along the ridge and in the plain. Was this crowding within the walls due to some special threat of attack, or was it caused merely by the knowledge that resources were no longer large enough to restore the fortifications to their former strength? The apparent tensions between Troy and the Hittites must have made the Trojans suspicious of incursions from the east; there is no reason to suspect that they particularly feared an Achaean attack, except for the decline in trade already mentioned. At any rate the rumour of the earthquake must have spread far and wide – not because earthquakes were so unusual, but because Troy's walls, especially in their careful finish and appearance, were unique in the Aegean world. Moreover

---

[43] C. W. Blegen *et al.*, *Troy III*, p. 16; *Troy IV*, p. 8.

her wealth, evident even in the treasures of the second city and surely increased during the 600 or 700 years of settled prosperity enjoyed by the sixth, was famous. Was all or most of it dissipated at the time of the earthquake? We cannot tell; but to the Achaeans of the mainland it might well seem that Troy was still rich, although not so rich as before, and now for the first time vulnerable to attack.[44]

How the fortress was actually besieged will again never be known. The general picture given by the *Iliad*, even apart from its exaggeration of time and numbers, is unlikely to be accurate. According to the *Iliad* it was only in the tenth year that the Trojans and their allies sallied far into the plain. Yet the need for supplies must have sent them constantly afield in small numbers, and indeed the poem occasionally envisages this; for Lycaon was captured by Achilles while cutting fig-branches for chariot-rails in one of Priam's orchards by night, and Aeneas was nearly caught by Achilles when with his herds on the foothills of Ida.[45] Achilles on this occasion was on a raiding expedition against Lyrnessus and Pedasus; at other times he had crossed to the islands, and Tenedos and Lesbos are among places he had ravaged – twelve cities by sea and eleven by land according to the hero himself,[46] in 'sleepless nights and bloody days' that won him (or Agamemnon) women and treasure.[47] This tradition of subsidiary raids in and around the Troad is curiously specific and certainly not implausible. Can we believe, on the other hand, that the minor Trojan sallies had never led to a major clash of arms, due perhaps to a hastily-mounted rescue operation from Troy?

The idea of an uninterrupted blockade is difficult in other respects. Neither the heroic mentality nor the heroic system of rewards was well suited to continuous vigilance. Each time booty was brought back into the camp (not to speak of the arrival of wine-ships as at the end of book 7) it presumably had to be apportioned in a careful and time-consuming process at which all the chieftains might insist on

---

[44] There may be a hint in the *Iliad* itself that the destruction of Troy VI was well known: according to 21, 446f. Poseidon had 'built a broad and very beautiful wall for the Trojans around their city, that it might be impregnable'. Laomedon refused to pay the stipulated reward and drove off both Poseidon and Apollo with threats. They are amazingly implied not to have retaliated (21, 456f.); but it is probable that in fuller versions of the story Poseidon, as god of earthquake and tidal wave, destroyed or breached his handiwork in retribution, cf. 7, 445–63.

[45] 21, 35–8; 20, 90–2.   [46] 9, 329f., cf. 128f., 11, 625   [47] 9, 325f.

being present. It is probable, too, that special feasts would follow, and on such occasions as these the Trojans would be free to steal into the plain, gathering food and other supplies. The fuss made over setting a night watch in the tenth book of the *Iliad* may give a hint about the general level of nocturnal security.

As for the fortress itself, the main problem for the historian is its size. Not so small as many surprised modern descriptions suggest, it could still hold few more than 3000 people under siege conditions. It had been extended in Troy VI to accommodate a mere thirty or so free-standing and spacious buildings; Troy VIIa had crammed in a great deal more, filling up in the process many of the 'wide streets' recorded in the Homeric epithet. Significantly, traces of VIIa houses have been found close outside the wall and even straddled across the Eastern gate.[48] It is possible, then, that a maze of small houses clustered round most of the circuit of the walls and provided an outer line of defence; and that people would continue to live in them, even under blockade, to withdraw into the fortress itself only under direct attack. How the fortress finally fell we can hardly conjecture. The story of the Horse is too obscure, and none of the attempts to explain it (for example as a siege-machine) carry much conviction. It might have been a displaced memory of the earthquake that breached Troy VI only a couple of generations before the fall of Troy VIIa; but that is quite uncertain, perhaps improbable. Possibly the death of their greatest fighter did indeed demoralize the Trojans and their allies, as the Homeric tradition implies.

Some organized encounters in the plain there must surely have been, and here the Homeric picture needs careful examination. On the one hand it envisages a massed march-out of troops, great 'ranks', 'columns' or 'phalanxes' (στίχες, πύργοι, φάλαγγες) of anonymous warriors, who clash with the enemy, similarly imagined, all over the battlefield. On the other hand the outcome of the battle is seen as depending primarily on a series of individual encounters between the main chieftains on either side. More explicitly, these chieftains are envisaged as either pairing off in duels, or being filled with might in a spasm of individual and personal triumph over the mass of the enemy. Such ἀριστεῖαι are reserved only for the greatest, for Achilles or Patroclus, Diomedes or Hector, Aeneas or Agamemnon. In these cases the hero is usually inspired by a god, which warns us

[48] C. W. Blegen *et al.*, *Troy IV*, pp. 120–2.

that the bounds of reality are liable to be overstepped. In fact we know that if the main heroes are involved in mass fighting, in which spears are thrust and hurled and arrows shot all over the place, then they cannot be invincible or anything like it. In the *Iliad*, however, minor figures like charioteers – even so famous a one as Hector's Cebriones – fall victim to shots aimed elsewhere, but the greatest heroes never succumb to such accidents. Partly, of course, this is because the singers cannot afford to lose many of their main characters by death, at least before the poem nears its end. Agamemnon, Diomedes, Odysseus, Menelaus, Hector or Glaucus can be temporarily disabled, but it is only Sarpedon and Patroclus, of the greatest figures, who fall, before the death of Hector himself. On the Trojan side the numerous sons of Priam form a useful reservoir of noble but mostly unimportant victims for the predominantly victorious Achaeans.

Poetry has taken its liberties in all this, yet one realistic tactical question remains to be asked. How far was the duel between chieftains, whether formally arranged as the result of a challenge as in the third and seventh books of the *Iliad*, or arising more accidentally out of the confrontations of battle, an important part of actual late Bronze Age warfare? Legend naturally fancies the idea, which recurs in certain semi-historical encounters of later Greek history; but was there any historical reality behind it? Of course, if a war started because of a personal dispute, as the Trojan war is held to have done, then in the event of stalemate a duel between the parties primarily involved, like that between Menelaus and Paris in *Iliad* 3, is one conceivable solution – although it must have been an uncommon one. What, though, of the pairs of heroes engaged in single combat in the midst of a general battle, when the death or flight of the loser tends to fill the whole army with φόβος, the panic desire for flight?

First, it is probable that if a king were killed then his own contingent, at least, would be demoralized and in any case would be obliged to escort the corpse to safety as soon as possible. Thus Sarpedon's companions carry him out of battle when he is wounded at 5, 663f., and his whole Lycian contingent panics and withdraws when it sees him slain and irretrievable at 16, 659f. That kind of loyalty and those burial customs, with that kind of effect on morale, are clearly represented in the *Iliad* and accord well enough with the probable structure and social obligations of the separate contingents. But, beyond that, can the defeat of one man – unless it be an Achilles or a Hector – have so instantly affected the whole army? That is to say, are the scenes of mass fighting in the *Iliad* (with warriors fighting shoulder to shoulder in a manner which makes it hard in two or three cases to resist the idea of infection, at a late stage of the tradition, from the new hoplite tactics) hopelessly exaggerated? Here the question of chariots enters. If chariots – and, perhaps, complete sets of bronze armour – were possessed only by the kings, by which I mean the main leaders of each contingent, then it might have been possible for the few chariots on each side to have brought their occupants into conflict somewhat apart from the infantry *mêlée*. The rôle of the chariot in the *Iliad* is, in any event, a distorted one; I have argued at length elsewhere that horses could not have been brought into the centre of the battle, where they would have been extremely vulnerable, merely to save a nobleman from walking around too much.[49] Either chariots must have been used as a genuine fighting force, as they are remembered by Nestor as having been used in the past, or they were essentially behind-the-lines transport. The latter function is not really very favourable to the heroic-duel type of fighting, and I am inclined to think that the isolation of the main heroes, and their tremendous physical effect on the course of the fighting as a whole, is a poetical device rather than a real and common element of late Bronze Age tactics.

A complementary problem concerns the nature and constitution of what Homer terms the λαός (on which compare the title *ra-wa-ke-ta*, λαγέτας, from the Pylos tablets).[50] The problem has been acutely tackled by Jeanmaire, who concluded that λαὸς 'Αχαιῶν, υἷες 'Αχαιῶν and κοῦροι 'Αχαιῶν are equivalent expressions and imply the whole army; that κοῦρος denotes the noble warrior, the free young man; and that λαός connotes the political community as well as the noble fighting men.[51] Yet I do not believe that the

---

[49] G. S. Kirk, *CAH* 2 (1975), 839f.; *The Songs of Homer*, pp. 124f. J. K. Anderson, *AJA* 69 (1965), 349ff.) has observed that according to Diodorus the people of Britain and Gaul used chariots in a manner superficially similar to that described in Homer. Yet the underlying differences are serious, and nothing that Anderson says removes the impossibility in practical terms of many of the equine circumstances described in the *Iliad*. See now P. A. L. Greenhalgh, *Early Greek Warfare* (Cambridge, 1973), pp. 12–17.

[50] See M. Lejeune in J.-P. Vernant (ed.), *Problèmes de la guerre*, p. 31.

[51] H. Jeanmaire, *Couroi et Courètes*, pp. 26f., 36, 43ff., 54.

solution can be so neat as that, or that, as presented, it is a complete one. There is almost certainly some confusion in the tradition about the possible applications of the term λαός. Most commonly in the *Iliad* it refers to the army, or to a particular contingent of the army, as a collective military unit with no further social or political implications. That is simple enough. Yet there are difficulties in equating the army simply with the κοῦροι envisaged as young noblemen (that is, not βασιλῆες). Twice there is an opposition between λαός and ἡγεμόνες, the leaders. This calls to mind the sharp distinction drawn at 2, 188ff. and 198ff., where Odysseus restrains each βασιλῆα καὶ ἔξοχον ἄνδρα ('king and eminent man') politely, but sets about each δήμου τ' ἄνδρα, 'man of the community', with his staff. These two categories compose the whole λαός. But can these 'men of the community' who are so roughly treated actually be young noblemen, attached to the king as something like vassals? Are they not more probably envisaged at this point as ordinary men, certainly not noble though probably above the status of δμῶες or θῆτες? What, for example, is the status of Thersites? He bears no patronymic or further identification, but came to Troy 'together with the Atreidai'.[52] If this implies that he belonged to Agamemnon's own contingent, then he was part of the πλεῖστοι καὶ ἄριστοι | λαοί who accompanied him.[53] Yet Thersites' treatment, and the scorn with which the rest of the army regards him, suggest much more that he was a member of the λαός in a different sense, represented by the λαοὶ...ἀγροιῶται, 'country folk' or 'rustic troops' of Nestor's reminiscence at 11, 676, or the λαοῖσιν, 'work-people' or 'household dependents', of the tanning simile at 17, 390.

The *Iliad* in fact does not envisage slaves before Troy, except for a few war-captives about whom (with the exception of concubines) little is heard. Even the stewards who give out food, who remain by the ships and have no normal part in the fighting, are free men who can attend the assembly to hear Achilles retract his wrath.[54] The oarsmen of the ships in the Catalogue are the very λαός who fill the ranks of warriors. Indeed it is precisely the implied size of this λαός, and the suggestion of mass fighting and mass formations, that complicate the picture both of the βασιλῆες and their effect on the

[52] 2, 248f.
[53] 2, 577f.
[54] 19, 42–6.

action and of the maintenance of the expedition as a whole. Either the Achaean expedition was a large affair with grooms, stewards, sweepers and the rest who were probably *not* free, let alone noble, and with a large army of free men in which the exploits of the leaders would be comparatively inconspicuous; or it was a do-it-yourself venture on a very small scale in which the menial tasks were all performed by the younger men, mainly the ἑταῖροι, but all were free and all were noble in the sense of belonging to the great princely families. In this latter case the great anonymous λαός deployed in mass movements was a fiction, and the feats of the greatest heroes would indeed dominate the field of warfare in scattered encounters. Our *Iliad* combines elements of both conceptions (and no doubt of others) to form a picture that is vivid and dramatic but, in both tactical and sociological terms, quite unrealistic.

It remains, in the consideration of tactics before Troy, to consider one other effect of cultural stratification in the text of Homer. Long-range fighting is largely ignored. The Locrians are slingers and archers, at least at 13, 712ff.; but heroic stone-throwing is confined to the use of huge boulders, and named archers are few and for the most part outsiders in one sense or another – Pandarus and Paris among the Trojans, the bastard Teukros among the Achaeans. The dichotomy between Odysseus the spearsman in the *Iliad* and Odysseus the archer in the *Odyssey* is equally significant, for the hero of the *Odyssey* is a backwoodsman, a figure from the confines of the Achaean world who deals in poisoned arrows. There is a feeling in the *Iliad* that the fighting of long ago was even more static. Ajax with his ancient tower-like shield is the exemplar of the great defensive fighter. Hector in an old or archaizing passage at 7, 238ff. claims 'I know how to wield my dry ox-hide to left, to right – that for me is ruthless fighting...I know how to dance for hostile Ares in fixed fight.' But he also knows 'how to dart into the moil of swift chariots' (240): here again is the hint of archaic memory, for, although the common Iliadic picture is of chariots as a means of transport even in battle, there are rare scenes where a chariot-charge is dimly envisaged and others in which a hero fights from his moving chariot. In Nestor's well-known advice at 4, 303ff. the Achaeans are urged to keep together in their chariots; whoever comes upon an enemy chariot should thrust out from his own with his spear – thus did the men of old (οἱ πρότεροι) sack walled cities. The combination of static foot-fighting and mobile and aggressive chariot tactics in these references to pre-Trojan warfare is somewhat paradoxical, and possibly the tradition, which is exceptionally vague on these points, has got its chronology confused. The absence of archery as an important factor in warfare is another ambiguous factor. It may reflect an actual phase in the late Bronze Age, or it may be due, somewhat like the misunderstanding over chariots, to a declining use of the bow in the early Iron Age. That is suggested by the rarity of surviving arrowheads, but seems unlikely for the more irregular type of warfare we envisage for that period. On the whole the evidence is too indefinite for us to say whether the small part played by long-distance and mobile warfare in the *Iliad* reflects a historical stage in the late Bronze Age, or whether it is due to poetical selection and the desire of the singers to concentrate on truly 'heroic' encounters, in which sheer strength and nerve were best revealed in close fighting.

The Homeric poems mention other types of warfare, too, sometimes in considerable detail and with a more synoptic vision than was applied to the more massive scene before Troy. Achilles' raids have already been noted, and they might reflect attacks not restricted to the late Bronze Age or to the Troad and north-east Aegean. More important is the kind of information given in Nestor's reminiscences, which describe two small and localized wars in Greece itself – wars that more probably reflect the breakdown of the Achaean empire or the conditions of the early Iron Age than the era of the great palaces. At 7, 132ff. Nestor recalls an encounter between the Pylians and Arcadians near the banks of the Celadon and Iardanus, close by the walls of Pheia; it was settled by a duel with the huge Ereuthalion, who issued a formal challenge which Nestor accepted and won. Then at 11, 670ff. he reminisces in greater detail over a war between the Pylians and Eleans 'about cattle-rustling', ἀμφὶ βοηλασίη. Fighting in defence of his cattle, Nestor felled the Elean Itymoneus and routed his rustic troops. The Pylians gathered booty in their turn, many herds of cattle, sheep, pigs, goats, and mares, and led them back to Pylos by night. The next morning heralds summoned the creditors of the Eleans; Neleus himself took a whole herd of cattle and a flock of sheep because of a notable bad debt – four prize-winning horses with their chariots, which had been sent to Elis for the games and been detained by Augeas. Soon an Elean army with chariots invested the Pylian town of Thryoessa in reprisal. The Pylians marched out again and routed them, inspired by the young Nestor who captured an enemy chariot and with it destroyed nearly the whole Elean chariot force. Only the young Molione twins got away; later Nestor met them in more peaceful circumstances in a chariot-race at the funeral games of Amarynceus.[55]

There are clear signs of conflation, confusion and exaggeration here, as well as strong elements of realism. Parts of the story, especially the chariot-contest in Elis (an apparent predecessor of the Olympic games), seem to reflect post-Bronze-Age conditions. Other parts may go back to the late Bronze Age – though when are Pylians and *Arcadians* likely to have clashed? Perhaps in the period of disruption at the end of the Achaean epoch, when Arcadia became a place of refuge from the Dorians? Less probably, at any rate, in the generations that bounded the Trojan war, since between about 1300 and 1200 B.C. the Pylian palace at Ano Englianos flourished undisturbed and unfortified. Many of the details are in fact timeless. Cattle, sheep, pigs, goats and horses were vital commodities even in the greatest days of Mycenae, and Achilles himself can refer to the raiding of cattle and sheep as natural and normal.[56] Yet the absence from Nestor's tale of more heroic prizes, like fine armour or great lumps of valuable metal or beautiful and industrious women, may indicate that its origins lay not in the heroic background itself, or even in the Dark Age centres that transmitted the heroic *ethos* in heroic song, but in some humbler and more regional poetical tradition, presumably of the western Peloponnese, either of the same Dark Age or of the succeeding Late-Protogeometric renaissance.

Still other types of warfare are described in the *Odyssey*: first and most obviously the civil strife in Ithaca, which culminated in a massacre and almost started a war between the small states of north-western Greece. In itself civil war is, again, timeless; but the particular circumstances of the *Odyssey* – the disruption and evident lack of communication that followed the capture of Troy, the uncertainty about what would greet the heroes on their return home, the dynastic and constitutional confusions – are too strongly redolent of conditions as they must actually have been in an age of disintegration to be attributed solely to the accidents of conflation and misunderstanding in a poetical tradition. Another consequence of the decline of the palace-societies is seen in the false tale (fictional in its context, but at least meant to be plausible) told by Odysseus to Eumaeus in the fourteenth book.[57] Odysseus describes himself as a restless Cretan who delighted in ships, spears, arrows and warfare. Even before the Trojan expedition he had made nine successful raids overseas, and after his return from Troy, where he had served reluctantly, a mere month at home had been enough to send him off again to the Nile delta with nine ships. Whether he intended to trade there, as Menelaus traded on his way home from Troy,[58] or whether he was cautiously preparing an attack, is not made clear;[59] at all events his crews got out of hand, fell on the Egyptians in their fields and carried off their wives and children, but were soon defeated by a mixed Egyptian chariot and infantry force. Can this story contain a memory of the Land and Sea raids on the Delta in the early years of the twelfth century B.C., only a generation or so after the probable fall of Troy VIIa? We cannot be sure; but at least this tale and the episode it describes are not 'heroic', but suggestive of an era when values were rapidly changing. The Cretan princeling is a bastard child, resentful, unco-operative and anti-social. Inconspicuous at Troy, he comes into his own as a privateer. He has more in common with Thersites than Idomeneus, whom he resents – more still, perhaps, with the resourceful but sometimes unheroic hero of the *Odyssey* himself.

It must be admitted that these stories of border-skirmishes, of cattle-raids, of private adventures, which seem to have no strong connection with the world ascribed to Agamemnon and his companions, are vastly overshadowed in the total Homeric scene by the more monumental and more heroic fighting before Troy. The description of that warfare, confused and inconsistent as it sometimes is, seems nevertheless to contain a surprising amount that is appropriate to what is objectively known of the late Bronze Age in Greece, and very little that can be firmly connected with, or is at all appropriate to, any subsequent period before the end of the eighth century B.C. The evidence of language, together with the misunderstanding of subjects like the use of chariots in war, strongly suggests that little in the way of detailed and unambiguous memory – which means, in effect, memory preserved in poetry – survived the destruction or

[57] *Od.* 14, 199ff.   [58] *Od.* 4, 90.   [59] *Od.* 14, 259ff.

abandonment of the Achaean palaces. Yet the sheer amount of information in the poems – information which, confused or not, can hardly have been either derived from the early Iron Age or invented in it – suggests, with other factors, that a vast mass of rather confused and vague memories *did* survive, to be enshrined in the growing poetical tradition as songs about the last great Achaean *geste* grew in popularity. That mass of imprecise recollection is of the highest importance; the provable imprecision was mainly over details (the way in which a helmet or a breast-plate with its fittings or a large *megaron* was constructed, the rôle of archers), but the general outline of the recollection may have been broadly correct.

My conclusion has been that the general outline *is* in many respects valid, at least so far as warfare is concerned. The support for this conclusion lies partly in our knowledge of the oral tradition and our estimate of what it would accept or reject in its formative stages; partly in the comparison with other oral traditions and their treatment of people, attitudes and categories of events; and partly in the relative accuracy of the Homeric poems over certain confirmed and individual characteristics of the late Bronze Age: the Achaean geography of the Catalogue, the knowledge of great Achaean palaces (although not of their detailed operation) and their approximate relationships, the awareness of certain pieces of armament. Even the apparent knowledge of Troy and its surroundings, beloved and mis-applied by Unitarian critics of the past, has its legitimate impli-cations. Men may have hung on in the ruins of Mycenae or Asine in the Submycenaean age, but the days of real fortresses and real sieges were past; yet the *Iliad* can give a picture that in many details (the crowding of non-combatants along the walls, the rapid opening of the gates to receive fugitives, the protection offered by spearsmen on walls and towers, the multiplicity of entrances, the awareness of weak spots in the defences, the position of the *megara* of the king and his family) seems realistic and accurate, at any rate beyond any plausible powers of purely imaginative reconstruction in a post-fortress age. Moreover the sheer geographical description of Troy (not in extravagances over hot and cold springs, but in its exact relation to plain, rivers, mountains, islands) contains that mixture of accuracy and inaccuracy which seems typical of a complex oral tradition of the kind I have suggested. The geography could, to be sure, be reported by Aeolic settlers, but so much else goes back to pre-colonial days that this kind of explanation is unlikely to be wholly correct.

Finally I repeat an important distinction. For the day-to-day operation of the palaces whose remains we can study, and for the titles, relations, activities and attitudes of their administrators, the Homeric poems are not good evidence. For the history of late Bronze Age warfare, on the other hand, their value is likely to be greater.

4

THE ORAL AND THE
LITERARY EPIC

I DO WE NEED A SPECIAL 'ORAL POETICS' IN ORDER TO UNDERSTAND HOMER?

Current Homeric scholarship, after a great surge forward in the wake of Milman Parry, seems to be rather in the doldrums. But there are still substantial gains to be made through the closer study of expression and style on the one hand, thematic structure on the other. It is with the former that I shall be primarily concerned here, and through the study of poetical language in particular that I hope to justify resurrecting the familiar comparison with Virgil and Milton in §2. The general conclusion will be that the differences between oral and literate expression, although considerable, are not necessarily so profound as is widely assumed; and that the oral epic, at least at the unmatched level of Homer, can display some of the supposedly distinctive subtleties of written poetry.

The special marks of a long oral poem are its heavy dependence on standardized phraseology and rhythmical cola, and, analogously, on a highly formalized thematic structure. The Homeric poems are far more formular in their language than any others known to us, and paradoxically they owe much of their superiority to this. Their broad themes and detailed motifs are likewise deployed in standard patterns and sequences, as has been demonstrated by Fenik for battle-scenes and Lohmann for speeches.[1] Such conventionalized arrangements tend to escape the listening ear or the casual eye, but when identified and closely examined they often reveal, as does the formular phraseology, signs of flexibility and imaginative adaptation on the part of the main singer and, no doubt, his close predecessors. The Homeric poems are, apart from anything else, the product of remarkable creative composition. Yet no criticism that overlooks the strongly formular tendencies of their language and

---

[1] B. C. Fenik, *Typical Battle Scenes in the Iliad*, *Hermes* Einzelschriften XXI (Wiesbaden, 1968); D. Lohmann, *Die Komposition der Rede in der Ilias* (Berlin, 1970).

theme-structure can be regarded very seriously, since it ignores one of the main factors determining the poet's intentions.[2]

Excessive attention to the formular aspects of Homer can be just as destructive as their total neglect – as for example, until just yesterday, by most German and Italian experts. Much of the recent publication on Homeric diction has been both turgid and linguistically insecure. One obstacle lies in the material itself, for the presentation even of relevant information about the formular status of a Homeric verse or passage is a difficult matter – it tends to become either unintelligibly concise or unreadably laborious and prolix. Books about the formulas make heavy going with their statistical tables and apparent soullessness; that applies even to so good a treatise as J. B. Hainsworth's *The Flexibility of the Homeric Formula* (Oxford, 1968), and Milman Parry's classic, *L'Épithète traditionnelle dans Homère* (Paris, 1926), makes an almost unique exception. Fresh critical commentaries on the *Iliad* and *Odyssey*, especially the former, are badly needed, but these problems of how to present the indispensable formular information in a less than repellent way are a difficulty for author and publisher alike. On balance the recent critical emphasis on the formular quality of much of Homer's language has made it harder, rather than easier, for the interested amateur to come to close grips with this kind of poetry, and this despite the fact that the basic principles, at least, are simple and easily understood.

It was mainly this formular quality that led Parry's followers, J. A. Notopoulos and A. B. Lord, to claim that a completely new set of rules of criticism, an actual 'oral poetics', was needed for the proper understanding of Homer.[3] Both language and plot, it was

---

[2] This restricts, although it does not entirely negate, the otherwise interesting book by H. A. Mason called *From Homer to Pope* (London, 1972). Its author will not be surprised to find a Classical critic expressing disagreement with his methods and conclusions when he himself asks whether 'anybody capable of grasping textual problems...ever said anything mildly impressive about the poetry' (p. 4). Indeed he asserts quite bluntly that 'the effective life of the Classics has... had to run outside the universities ever since Shakespeare's day' (p. 5). Something similar had been said by Pope and, more to the point, Matthew Arnold, and it is up to Classical scholars to demonstrate without rancour that such strictures, if they were ever deserved, no longer are so. One need do no more, in fact, than point to the discovery of Homer's orality, a discovery made and developed within the universities and now belatedly being latched on to, and sometimes misunderstood, by literary critics.

[3] J. A. Notopoulos, 'Towards a poetics of early Greek oral poetry', *HSCP* 68 (1964), 45–65; cf. *TAPA* 80 (1949), 1–23; A. B. Lord, 'Homer as oral poet', *HSCP* 72 (1968), 1ff., especially p. 46.

implied, would respond to the new kind of poetics and required it for their full appreciation. This idea of a need for special criteria for judging oral as opposed to written poetry has been much in the air for the last thirty years and has been discussed in rather vague terms all over the place, in relation primarily to Homer but also to other oral poetry whose qualities are less pure but not completely distinct.

The trouble is that none of its exponents has been able to indicate in any useful way what the new 'oral poetics' might consist of. What *sort* of rules, one might inquire without being unreasonable, is it likely to contain? Rules, it seems, that will cover three main topics: first the use of formular phrases, secondly standard themes and typical scenes, thirdly the special devices of repetition, foreshadowing and ring-composition. Well, there is nothing surprising here – and not much that makes the sort of rules envisaged seem either clearer or more viable. The formulas have been quite intensively studied already, although without leading to any firm conclusion about their 'true' limits and consequently about the precise kind and degree of formularity in Homer's compositional and narrative technique. The idea of the formula has proved valuable, but it is a waste of time to try and press it too hard. As for theme-structures, their study has at times been interesting and useful, but it can never – as many contemporary monographs depressingly show – be susceptible of exactly defined canons and definitions. *Repetition* tends to be used in particular but unsurprising ways in an oral poem; *foreshadowing* may be necessary for following a very long one (although it is not, as it happens, prominent in the *Iliad*); *ring-composition* is a common structural device in all forms of large-scale literature, oral included. None of these is unique to oral literature, and in no case can the critic make his modes of analysis sufficiently definite and specific to justify talking of an oral poetics, or implying that the process of criticism can be reduced to invariant forms.

It remains true that the perception that the *Iliad* and *Odyssey* are in essence oral, that they have been built up by singers who assimilate the work of other singers and then elaborate, refine or combine it, is obviously important for understanding Homer's *kind* of poetry and the special aims and limitations its author or authors may have had. The whole matter has been helpfully adumbrated by J. B. Hainsworth in his article 'The criticism of an oral Homer', and can

I believe be carried further.[4] Hainsworth usefully distinguishes the effects of oral performance (whereby the singer must be ready to curtail or expand in accordance with the mood and response of his audience and the exigencies of time and space) from detailed diction and theme-deployment on the one hand, large-scale structure on the other. The last, he maintains, is not heavily affected by orality or literacy.

This matter of large-scale structure is perhaps not quite so simple as that. The unity involved in a long oral poem can certainly be less than that of a work designed to be read. The poem may move forward in more or less autonomous sections; its overall content may be a compound of tonal detail (for instance the fighting in the *Iliad*) and a dramatic organizing theme (the wrath and withdrawal of Achilles). The listening audience savours immediate action rather than a complicated and only gradually emerging situation – although it may be prepared to tolerate the latter from the lips of a great artist. And yet such considerations as these are so general and obvious, but also so erratic in their possible application to any particular part of an oral poem, that they cannot possibly constitute a firm set of special rules concerning this aspect of orality. Much of the old 'Homeric Question', it is true, fades away once one takes note of such tendencies; but they remain important for only so long as they are regarded as fluid and to some extent unpredictable. In any event Homer's intentions and status are unique among those of oral poets. The rules one might construct to cover the regular singer entertaining an audience on a single occasion would not in any case apply to him, and *vice versa*; and we cannot even plausibly guess the circumstances in which the *Iliad* or *Odyssey* was first delivered or perfected, or exactly how they both survived (no doubt with slight further development) until the time of their first adequate recording as written texts.[5]

The more detailed thematic and episodic structure of medium-scale oral poetry – for example a single Homeric book – better reflects mnemonic and narrative techniques that are specially helpful to the singer who reproduces his poetry from memory and cultivated verbal instinct.[6] Ring-composition, standard theme-

---

[4] *JHS* 90 (1970), 90–8.   [5] See further pp. 132f.

[6] Words like 'mnemonic' and 'memory' are becoming taboo in relation to oral poets. Of course these poets do not exactly memorize songs from others (even if

sequences, repetitions and doublets are useful to the composer of any complicated work, and the critic properly remembers that they are especially pertinent to the oral poet. Yet the tracing of patterns of correspondence or reversal over distant stretches of a major work is notoriously precarious. The dangers are illustrated not only by C. H. Whitman's ingenious relating of the first and last books of the *Iliad* but also by structural and numerological analyses of Latin poetry.[7] A newer peril within the field of Homeric scholarship is presented by the proliferation of treatises on the recurrence of special themes – conferences and conversations, rebuke and encouragement, mutilation, lamentation, burial and so on. A. B. Lord has rightly emphasized the need for looking at standard themes as an important element in oral poetry, and B. C. Fenik in his *Studies in the Odyssey* (Wiesbaden, 1974) has stressed the importance of theme-repetition in that poem. Now, as often happens, a new generation of learned exploiters is in danger of driving the idea into the ground. We can nevertheless take it for granted that oral poets do indeed use themes in the way demonstrated in palmary fashion by Fenik for the battle-poetry of the *Iliad*, that much of their apparent complexity depends on the variation and redeployment of a limited range of standard ideas and actions, and that in this respect the oral poets were merely accentuating, for good practical reasons in the main, some of the basic creative and organizing tendencies of all narrative whatsoever.

Now for the formular phrases themselves. Let us not ask questions like precisely how many of them there are in Homer, for the answers would be as misleading as they would be indigestible. But rather, what does the undoubted use of many formular and repeated phrases do, in broad terms, for the Homeric style? I would like to distinguish two particular effects.

First, it is notable that within certain topics the formulas are exceedingly limited in their range of content, and as a consequence that they limit not only the expression but also the underlying thought itself. Formulas for speaking and answering (to take an

they sometimes think they do), any more than they exactly improvise (another taboo term) – but there are *elements* of both memorizing and improvising in what they do. See p. 137.

[7] C. H. Whitman, *Homer and the Heroic Tradition* (Cambridge, Mass., 1958), chapter 11, especially pp. 257–60; G. E. Duckworth, *Vergil and Classical Hexameter Poetry* (Ann Arbor, 1961).

extreme example) form a well-known system. That is convenient for the poets, but it prevents them from identifying special ways in which a particular character might reply in particular circumstances. Many of the details of warfare, too, or of common actions like launching or beaching a ship, have become strongly formalized, and this limits the poets' imagination – as well as, on the positive side, giving such scenes a familiar, comforting and almost paradigmatic air. For most subjects the formular system is far less rigid and the degree of special invention or fresh elaboration and variation correspondingly higher. The flexibility of Homeric formulas (that is, their capacity for minor adaptation in reference and implication as well as in metrical and syntactical value) helps prevent the style from seeming repetitive or flat, although a few stretches, especially in the *Odyssey*, do not entirely escape that danger. Indeed the interplay between regular and adapted versions of a formula, little less than that between formular and non-formular language, constitutes part of that complex of tensions that makes the supposedly plain style of Homer so elaborate, subtle and rewarding for those who are intimately familiar with it.

The second effect of a formular style with which I am concerned is both harder to define and easier to caricature. The expression of experience in strictly categorized terms has peculiar effects on one's vision of the world itself. If streets are always broad, leaders always god-like and ships always swift (at least when the singer chooses to place them in the first half of his verse), that admittedly helps to establish the subjects of such poetry as lying in the past, as being 'heroic'; for in the real world there are slow ships and narrow streets and hopeless muddlers among generals and politicians. But it also does something quite different, by extracting and encapsulating the essence of things and people as the poets have come to see them and establishing this particular quality at the expense of other possible ones. Such a process encourages a rather rigid assessment of human experience, and that may have suited the outlook of the Mycenaean heroic age as well as the convenience of poets who chose to transmit and transform it. One must be careful not to exaggerate here, as Adam Parry came close to doing when he suggested that the use of formulas reflects a uniformity of experience in which thought, speech and action are reduced to the most concrete possible terms. That could begin to verge on the erroneous view that Homer's thought is totally non-abstract, 'mythological' even.[8] In any case it is important to remember that the formular element in the language of Homer comprises a large variety of word-patterns and verbal phrases, not just the noun–epithet groups that are its most extreme and striking application.

These generalizations may be illustrated by two passages that are not untypical of formular capacities. First *Iliad* 16, 477–91:

> Then again Sarpedon missed with shining shaft
> and over Patroclus' left shoulder went the point
> of the spear, and did not hit him; and he rose up second with the
>   bronze,
> Patroclus did; *his* missile did not fly from hand in vain   480
> but hit where lungs are pressed round dense heart.
> He toppled as when some oak or poplar topples
> or tall pine that woodcutters in the mountains
> have cut out with fresh-sharpened axes to be a ship's timber;
> so did he lie stretched out in front of his horses and chariot,   485
> roaring, clutching the bloody dust.
> As when a lion, coming among the herds, has slain a bull,
> a spirited tawny one, among the shambling cattle,
> and it dies groaning under the lion's jaws,
> so at Patroclus' hands did the leader of Lycian spearsmen   490
> rage as he died...

It is a heavily formular passage, not only in verses occurring elsewhere in Homer (479, 482, 483, 486) and noun–epithet groups ('shining shaft', 'dense heart', 'tall pine', 'fresh-sharpened axes', 'shambling cattle', 'leader of Lycian spearsmen'...), but also in its verbal phrases ('he toppled as when', 'missile did not fly from hand in vain', 'but hit', 'lie stretched out' – even the single words 'dies' and 'groaning' in 489, in these positions in the verse) and inconspicuous joining-phrases ('then again', 'and he second', 'so did he', 'as when', 'so at the hands of'...). And yet the overall effect is not, as one might expect as a consequence, stale and second-hand, but rather one of dignity and monumentality. This is an important fight, with Sarpedon a son of Zeus himself and Patroclus achieving a major victory that turns out to be the prelude to his own death; yet the conventions are maintained, thematic as well as

---

[8] Adam Parry, 'The language of Achilles', *TAPA* 87 (1956), 4; on 'mythological thought' see my *The Nature of Greek Myths* (Harmondsworth, 1974), pp. 279–89. Parry had some excellent things to say on the implications of a formular style in the article cited.

verbal – for example the exchange of spear-casts is soon over, with one miss and then the mortal hit. The special significance of Sarpedon's death is marked in another formular way by a pair of similes that are themselves typical in their class: the tree cut or blown down, the lion attacking cattle. Similes have their own conventionalized language that is perceptibly different from that of ordinary narrative, even apart from their distinct subject-matter; but here little effort is made to render them especially striking, and they are left to make their point without additional emphasis. The tree is to be a ship's timber – that is standard Homeric detail to make the comparison more vivid – and is related first to Sarpedon falling, then to his lying stretched on the ground. The multiple reference is slightly unusual, but that is all. The slain bull is elaborated by the two unremarkable phrases that constitute verse 488, but then his resemblance to the fallen warrior is sharpened by an unusual counterpoint of verbs; for the bull 'groans' like a man in 489, whereas 'roaring' of Sarpedon in 486 is more appropriate in ordinary language to the bull, although it is formular for fallen warriors in the epic. Through the passage as a whole the progress of thought is straightforward, linear, cumulative in the oral manner. 'Of the spear' in 479 is a runover word that leads on to an important accession of meaning, and so too is 'Patroclus (did)' in the following verse – a specification that is not essential for comprehension. One could say of this passage almost exactly what I wrote about a very different kind of scene from the *Odyssey* on pp. 5f.: 'The words, the phrases, the rhythms are familiar, but the style...is relaxed, effortless, and faintly muted rather than stale, redundant or mechanical. The familiar words and phrases and rhythmical cola, acquired from the singers of older generations and refined of needless excrescence or pointless variant, are cast up anew...clustered with the heroic past.'

My second illustration of the stylistic potentialities of a formular language exemplifies the resonances that can be created by varying an obvious or a standard use. Here, this time in Greek, is the powerful description from the thirteenth book of the *Odyssey* of Odysseus' return to Ithaca on the Phaeacian ship:

> εὖθ' οἱ ἀνακλινθέντες ἀνερρίπτουν ἅλα πηδῷ,
> καὶ τῷ νήδυμος ὕπνος ἐπὶ βλεφάροισιν ἔπιπτε,
> νήγρετος ἥδιστος, θανάτῳ ἄγχιστα ἐοικώς.   80

ἡ δ', ὥς τ' ἐν πεδίῳ τετράοροι ἄρσενες ἵπποι,
πάντες ἅμ' ὁρμηθέντες ὑπὸ πληγῆσιν ἱμάσθλης,
ὑψόσ' ἀειρόμενοι ῥίμφα πρήσσουσι κέλευθον,
ὡς ἄρα τῆς πρύμνη μὲν ἀείρετο, κῦμα δ' ὄπισθε
πορφύρεον μέγα θῦε πολυφλοίσβοιο θαλάσσης.   85
ἡ δὲ μάλ' ἀσφαλέως θέεν ἔμπεδον· οὐδέ κεν ἴρηξ
κίρκος ὁμαρτήσειεν, ἐλαφρότατος πετεηνῶν.
ὡς ἡ ῥίμφα θέουσα θαλάσσης κύματ' ἔταμνεν,
ἄνδρα φέρουσα θεοῖς ἐναλίγκια μήδε' ἔχοντα,
ὃς πρὶν μὲν μάλα πολλὰ πάθ' ἄλγεα ὃν κατὰ θυμὸν   90
ἀνδρῶν τε πτολέμους ἀλεγεινά τε κύματα πείρων,
δὴ τότε γ' ἀτρέμας εὗδε, λελασμένος ὅσσ' ἐπεπόνθει.

(13, 78–92)

In verse 86 the ship runs on safely and firmly through the sea, ἡ δὲ μάλ' ἀσφαλέως θέεν ἔμπεδον, so that even the hawk, the swiftest of birds, could not keep pace with it. The adverbs ἀσφαλέως, 'safely', and ἔμπεδον, 'firmly', are often used in those positions in the verse, and so tend to be formular. What is significant, however, is that the whole phrase ἀσφαλέως θέεν ἔμπεδον (although with the present tense θέει, an unimportant difference) occurs also in a simile at *Iliad* 13, 141. But there it is not a ship running through the waves but a great boulder, loosened from a mountainside by torrential rain, that rushes headlong doward spreading destruction and ruin – so that ἀσφαλέως has a completely different connotation, not 'safely and surely' but 'unstoppably, inexorably'. Was that disturbing echo in the mind of the Odyssean singer when he sang so finely of the Phaeacian ship cleaving the waves, 'carrying a man like the gods in counsel' (89), and yet there were destructive things to come, for Odysseus would find hardship and danger in Ithaca and the ship itself would be turned to stone by Poseidon as it reached home? Obviously one cannot answer with complete certainty; what can be said is that such tensions and echoes, conscious or otherwise, are an aspect of the formular style that the critic overlooks at his peril, even if he has to use a slightly subjective tact in distinguishing probable overtones from improbable ones. A second instance occurs a few verses later in 92 where Odysseus lies aboard sleeping, 'all sufferings forgotten' – λελασμένος ὅσσ' ἐπεπόνθει. Is it just poetical accident that this is an obvious variant of the formular pattern expressed in a famous passage of the sixteenth book of the *Iliad*, at 776, as λελασμένος ἱπποσυνάων, 'his horsemanship forgotten', a pathetic and sinister phrase as it is used of the slain charioteer Cebriones, precursor of Patroclus' own death?

There is a different oral technique that I believe to be only a little less important than formulary itself for the understanding of Homer's craftsmanship, even if it is no more susceptible than before to a new scientific poetics. It is a stylistic phenomenon that has sometimes been identified but rarely examined in detail; Milman Parry called it 'the adding style', J. A. Notopoulos 'the paratactic style', and in its cruder aspects it is a simple matter.[9] The point is that it has many less crude aspects. I prefer to call it something like 'the cumulative technique', and the basic facts are these. The more rudimentary kind of oral singer (and that includes most of them) tends to make each verse into an independent statement and to avoid the complications of enjambment (the continuation of the sentence from one verse into the next) and a subordinating syntax. The South Slavic singers of modern Yugoslavia, who have provided much that is helpful as well as a good deal that is obstructive to the understanding of how Homeric poetry works, are distinctly of this kind:

> Men's heads rolled and dead limbs twitched.
> The wounded and dying groaned.
> One said, 'Woe, woe, do not tread upon me, comrade!'
> And another wailed, 'Raise me, comrade!'

and so on; the singer is one of the best of the Novi Pazar poets, Salih Ugljanin.[10] More advanced traditions, on the other hand, do not restrict each verse to a sentence and each sentence to a verse. Homer, in particular, is far more complex and skilful in his variation of sentence-length, his ability to overrun the verse-end when he wishes, his deployment of different rhythmical cola and subordinate clauses. At the same time he clings by necessity to the singer's preference for simple linear narrative, in which the main concept is expressed first and subsidiary limitations or elaborations are accumulated in successive statements and verses.

It is a real and important question how far this linear and cumulative approach to the expression of meaning either reflects or actually helps determine a particular view of the world. The

---

[9] See pp. 152ff., 167ff. for a more technical discussion of this phenomenon with special reference to *Iliad* book 16.

[10] See M. Parry and A. B. Lord, *Serbocroatian Heroic Songs*, I (Cambridge, Mass., 1954), 111.

question is analogous to the one put to the use of formulas. Fixed epithets, for example, may sometimes entail a certain limitation of vision; is it conceivable that the paratactic tendencies of oral composition helped to perpetuate a non-synthetic view of the world, or a loose and erratic connection between subjects or events and their attributes or consequences? If that were one result of the oral style then a completely different critical reaction might indeed be called for, one that might be thought to justify the title of an oral poetics. That is an intriguing idea, but unfortunately two difficulties remain. First, the fixed set of criteria implied by 'poetics' would be even less appropriate to such an abstract consideration than to the more concrete aspects of oral technique that have already been outlined. Second, although I should not wish to reject as absolutely impossible the notion of a paratactic or cumulative *Weltanschauung*, this is an excessively vague concept that requires more thought and refinement than it has received so far before it can be taken seriously. It can therefore be left as an interesting possibility by those who wish to proceed to more immediate matters, in particular the operation of the cumulative style in Homer's poetry itself.

For a clear but crude illustration of the cumulative technique in action one can turn to passages like the Arming of Agamemnon at the beginning of the eleventh book of the *Iliad*. Each item of armament is described in a single verse and then elaborated in a cumulated succeeding verse, often with the help of a runover epithet; for instance

> first round his calves he placed greaves
> – beautiful ones, fitted with silver ankle-guards.
>
> (16, 17f.)

Perhaps we can take such basic applications for granted and proceed to a subtler and indeed more typical passage that describes the death of the Trojan Hippothous at the hands of Ajax as he tries to drag away the corpse of Patroclus:

> Ἤτοι τὸν Λήθοιο Πελασγοῦ φαίδιμος υἱός,
> Ἱππόθοος, ποδὸς ἕλκε κατὰ κρατερὴν ὑσμίνην,
> δησάμενος τελαμῶνι παρὰ σφυρὸν ἀμφὶ τένοντας,   290
> Ἕκτορι καὶ Τρώεσσι χαριζόμενος· τάχα δ' αὐτῷ
> ἦλθε κακόν, τό οἱ οὔ τις ἐρύκακεν ἱεμένων περ.
> τὸν δ' υἱὸς Τελαμῶνος ἐπαΐξας δι' ὁμίλου
> πλῆξ' αὐτοσχεδίην κυνέης διὰ χαλκοπαρήου·

79

ἤρικε δ᾽ ἱπποδάσεια κόρυς περὶ δουρὸς ἀκωκῇ,   295
πληγεῖσ᾽ ἔγχεΐ τε μεγάλῳ καὶ χειρὶ παχείῃ,
ἐγκέφαλος δὲ παρ᾽ αὐλὸν ἀνέδραμεν ἐξ ὠτειλῆς
αἱματόεις· τοῦ δ᾽ αὖθι λύθη μένος, ἐκ δ᾽ ἄρα χειρῶν
Πατρόκλοιο πόδα μεγαλήτορος ἧκε χαμᾶζε
κεῖσθαι· ὁ δ᾽ ἄγχ᾽ αὐτοῖο πέσε πρηνὴς ἐπὶ νεκρῷ,   300
τῆλ᾽ ἀπὸ Λαρίσης ἐριβώλακος, οὐδὲ τοκεῦσι
θρέπτρα φίλοις ἀπέδωκε, μινυνθάδιος δέ οἱ αἰὼν
ἔπλεθ᾽ ὑπ᾽ Αἴαντος μεγαθύμου δουρὶ δαμέντι.

(17, 288–303)

Verse 289 states that he was dragging him by the foot; 290 expands
this by telling how he did so, by tying his shield-strap round
Patroclus' ankle and tugging on that – not exactly an unnecessary
elaboration, but a cumulated clause that provides, in a way that is
both logical and pleasing, an intenser vision of the crucial action.
The following verse, 291, begins with a pure elaboration, an almost
ruminative cumulation built upon the initial action: 'to please
Hector and the Trojans'. The information is of course unnecessary,
since all the Trojan allies were fighting for more or less that reason;
but the harmless redundancy leads on, as part of the same verse,
to something far more concrete and pointed:

> but swiftly upon him
> came evil that no one could fend off, wish it as they may,

an addition that brings a definite accession both of meaning (namely
that Hippothous' attempt resulted in his own death) and of emotional colouring (that the evil was inexorable, that his friends wanted
to save him but had to stand by helplessly). Next, Ajax pierces
Hippothous' helmet with his spear-point. That occupies two verses,
293f.,

> the son of Telamon rushing up through the battle-throng
> struck through the bronze-cheeked helmet from close by,

and there follows a cumulative and elaborative verse that once again
describes in vivid detail what has already been stated more abstractly
and in terms of general effect:

> and the horse-hair-plumed helmet shattered about the spear-tip.

Next comes an afterthought, or so it seems – not least because of the
steady, progressive, whole-verse mode of composition at this point:

the helmet shattered,

> struck as it was by great spear and stout hand.
>
> (296)

Yet the addition has the important purpose of emphasizing the heroic status of the whole encounter and the noble force, not exceptional but none the less devastating, of the blow. Two pairs of verses follow in which the sense could be regarded as complete in the first verse but is carried on by a runover-word cumulation in the second (αἱματόεις in 298 and κεῖσθαι in 300); but in neither case, although the degree of enjambment differs, is the cumulation merely decorative. It starts as such, but then leads into an integral accession of meaning and an indispensable drawing-out of the narrative thread. In other words the cumulative runover technique, itself a special manifestation of the general cumulative style, is being used as a subtle extension of the range of enjambment and a means of combining inessential although usually desirable decoration with the essential onward flow of events. That is a typical but nevertheless slightly curious characteristic of the Homeric style, one that is seldom noted perhaps because it is felt to be too obvious. But it is not really obvious at all, at least in its more tenuous implications – for example that the combination of apparent afterthought (the leisurely piling-up of often conventional detail) with what will turn out to be a definite advance in the concrete situation results in an unusual, evocative and intriguing blend of the practical and the reflective.

Finally in this same inconspicuous but affecting passage one may observe how the lightly adumbrated pathos of 'wish it as they may', ἱεμένων περ, back in 292 is accentuated in the closing verses, 300ff., where Hippothous lies stretched over the corpse of Patroclus

> far from deep-furrowed Larisa, and to his parents
> he paid not back the cost of his rearing, but short was his lifetime
> at the hands of great-spirited Ajax when he was struck down by
>   his spear.

Even in translation one can assess something of the complexity of these verses compared with the whole-verse sentences that described his actual death: not particularly cumulative poetry at this point, but elaborate poetry most carefully worked out.

The cumulative technique also operates on a larger scale, and its implications and occasional ambiguities are demonstrated by the famous scene in the third book of the *Iliad* in which Helen is asked by Priam, as they sit overlooking the battlefield from the Scaean gate of Troy, to identify for him some of the leading Greek heroes. It is a commonplace that this activity properly belongs to the first year of the war rather than the last, and that Priam must have had opportunities to learn by now which is Agamemnon and which Odysseus. That is a mild casualty of the process of orally composing, literally 'putting together', a monumental epic out of shorter elements. It is artistically unimportant, although in a minor sense Homer may be said to nod. Yet he had good reasons, no doubt, for wanting some such scene in this position in his poem; primarily perhaps, as Adam Parry thought, to show Helen and her feelings of nostalgia and her present standing in Troy as Priam's daughter-in-law.[11] All that is important for the shape and impact of the poem as a whole. But it is not that familiar anomaly that requires further discussion now, or anything so portentous as an oral poetics to assess. What I want to stress, rather, is the ultimate critical mystery of this kind of passage, cumulative in the large sense: its irresolvable ambiguity in terms of agglomerative accident and strictly artistic intention. Adam Parry took the scene as an instance of extremely careful construction, and went on to suggest – too optimistically in my opinion – that the whole epic consists of a more or less unbroken sequence of similarly carefully-constructed scenes: see p. 142 below. Yet the main problem is as follows. Helen is asked to identify first King Agamemnon himself and then, in a dramatic contrast of physical types, Odysseus. The conversation about the former covers twenty-five verses, that about the latter some thirty-four, involving Antenor as well as Priam and Helen. But then Priam sees Ajax and asks who *he* is, outstanding as he appears to be with his massive head and shoulders (3, 226f.). We expect, for this Achaean hero of the very first rank who plays a vital part in the fighting throughout the poem and is one of the most conspicuous dangers to the Trojan cause, a description commensurate with those already devoted to Agamemnon and Odysseus. Instead the scale of discussion changes most drastically, for Helen dismisses him in a single verse, 'This is huge Ajax, bulwark of the Achaeans', and then carries straight on

---

[11] 'Have we Homer's *Iliad*?', *YCS* 20 (1966), 198; for further discussion of Parry's views on this passage see pp. 142f. below.

with a gratuitous description, in the sense that it has not been requested by Priam, of the Cretan prince Idomeneus, a far less important (although by no means a minor) hero in the *Iliad*. 'And on the other side', she says, 'stands Idomeneus among the Cretans, like a god, and around him are gathered the Cretan leaders. Often valiant Menelaus entertained him in our house, whenever he came from Crete. But now', she continues (and I summarize slightly), 'I can see all the other Achaeans, whose names I could tell you, but Castor and Polydeuces, my own brothers, I cannot see. Either they cannot have come to Troy from Lacedaemon, or they are not fighting because they fear reproach on my account' (230–42).

'These were her words', the poet comments, 'but the life-giving earth already possessed them back in Lacedaemon, in their own dear native land' (243f.). The pathos of this conclusion – of Helen's isolation and ignorance of their tragic and unusual death – is justly renowned; but the question that needs to be put to the whole episode is a different one. It concerns Ajax; just why did Homer dispose of him so perfunctorily in a single verse? Why mention him at all, in that case, since the treatment of the Achaean warriors is in any event selective? And why pass on so rapidly to the lesser figure of Idomeneus and then accord him four times as much detail, in crude measure, as the more important Ajax? One reason might be that Idomeneus leads Helen's thoughts back to her life in Lacedaemon where he was such a frequent guest, and through Lacedaemon she comes to think of her brothers. But that still does not account for the apparently offhand brevity of her reply about Ajax. Perhaps part of the description of him dropped out in the course of transmission? An unlikely explanation, this, especially because the Athenians controlled the text through the crucial sixth century B.C. and were always anxious to stress the role of Ajax, who as their neighbour provided their best link with the heroic world of Troy. Suppression might in theory have occurred during the more immediately post-Homeric era, but on the whole the tendency then was for further expansion and elaboration.

There is a different kind of explanation that is intrinsically more satisfying, especially to modern readers, although not altogether free from difficulty. That is, perhaps the brevity of the reference to Ajax is intentional and psychologically quite subtle: Helen begins to become anxious about her brothers at just about the time when

Priam inquires about Ajax, so that she diverges to Idomeneus, partly in order to avoid the long description that Ajax warrants but partly because he provides a link to Lacedaemon and enables her to externalize her concern. Is this too modern a reading of the passage, crediting Homer as it does with a minute observation of human, especially feminine, psychology that cannot be closely paralleled elsewhere in the poems except perhaps in the Nausicaa episode of the *Odyssey*? No definite answer can be given, but what is important for both reader and critic is that we certainly cannot absolutely reject the interpretation. We cannot do so largely because of the ultimate impenetrability of the cumulative style in its broader aspects – because of the impossibility of surely distinguishing, in most cases, between Homeric cumulations, pre-Homeric ones already developed in the tradition, and even, occasionally, the more skilful among the elaborations carried out by post-Homeric singers and rhapsodes. Moreover we often cannot tell when a cumulation that is made in the first instance almost automatically, for obvious reasons of decoration and elaboration, has been developed further to express and develop a substantially fresh insight.

Catalogues of any sort – and the scene with Helen and Priam starts out as one – are particularly hard to assess in this respect, because they are by nature equally receptive of cumulative elaboration and simplifying abbreviation. The Catalogue of Ships in the second book of the *Iliad* is a notable instance; so is the list of heroines encountered by Odysseus in the underworld-scene of the eleventh book of the *Odyssey*; so too are the funeral games for Patroclus in *Iliad* book 23 and, an especially fascinating case, the list of scenes depicted on the shield made by Hephaestus for Achilles at the end of *Iliad* book 18. Here one can probably detect an original and simple intention of describing typical scenes from a city at peace and a city at war. This intention has become complicated and confused in the text we possess. The result is not aesthetically very disturbing, especially for an oral audience that is moving on with the singer and not checking back and forth like the careful reader or scholar. But again there are several points at which we cannot tell exactly what has happened, what Homer's intentions really were, and how much the naturally cumulative inclinations of the oral approach have become complicated by the accidents of transmission or the ambitions of post-Homeric singers and literate reciters.

The oral and the literary epic

For among the idiosyncrasies of traditional oral poetry are these: that it develops autonomously over generations; that each singer in the evolving tradition assimilates much from the past, from his pre-decessors and masters, but contributes something of his own for better or for worse; and that when a megalomaniac genius like Homer enters the scene almost anything can happen. I have written above of the ultimate *impenetrability* of a complex oral tradition, and that is something the more persistent type of modern interpreter might care to bear in mind. The critic will function best only if he has a full and sensitive knowledge of the formular and cumulative style and its implications, as well as of other technical elements to which references will be made in §3; and only if he lacks the ambition to make doctrinaire or scientific rules for oral poetry such as are implied by the whole concept of an 'oral poetics'. Literate taste alone, in these circumstances, is a fatal guide – but so too is a simplistic and inflexible view of the nature of oral poetry, which varies, it seems, from place to place, from performance to per-formance, from generation to generation and from culture to culture.

2 FROM HOMER TO VIRGIL AND MILTON

It may be profitable now to look at the most important of Homer's imitators, Virgil and Milton. The comparison is a familiar one, and so is the attempt to distinguish sharply between the two kinds of epic they, and Homer, represent. 'Primary and secondary', 'authentic and literary', 'naive and sophisticated': these are some of the favoured dichotomies, still occasionally used today and still mis-leading in different ways. 'Oral and literate' is slightly safer, but even those who restrict themselves to this kind of terminology sometimes share the old failure to see that some oral poetry can be complex, sophisticated and indirect just as some written epic can be superficial and naive.

Consider the following from C. M. Bowra's *From Virgil to Milton* (London, 1945):

If the oral epic triumphs through its simplicity and strength and straight-forwardness, through the unhesitating sweep of its narrative and a brilliant clarity in its main effects, the written epic appeals by its poetic texture, by its exquisite or apt or impressive choice of words, and by the rich significance of phrases and lines and paragraphs. Homer sweeps us away by the

85

irresistible movement of lines through a whole passage to a splendid climax (p. 5).

It is magnificent in its way, but largely untrue when one thinks hard about Homer: Bowra's criticism at its wordiest and least effective. Here is something better, a page later: 'The writers of literary epic see their subject through a haze of learned associations; they do not come to it directly as to a part of their daily lives' – it is too general, but at least it is roughly true of Virgil. But now once again the romantic simplification follows: 'Their distance from it [that is, literary writers from their subject] deprives them of the noble simplicity which is so natural to Homer.' I defer to §3 the ultimate assessment of Homer's simplicity, noble or otherwise; meanwhile we have a clear demonstration of the tendency, by no means restricted to Bowra and not abandoned by him even in his later work, to regard oral epic as an essentially homogeneous *genre* and literate epic as necessarily learned and carefully allusive and symbolic. Bowra himself gave a good example of the confusion when he went on to characterize the death of Roland in the *Chanson de Roland* (which he erroneously judged to be primarily oral) as 'simple and clear' – it is very far from that – in contrast with Virgil's description of the death of Dido which is 'heavy with meaning and clouded with symbolism' (p. 6), an evaluation I should now like to examine by considering a portion of Virgil's text.

Not the least profound element of the Dido episode in *Aeneid* 4 is her famous address to Aeneas on parting. Before criticizing it in detail I should admit that my general thesis about the *Aeneid* will be that, notwithstanding its power and charm, its extraordinary linguistic virtuosity and its reverberant central theme, it does not really possess all the mysterious and symbolic virtues its commentators habitually claim for it. Here is V. Poeschl in his widely-used *The Art of Vergil* (English translation, Ann Arbor, 1962): 'In Vergil's poetry everything participates in the inner drama and reflects the poet's awareness of the stirrings within his characters and of the destiny inherent in the events. Everything – landscape, morning, evening, night, dress and arms, every gesture, movement and image becomes a symbol of the soul' (p. 3). The author, although he is often considered to exaggerate a little, is respectfully regarded by Latinists; but this is wild stuff indeed. Even the austerer

86

critics have acquired the habit of making pretentious and un-
substantiated claims for Virgil's subtlety and symbolism – so much
so that the world of Homeric criticism begins to look a sane place by
comparison. But now for the passage itself:

> 'nec tibi diva parens generis nec Dardanus auctor,   365
> perfide, sed duris genuit te cautibus horrens
> Caucasus Hyrcanaeque admorunt ubera tigres.
> nam quid dissimulo aut quae me ad maiora reservo?
> num fletu ingemuit nostro? num lumina flexit?
> num lacrimas victus dedit aut miseratus amantem est?   370
> quae quibus anteferam? iam iam nec maxima Iuno
> nec Saturnius haec oculis pater aspicit aequis.
> nusquam tuta fides. eiectum litore, egentem
> excepi et regni demens in parte locavi.
> amissam classem, socios a morte reduxi   375
> (heu furiis incensa feror!): nunc augur Apollo,
> nunc Lyciae sortes, nunc et Iove missus ab ipso
> interpres divum fert horrida iussa per auras.
> scilicet is superis labor est, ea cura quietos
> sollicitat. neque te teneo neque dicta refello: 380
> i, sequere Italiam ventis, pete regna per undas.
> spero equidem mediis, si quid pia numina possunt,
> supplicia hausurum scopulis et nomine Dido
> saepe vocaturum. sequar atris ignibus absens
> et, cum frigida mors anima seduxerit artus,   385
> omnibus umbra locis adero. dabis, improbe, poenas.
> audiam et haec Manis veniet mihi fama sub imos.'
>
>   (*Aeneid* 4, 365–87)

'No goddess was your parent,' it begins, 'nor Dardanus the ancestor
of your race, traitor, but the hard rocks of craggy Caucasus engendered you and Hyrcanian tigresses gave you suck.' A rhetorical
commonplace, as is correctly observed by R. D. Williams, a sensible
and sober critic.[12] But this is not, according to him, because Virgil is
addicted to a rhetorical style in speeches and at moments of high
emotion. On the contrary, it is because Dido 'has nothing personal
to say to Aeneas now, and she has recourse to a formally elaborate
imprecation'. I wonder whether this is truly so, and whether a
contrast is really implied – as Williams and others suggest – with
her first words to Aeneas three books earlier, when she inquired of
him with equal rhetoric if he was indeed the son of Venus and
Anchises. Anyway, the rhetorical trope is immediately followed in

---

[12] *The Aeneid of Virgil, Books 1–6* (London, Macmillan, 1972), p. 365.

verses 368–71 by some explicitly rhetorical questions ending with the frigid locution 'quae quibus anteferam?', 'to which of these should I give priority?'. Only with 373f.,

> eiectum litore, egentem
> excepi et regni demens in parte locavi,

'cast up on the shore, in dire need, I took you in, and in my madness gave you a share of the kingdom', does some genuine feeling begin to reveal itself, and even here it is diminished by the prosaic and abstract formalism of 'placed you (*locavi*) in part of my kingdom'. This seems significant, since it suggests that Dido's rhetoric at this point is as likely to be the product of an automatic tendency of Virgil's style as of a special psychological insight.

An ironic and ingeniously compressed reference in 376f. to some of Aeneas' excuses culminates in the epigrammatic Epicureanism of 379, 'scilicet is superis labor est', 'yes, no doubt that is the kind of work gods do'. After this crowning irony she tells Aeneas to get out, and hopes he will be stranded on a rock at sea and repeatedly call on her name:

> spero equidem mediis, si quid pia numina possunt,
> supplicia hausurum scopulis et nomine Dido
> saepe vocaturum.
>
> (382–4)

R. D. Williams comments that the wide separation of 'mediis' in 382 from 'scopulis' in 383 'seems to aid the hoped-for isolation of her shipwrecked lover, far from human aid'. But is the gap so wide for Virgilian Latin? The sentence is carefully constructed, but I presume to doubt whether anything of the kind suggested by Professor Williams was in the poet's mind. Verse 384 continues with Dido's threat to pursue Aeneas, even in her absence, with black fires, 'atris ignibus'. The ancient commentator Servius saw here an implied reference to her own funeral pyre, although the primary image is certainly of the torches carried by the dark Furies of vengeance. Admittedly Dido says later, at 661f., that Aeneas will sight the flames of her pyre from far out at sea, and Servius may, as most modern critics think, be right. But 'atris' remains visually pertinent only to the image of Dido as Fury, and so complicates and diminishes the association with the funeral pyre – even if 'black' evokes death, as it may. It could be concluded that in any case the verbal ingenuity at this point is just too much for mystery, power or pathos; although those, as it happens, are soon supplied:

> et, cum frigida mors anima seduxerit artus,
> omnibus umbra locis adero.

'And when frigid death has separated limbs from soul, I shall haunt every place as a shade.' Even here the diction, although simple, remains a little stilted in the 'artus' of 'anima seduxerit artus' and in 'omnibus...locis adero'; for by translating this as 'haunt every place' rather than literally 'be present in every place' I have improperly done what commentators and translators often do, and ascribed to Virgil an emotive phrase where he actually uses a prosaic one. But the poetry is undeniably melancholy and sinister, truly loaded with significance, free at last from the floridity of rhetoric. The expression is relatively direct, and in spite of prosaic touches full of artistry: the confluence of metrical stress and word-accent, the fitting of 'frigida' within the second metrical foot and its close link with dire monosyllabic 'mors' before the main caesura, the assonance of 'omnibus umbra' – all these conspire to produce a sense of fluent inevitability that is then deliberately broken by the harsh 'dabis, improbe, poenas', 'you shall pay, villain, the penalty'.

My purpose in analysing this famous passage once again is to suggest that, skilful as it is, it is not strikingly full of mysterious power and symbolic allusion – not more so, indeed, than a great deal in Homer; but that its effectiveness depends primarily on a careful virtuosity in metre, word-music and diction combined with a strongly rhetorical tone over much of its extent.

Take by contrast a simple narrative passage from *Aeneid* 1, 208–22. Aeneas and his followers are exhausted as they reach the shores of Carthage; Aeneas addresses them with simulated confidence and 'presses his sorrow deep down in his heart', 'premit altum corde dolorem' (209) – Virgil is good at this kind of psychological comment, which the Homeric poets would only rarely attempt. Then at 210ff.

> illi se praedae accingunt dapibusque futuris:
> tergora diripiunt costis et viscera nudant;
> pars in frusta secant veribusque trementia figunt,
> litore aëna locant alii flammasque ministrant.

'They gird themselves for the prey [that is, for the stags Aeneas has just shot] and for the feast to come; they tear the hide from the ribs and lay bare the entrails; part cut them into small pieces and fix them quivering on spits, others place bronzes [that is, bronze cauldrons] on the shore and look after the flames'. How literary and un-actual Virgil has managed to make this typical scene by the very language he chooses! He has indeed, as Bowra suggested, seen the events through a veil of tradition and learning and abstract and rhetorical diction. It is obviously a Homeric scene in origin, but I cannot agree with R. D. Williams (in his note on the passage) that 'This elaborate description of the preparation for a feast is very much in the Homeric style'; in fact Homer's manner of describing the preparation of a meal is far more telling and appropriate, as one can see by looking, for example, at *Iliad* 1, 458ff. 'Girding themselves for the prey' and 'the feast to come' provide a curiously stilted introduction to the Virgilian account; phrases like 'viscera nudant' and 'flammasque ministrant' are neatly concise but at the same time distractingly indirect; 'trementia', '(still) quivering', is by contrast simple and realistic, but then comes the artificial 'aëna', 'bronzes', for bronze cauldrons; and the variation of 'pars' and 'alii' and the overworked 'locant', with its meaning that is here either too abstract or too precise, are equally cerebral in effect.

The tone changes in what immediately follows, but then in an odd and ultimately a tactless way:

> tum victu revocant viris, fusique per herbam
> implentur veteris Bacchi pinguisque ferinae.
> postquam exempta fames epulis mensaeque remotae,
> amissos longo socios sermone requirunt...
>
> (214–17)

'Then they recall their strength by food, and stretched out on the grass take their fill of old Bacchus and rich venison. After their hunger is gone and the tables are removed they talk long of their lost companions and wish them back...' The rather jolly and typically Latin but meaningless alliteration of 'tum victu revocant viris', a neat but arch expression, hardly prepares one for the false lyrical note of 'fusique per herbam', literally 'poured over the grass' like languid Euripidean bacchants rather than demoralized survivors of a great storm at sea; or for the sterile periphrasis 'old Bacchus' for wine. More disturbing still, the *déjeuner sur l'herbe* changes with startling suddenness to something even more inappropriate, close to a sophisticated Lucullan banquet, with the 'mensaeque remotae' of 216: the tables are removed as though the Trojans were reclining in a comfortable Roman villa and the slaves came in to clear away. A metaphorical use, no doubt, but full of false echoes rather than mysterious power, let alone a great Poeschl-esque revelation of the human soul. After that, Virgil's description of their doubt and despair about the fate of their comrades comes as a relief – this is something he expresses rather well – and the scene ends with brilliant enjambment and rhetorical pathos:

> nunc Amyci casum gemit et crudelia secum
> fata Lyci fortemque Gyan fortemque Cloanthum.
>
> (221f.)

Despite his relatively plain vocabulary Virgil uses a highly artificial language – even more so in effect than Homer's, whose artificiality is of a different kind, arising as it does partly out of the formular style and partly from the conflation of forms and dialects in the course of an evolving oral tradition. Virgil is artificial, first, because of his brilliant but over-intense deployment of those linguistic airs and graces that were adumbrated in the self-conscious development of Latin as a literary language from Ennius on and sharpened by the virtuoso effects so dear to the Alexandrine taste. Second, through his *penchant* for rhetoric and rhetorical tropes, from which Homer is mercifully almost free. Moreover the abstract quality of Virgil's poetry, its inability to describe concrete experience in actual terms, its indirectness, is the reverse side of that famous profundity and mysterious use of symbol and association that are praised more often than they are precisely identified. The *Aeneid* is, to be sure, a great poem, greater perhaps in texture than in overall conception. Yet it ultimately creates a kind of monotony that undercuts the brilliant detail and the occasional reflective *tour de force*; for the same kind and degree of intensity are poured out on scenes of quite diverse feeling and emphasis. In Homer on the other hand – that 'direct' and supposedly naive and limited primitive – both tonal variation and the contrast of deliberately simple and deliberately complex passages are distinctly superior.[13]

---

[13] Brooks Otis in *Virgil: a Study in Civilized Poetry* (Oxford, 1963) admits some of the weaknesses of Virgil's 'subjective' style; for example 'we...lose the sense of the

4-2

One should not evade judging the *Aeneid* as a whole in relation to its central theme and purpose. Is it perhaps Virgil's great theme of Rome's destiny that elevates the epic, and the lack of some such theme that reduces Homer in the eyes of some critics to a lower level? Is it the case, as J. B. Hainsworth suggested in the article cited in n. 4, that 'Nor has Homer any great argument to advance, like Virgil or Milton, an element that is perhaps an essential part of the successful literary epic'? The first part of this statement must be true, in so far as Homer's main themes are ostensibly far more limited; but is it true that a good *literary* epic, even, must have a great – that is a 'grand', and therefore political, philosophical or theological – argument? Any epic, since this properly implies a very long poem, requires a central and unitary theme to sustain it; yet the theme need not be a grand one. The *Argonautica* of Apollonius is an unsuccessful epic, yet its weaknesses are not particularly engendered by its lack of 'great argument'; the tale of the Argonauts and of Jason and Medea had enough unity and importance to carry a great poem, had Apollonius only known how to make one. But it is obviously the moral quality of the themes of the *Aeneid*, and the *Divina Commedia* and *Paradise Lost* as well, that Hainsworth had in mind. It is in this respect that Virgil is the innovator and master, the model for all subsequent epic.[14] Yet is it *necessary* for the central argument to be grand, and in particular to be moral? Most professional critics now see literature as essentially a moral activity; William Empson went so far as to say that 'The idea that there actually couldn't be a moral debate in a literary work amounts to a collapse of the Western mind', and H. A. Mason's main question of the Homeric epics is this: 'are they great poetry and can they

character's objective reality' because the poet is 'constantly conscious of himself inside his characters' (pp. 31, 49). He still insists on its importance, although he is quite unable to define its 'true meaning and function' (p. 90).

[14] It is probably in theme rather than language that Virgil was Dante's true master, in spite of what Dante himself seems to have thought:

> Tu se' lo mio maestro e 'l mio autore;
> tu se' solo colui da cu' io tolsi
> lo bello stilo che m' ha fatto onore,

'Thou art my master and my author. Thou art he from whom alone I took the style whose beauty has brought me honour' (*Inferno* I, 85–7, tr. J. D. Sinclair). Yet the style of the *Divina Commedia* is alien to the highly artificial style of Virgil, being plain and direct, more similar in many ways to Homer's, although of course entirely unformular. Its artifice lies primarily in the complicated and quite un-Virgilian system of the *terza rima*.

perform poetry's greatest office, to make us, in a good sense, more knowing about Man?'[15] Admittedly, any long poem that has absolutely nothing important to say about human life is likely to be trivial; but Greek tragedy shows very clearly that important things can be said within the framework of a narrative based on figures of legend or myth who are not necessarily engaged in cataclysmic events like the foundation of Rome or the Fall of Man.

My personal feeling about the much-debated question of Virgil's grand theme is that Rome's destiny and Aeneas' part in it, although noble, are at odds with several of the poet's other intentions and methods and in particular with his thematic use of the *Iliad* and *Odyssey*. It would be agreed, at least, that *Paradise Lost* is finest where it does not try too hard to fulfil Milton's expressed intention to 'justify the ways of God to men'. The familiar difficulties about that poem, that Satan is far more interesting than God or his Son, that even Milton can become tedious when he tries to represent divine majesty in bloated passages about angelic choirs worshipping Jesus Christ, and that he is stronger in his lyrical descriptions of Adam and Eve in Paradise than in his reflections upon its loss – all these combine to suggest that, although a major epic needs a major theme, it does not have to be an overtly philosophical, political or theological one. Perhaps it is salutary to remember at this point that one of the most powerful and moral of all poems is of mixed oral and literary origins and has a theme that, like the *Odyssey*'s, is professedly biographical: the *Epic of Gilgamesh* (an epic admittedly only relatively), composed in Akkadian, but using Sumerian elements, in the second millennium B.C.

That brings us back to the *Iliad* before we return to *Paradise Lost*. What *is* the *Iliad*'s main theme? The wrath of Achilles, as it purports to be? Or the whole fighting before Troy? Neither answer is complete enough to be entirely satisfying, and the tendency has recently been to side with the English critics and look for something grander. 'If we should try to define the *Iliad* in a general way', wrote Adam Parry, 'we might think of a long poem dealing critically with the heroic conception of life', and that is echoed by Hainsworth: 'there shines through his narrative his vision of the heroic world'.[16] These

[15] H. A. Mason, *From Homer to Pope*, p. 10.
[16] Adam Parry in 'Have We Homer's *Iliad*?', pp. 191f ; J. B. Hainsworth in 'The criticism of an oral Homer', p. 93.

judgements are true, up to a point. Certainly it is the conflict of heroic and post-heroic values and attitudes that gives the *Iliad* much of its piquancy for the discerning modern reader, and I should be surprised if Homer himself were not aware of something of the kind. Nevertheless it was, for him, formally an attempt to give a central core and focus, through the wrath-theme, to a whole mass of inherited poetry about the war – to reduce a many-sided nostalgic vision of the Trojan *geste* to an artistic and logical unity. This is one important respect (to revert for a moment to the discussion in § 1) in which the critic needs to take a special view of an oral poem, especially a massive one that is the culmination of a highly developed and ancient tradition. For the motives of such a work are inevitably complex; such a work has no author who begins by crystallizing (over many years, perhaps, like Milton and Virgil) a deliberate and autonomous conception of what his central theme is to be in all its aspects and implications. The oral poem has a 'final' composer who is faced with a mass of pre-existing materials and who imposes, or elicits, a theme of which one main purpose must be simply to provide a kind of coherence – one that, as in Homer's case, can drop into the background over whole sections of the monumental product but that also possesses its own quite distinct unity of *genre* and subject. That is why it may be no less misleading to ask 'What is the theme of the *Iliad*?', or 'Has the *Iliad* a grand argument, and, if not, why not?' than to demand to be told 'Who, precisely, is the hero of *Paradise Lost*?'.

In the preface that Milton added to that poem in 1668 he defended his use of blank verse; rhyme, he wrote in this well-known passage, is 'to all judicious ears, trivial and of no musical delight; which consists only in apt Numbers, fit quantity of Syllables, and the sense variously drawn out from one Verse into another.' It is interesting to observe the stress Milton places on 'sense variously drawn out from one Verse into another'; that is, on variety of enjambment, of which Homer even more than Virgil was so great a master. Here is a passage from the second book of *Paradise Lost* that describes the fallen angels at leisure; some run races and engage in mock battles,

> Others with vast Typhoean rage more fell
> Rend up both Rocks and Hills, and ride the Air
> In whirlwind; Hell scarce holds the wild uproar.
> As when Alcides from Oechalia Crown'd

With conquest, felt th' envenomed robe, and tore
Through pain up by the roots Thessalian Pines,
And Lichas from the top of Oeta threw
Into th' Euboic sea.

(II, 539–46)

A Homeric as well as a Virgilian passage, obviously enough. Its
complexity of enjambment and the tension between the verses as
rhythmical and semantic units have given rise to an acute if sometimes precarious debate between two distinguished critics. Donald
Davie remarks of verse 540 that 'there is no expressive or dramatic
reason why "Air" should be separated in this way from "In
whirlwind" – a phrase which merely dangles limply into the next
line'; on which Christopher Ricks comments that 'this is surely to
miss the utter difference in tone between the two phrases "ride the
Air" and "In whirlwind" – a difference which is successfully
emphasized by the line-break. "Ride the Air" gives a momentary
suggestion of serenity, of strong and calm control. "In whirlwind"
shatters this into "wild uproar".'[17] This is, I believe, to say too much,
just as Dr Davie says too little. 'Ride the Air' needs modifying, and
Milton does so in an entirely Homeric use of runover-word enjambment. I doubt whether any 'serenity' was being set up, even momentarily – after all, they are rending up rocks and hills – in order
to be shattered. It is simply that, in Dr Davie's words, 'the swing of
the reading eye or voice around the line-ending is...turned to
poetically expressive use', as ideally it should be. In the Hercules
(Alcides) simile that follows Davie criticizes the abrupt interposition
of 'Through pain' in verse 244, and Ricks retorts that through the
separation of 'tore' from 'up' in the succeeding verse 'The agonized
word-order presents the knotted effort of Hercules'. Both ignore the
deliberately Grecizing word-order and the emphasis on 'Through
pain' by its careful positioning at the beginning of the verse: not
only *in* pain but *driven on by* pain and *through a veil* of pain; while the
heavy monosyllables, rather than the word-order, do indeed
reinforce the sense of intensity and effort. Finally Davie objects to
the cumulation of 'Into th' Euboic sea' on the ground that *where*
Lichas was thrown is unimportant. Ricks replies that *how far* he was
thrown emphasizes Hercules' great strength; but this too is not the

[17] Donald Davie, *The Living Milton*, p. 83, cited by C. B. Ricks, *Milton's Grand Style* (Oxford, 1963), pp. 44f.

whole truth, or even the important aspect of it, for Lichas being hurled into the sea close to Euboea is simply part of the learned allusion, which is completed in a natural and flowing way by a cumulative technique that is both relaxed and charming, reminiscent as it is of Homeric craftsmanship and reminding us that Milton composed in darkness, in his mind, not on to the blank page. If his style is like the 'deliberate unrolling of some vast material', as the Victorian critic R. W. Dixon is cited by Professor Ricks as saying, then it is essentially progressive and cumulative in the manner of the oral singer, although with expressive refinements derived from literacy and from the whole Virgilian background.

Milton's fallen angels have their own heroic bards, for

> Others more mild,
> Retreated in a silent valley, sing
> With notes angelical to many a harp
> Their own heroic deeds and hapless fall.
>
> (II, 546–9)

Yet

> Others apart sat on a hill retired,
> In thoughts more elevate, and reasoned high
> Of providence, foreknowledge, will, and fate,
> Fixed fate, free will, foreknowledge absolute,
> And found no end, in wandering mazes lost.
>
> (II, 557–61)

Here in this contrast is Milton's own implied assertion of the 'grand theme', of philosophy over poetry, of Virgil over Homer, of Aeneas seeking Rome's destiny over Achilles sitting in his hut and singing to Patroclus of something like 'their own heroic deeds'. And yet the whole brilliantly wrought scene, with its elaborate patterning and typically Miltonic mixture of the lyrical with the didactic, contains much that is Homeric in style (as well as a certain amount that is Virgilian), most clearly so, once again, in its cumulative technique; for example verse 559, 'Of providence, foreknowledge, will, and fate' is marvellously elaborated in a ruminative oral way by 560, 'Fixed fate, free will, foreknowledge absolute', and this sharpens the impact of the pungent and paradoxical yet magical climax of 561, 'And found no end, in wandering mazes lost'.

If Milton's cumulative technique has caused his critics some difficulty, I cannot forbear to cite one brilliant interpretative success to which Professor Ricks also pays tribute. In book VIII, 59–63, Milton says of Eve that

> With goddess-like demeanour forth she went;
> Not unattended, for on her as Queen
> A pomp of winning Graces waited still,
> And from about her shot Darts of desire
> Into all eyes to wish her still in sight.

A. Stein shows on p. 91 of his book *Answerable Style* (Minneapolis, 1953) that the 'desire' of the penultimate verse begins by looking like the blatantly sexual desire that Eve inspires, and herself feels once she has tasted the forbidden fruit; but is then revealed by the enjambed final verse ('desire...*to wish her still in sight*') as a still entirely innocent desire projected on to others that so lovely a creature should not go away. Does Homer anywhere offer such brilliant ambiguity and paradox, so haunting a foreshadowing of what is to come? I doubt it; and it is scarcely relevant that Milton's model here was assuredly, in part, the Odyssean description of Penelope descending the staircase of her palace 'not alone, but two maidservants followed with her', οὐκ οἴη, ἅμα τῇ γε καὶ ἀμφίπολοι δύ' ἕποντο (1, 331 = 18, 207), in itself superior to Milton's over-blown 'pomp of winning Graces'. Yet perhaps a faintly similar nuance can be found, for instance, at *Odyssey* 13, 80, quoted on p. 102, where the sleep that falls on Odysseus' eyelids once he boards the Phaeacian ship is 'beyond waking, sweetest, most closely similar to death'. The conjunction of sweet sleep and death is poignant and still unusual at this period, but it is also subtly symbolic of Odysseus' reaffirmed mortality as he returns from the half-divine Phaeacians, and the memory of divine bliss with Calypso rejected by his own choice, to the destruction of the suitors in Ithaca and the mature charms of the mortal Penelope.

Milton at his tenderest and most powerful overwhelms one with his concentrated virtuosity and intensity of vision, in a way that arguably surpasses anything that can reasonably be claimed for Homer. Here Satan takes possession of the serpent in order to approach Eve:

> him fast sleeping soon he found
> In labyrinth of many a round self-rolled,
> His head the midst, well stored with subtle wiles:

Not yet in horrid shade or dismal den,   185
Nor nocent yet, but on the grassy herb
Fearless unfeared he slept: in at his mouth
The Devil entered, and his brutal sense,
In heart or head, possessing soon inspired
With act intelligential; but his sleep   190
Disturbed not, waiting close the approach of morn.
Now whenas sacred light began to dawn
In Eden on the humid flowers, that breathed
Their morning incense, when all things that breathe,
From the earth's great altar send up silent praise   195
To the Creator, and his nostrils fill
With grateful smell, forth came the human pair
And joined their vocal worship to the choir
Of creatures wanting voice; that done partake
The season, prime for sweetest scents and airs: 200
Then cómmune how that day they best may ply
Their growing work: for much their work outgrew
The hands' dispatch of two gardening so wide.
And Eve first to her husband thus began:
    'Adam, well may we labour still to dress   205
This garden, still to tend plant, herb and flower,
Our pleasant task enjoined, but till more hands
Aid us, the work under our labour grows,
Luxurious by restraint; what we by day
Lop overgrown, or prune, or prop, or bind,   210
One night or two with wanton growth derides
Tending to wild. Thou therefore now advise...'
                                            (IX, 182–212)

All the inherited felicities of diction and style are here: assonance, alliteration, inversion, chiasmus, antithesis, paradox, euphuistic or consciously etymological epithets – 'many a round self-rolled', 'Nor nocent yet', 'Fearless unfeared', 'brutal sense' versus 'act intelligential', 'their vocal worship to the choir | Of creatures wanting voice', 'luxurious by restraint', and so on. Such refinements of the classicizing style are essential to Milton's poetry, as are the variations of tone from grandiloquent to hieratic to the touching simplicity, artificial in the best sense though it is, of Eve's prelude to Adam; but so too is the 'sense variously drawn out from one Verse into another' and the almost Homeric conjunction of a subordinating syntax with the steady progression of thought required by a semi-oral mode of composition. Underneath it all is the poet's unique conception of the scene itself, his clear and enchanting vision of all that happened, the gradation from the brute qualities of Satan and the serpent to the coming of ambivalent dawn (both pagan and Christian), then to Eve's fatal but irresistible plea about the inefficiencies of gardening when in love. This part of *Paradise Lost* towers above everything in Virgil and nearly everything in Homer. For what Milton uniquely possessed as an epic poet, to complement the grandeur of his theme and style and the seriousness of his epic vision as a whole, is a marvellous feeling of living force and sensuous beauty that finds expression in purely lyric terms. This lyrical quality is almost entirely beyond Virgil and shines out only fleetingly in Homer, most clearly in some of the similes but also, for instance, in that same scene of the carrying back of Odysseus on the Phaeacian ship. Yet it is also Milton's capacity for varying the tone and feeling of his poetry that makes him resemble Homer rather than the consistently intense and artifice-dominated Virgil. Admittedly he derives much of the artistry of his grand style from the Virgilian model as well as from the tradition of Latin prose rhetoric; but he has an unusual gift for exploiting the inner resources of language and at the same time preventing language from disguising thought – and in that he is entirely Homeric.

3 THE PLAIN STYLE RECONSIDERED

The last section considered some of the ways in which Virgil and Milton do and do not depart from the ancient oral exemplar of the *Iliad* and *Odyssey*. Against that background of Homer's literate descendants it is worth looking again at his diction and style – the plain style as it is often assumed to be – to see whether it is really so restricted by its formular and cumulative procedures, and by the lack of Virgilian rhetoric and word-music and the elaborateness of Milton's Grand Style, as to be enthralling mainly at the narrative level; or at most through what Bowra termed 'the irresistible movement of lines through a whole passage to a splendid climax'.

It is convenient to start from a more recent piece of Bowra's criticism, from the book that he left not quite complete at his death.[18] I shall interpose my own italicized comments and disagreements in the course of this unusual attempt to talk seriously about the style and language of Homer:

[18] C. M. Bowra, *Homer* (London, 1972), pp. 29f.

The oral and the literary epic

The Homeric style is beautifully straightforward and easy to follow [*yes*], and this is largely because it is formulaic [*no: it is largely because it is progressive*]. The fundamental formulae often consist of half-lines, which may be combined with others equally short to achieve a joint result, and these results are for this very reason easy to grasp [*actually formular verses are probably not much easier to comprehend, although they are easier to compose, than others*]. We know the parts, and the sum of them presents no difficulty [*does not follow; the same should be true of difficult sentences compounded out of simple words*]. Moreover, because the short phrase is ultimately the primary unit of composition, sentences are usually short, and more often than not end with the end of a line [*does not follow; moreover there are no less than 45 sentences of 4 or more lines in the 867 lines of Iliad 16, for example, and in fact most Homeric sentences are of two or more lines, that is, not strikingly short at all*]. Even when a word is carried over to the next line, it is not very important and tends usually to amplify what is already clear [*I am afraid this is a gross distortion of the runover-word technique and the cumulative style*]. Long sentences are rare [*I have already commented on that*]; paragraphs are made out of simple units [*what is a paragraph? it has no meaning in Homer*]. The speed and lightness of Homeric poetry, so alien to the deeply meditative and associative language of Virgil [*on which see the preceding section*], come from the formulae, and particularly from their being so well concentrated and polished by time and use [*again, speed and lightness depend primarily on the progressive style and the predominantly dactylic metre. The 'polish' of the formulas helps, but even predominantly non-formular passages, of which there are many, can be fast and light*]. There is nothing otiose in them [*except for a good deal of the formular elaboration itself, although I concede that it depends what one means by 'otiose'*], and their meaning is immediately clear. This clarity is a great source of strength... and...Homer again and again gives lines which for their sheer simplicity of strength, their immediacy of attack and surety of aim, go far beyond most literate poets [*a bit vague, but perhaps Homer's lucid and progressive expression of meaning does result in unusual forcefulness*]. This manner suits his matter, and is part of his triumph [*the material is not so straightforward as all that, and neither, as we shall see, is the manner of expressing even quite simple content*].

To justify and supplement these rather dogmatic amendments let me outline some concrete and substantial elements of Homeric craftsmanship and illustrate them from passages selected almost at random.

Homer's language is most obviously artificial because of its remoteness from any spoken language; otherwise his artifice does not obtrude itself, and does not depend heavily on a multitude of rhetorical expressions or on consciously elaborated word-music as in Virgil, or on the sublime magniloquence of Milton at his most typical. Yet artifice there certainly is. It lies in a whole set of complex tensions and counterpoises that include the following: tension between the two basic metrical elements, namely dactyls and spondees; between stress on the first long syllable of each of these elements and the natural accent of individual words, depending on their number of syllables; between phrases or sense-units and the individual cola, that is, the longer rhythmical units of which the hexameter verse is constructed; between adjacent verses of different colon-constitution – for the most regular form of Homeric hexameter entails four cola separated by word-break in or just before the second foot, in the third foot, and before the fifth foot or less commonly in the fourth. Other tensions exist between short simple sentences and longer more complex ones, and between enjambed and unenjambed verses; and equally in those delicate contrasts between formular and non-formular, cumulative and non-cumulative that were indicated in § 1. Each of these tensions or counter-points is combined with and modified by some of the others, and the result is a fertile and complex variety that outweighs by far the relative lack of refinement in word-order. Occasionally these phenomena are deliberately manipulated to produce a special effect. More often, one may guess, they are the product of unconscious development of the resources of an established phraseology and an inherited rhythmical instinct. In either case they are largely responsible for the tautness and limpidity of Homeric verse.

Take for example the continuation of the passage quoted on pp. 76f. in which Odysseus is ferried back to Ithaca; this describes the harbour of Phorcys where he is landed:

> Φόρκυνος δέ τίς ἐστι λιμήν, ἁλίοιο γέροντος,
> ἐν δήμῳ 'Ιθάκης· δύο δὲ προβλῆτες ἐν αὐτῷ
> ἀκταὶ ἀπορρῶγες, λιμένος ποτιπεπτηυῖαι,
> αἵ τ' ἀνέμων σκεπόωσι δυσαήων μέγα κῦμα
> ἔκτοθεν· ἔντοσθεν δέ τ' ἄνευ δεσμοῖο μένουσι   100
> νῆες ἐΰσσελμοι, ὅτ' ἂν ὅρμου μέτρον ἵκωνται.
> αὐτὰρ ἐπὶ κρατὸς λιμένος τανύφυλλος ἐλαίη,
> ἀγχόθι δ' αὐτῆς ἄντρον ἐπήρατον ἠεροειδές,
> ἱρὸν νυμφάων αἳ νηϊάδες καλέονται.
>
> (*Odyssey* 13, 96–104)

The verse is primarily dactylic, with occasional spondaic sequences that can be significant for sense or emphasis, for instance Φόρκυνος in 96, δυσαήων in 99. The tension between metrical stress and word-accent is strongly marked in 102 but neatly resolved in the culmiating word, ἐλαίη, where the two coincide. The punctuation of 96–101 is an indication of the harmonious variation of internal stop and sentence-length, and the three last verses are uninterrupted and very lightly enjambed to provide both contrast and the resolution of tension. A different and more obvious artifice, more Virgilian in character, shows itself exceptionally in the emphatic word-music of 103 with its accumulation of similar vowel-sounds and in the brief rhetorical antithesis of ἔκτοθεν· ἔντοσθεν δέ in 100. For the counterpoint between sense-units and rhythmical cola it is convenient to look back at the preceding verses, 90–5:

> ὃς πρὶν μὲν μάλα πολλὰ πάθ᾽ ἄλγεα ὃν κατὰ θυμὸν
> ἀνδρῶν τε πτολέμους ἀλεγεινά τε κύματα πείρων,
> δὴ τότε γ᾽ ἀτρέμας εὗδε, λελασμένος ὅσσ᾽ ἐπεπόνθει.
> εὖτ᾽ ἀστὴρ ὑπερέσχε φαάντατος, ὅς τε μάλιστα
> ἔρχεται ἀγγέλλων φάος Ἠοῦς ἠριγενείης,
> τῆμος δὴ νήσῳ προσεπίλνατο ποντοπόρος νηῦς.   95

These are all 'ideal' four-colon verses; the sequence is an unusually long one, but the first three provide a kind of coda to the whole first half of the poem and are therefore appropriately lapidary in construction, while the next three herald the arrival in Ithaca itself. The new scene is distinguished by a less straightforward distribution of rhythm and meaning:

> τῆμος δὴ | νήσῳ | προσεπίλνατο | ποντοπόρος νηῦς.   95
> Φόρκυνος | δέ τίς ἐστι ⋮ λιμήν, | ἁλίοιο γέροντος,   96

where the former verse maintains the classic form and the latter extends it by the surge of sense across the main caesura, to begin a run of rhythmically more complex verses that accord perfectly with the condensed and variegated aspects of this ideal harbour.

If one doubts the ability of oral composers to create such effects deliberately one has only to look at what they can do in more obviously extreme cases. Here for example are seven verses from a brilliant scene of confused fighting in *Iliad* 16 (on which see also pp. 168f. below):

> Πηνέλεως δὲ Λύκων τε συνέδραμον· ἔγχεσι μὲν γὰρ
> ἤμβροτον ἀλλήλων, μέλεον δ᾽ ἠκόντισαν ἄμφω·
> τὼ δ᾽ αὖτις ξιφέεσσι συνέδραμον. ἔνθα Λύκων μὲν
> ἱπποκόμου κόρυθος φάλον ἤλασεν, ἀμφὶ δὲ καυλὸν
> φάσγανον ἐρραίσθη· ὁ δ᾽ ὑπ᾽ οὔατος αὐχένα θεῖνε

The oral and the literary epic

Πηνέλεως, πᾶν δ' εἴσω ἔδυ ξίφος, ἔσχεθε δ' οἷον
δέρμα, παρηέρθη δὲ κάρη, ὑπέλυντο δὲ γυῖα.

(Iliad 16, 335–41)

There is no need to stress the wonderful skill that such a violent
manipulation of the rhythmical verse-norm must imply, or the
deliberateness of its application to a description of violent and
staccato action. One suspects that it is only feasible because the
progress and continuity of the action is simple and uninterrupted,
as is the normal case with Homer; the subtleties of rhythm, sentence-
length and enjambment do not extend to, and would perhaps be
excluded by, an artificially subordinating syntax. This basic
simplicity has a further manifestation that may have done much to
foster the illusion that Homer's is in any serious sense a 'plain' style:
on the whole each verse tends to contain just one single idea that is
strictly relevant to the advancing narrative, or even no more than
a single basic element of a proposition. The rest of the verse then
tends to consist of various kinds of elaboration, adjectival or adverbial
for the most part. There are naturally many exceptions to this
generalization, which is nevertheless more than a mere commonplace (and more significant than the observation that often the
important part of the sense comes in the first half of the verse); for
if true it makes the detailed refinements of diction and style much
easier to credit in the case of an oral composer. One can see the
phenomenon clearly enough even in English translation:

> While the sun was traversing the middle of the sky
> Then both sides' weapons struck home and the troops kept falling;
> But when the sun turned downward toward the time of unyoking
> Then the Achaeans prevailed even beyond their portion.
> They dragged hero Cebriones out of the spear-casts,
> Out of the tumult of Trojans, and took the armour from his shoulders,
> And Patroclus with hostile heart leapt upon the Trojans.

(Iliad 16, 777–83)

In unelaborated basic-English form the thought-sequence is as
follows, verse by verse: / Day long / fighting continued; / toward
evening / Achaeans prevailed, / got Cebriones' corpse / and stripped
it. / Patroclus attacked. / All else is elaboration and detail – essential
for making basic Greek into poetry, but the point is that the sense-
structure remains extremely simple and linear and allows the poet
to refine his words as he goes along.

Brooks Otis in his book on Virgil, significantly sub-titled 'A Study in Civilized Poetry', remarks of Homer that 'he was, as the later Greeks put it, imitating life and imitating it in a great but also a direct and simple way': a judgement that somewhat extends the implications of Homer's plain style.[19] *Simplicity* I have shown to exist in certain basic ways essential to the oral poet, but in Homer's case it is combined with enormous complexity in the use of words, rhythms and phrases as well as in the specifically oral techniques of formularity and cumulation. *Directness* is slightly different, but we may be inclined to suspect it as an authentic keynote of Homeric poetry now that the simplicity of expression has turned out to be so ambiguous. In what remains I shall be concerned with indicating some of the ways in which Homer is not so directly *imitative* of life as Professor Otis and others may believe.

The idea that Homer simply imitates life without penetrating far beneath its surface is an ancient one that was given fresh expression in the famous first chapter, on 'Odysseus' Scar', of Erich Auerbach's book *Mimesis* (Princeton, 1953). Starting from the scene in which the poet interrupts Eurycleia's recognition of her master through the scar on his foot by recounting at length how he had received the wound when still a boy, Auerbach concluded not only that Homer is uninterested in suspense (a judgement that has elements of truth but is not the whole truth) but also that there is, in his term, no 'background'. Nothing is hidden or kept back, everything is brought out into the open, into the foreground, everything is described, and as much formal importance is assigned to minor details as to the main actions. The feelings of the characters are not analysed and interpreted, as they are for instance by Virgil, but are externalized in speeches. Auerbach contrasts this kind of relentless realism (as he judges it to be) with the internalized view of events exemplified in the Old Testament tale of Abraham and Isaac. Here everything is mysterious and obscure; it is not even clear where God and Abraham are envisaged as being, the syntactical connection of events is rudimentary, and speech is used to suggest an inner meaning rather than to express, fully and openly, a specific attitude of mind. Homer, on the other hand, is concerned with 'delight in physical existence' (p. 10), or in Schiller's words 'simply the quiet existence and operation of things in accordance with their natures'. That is why there

---

[19] Brooks Otis, *Virgil: A Study in Civilized Poetry*, p. 5.

The oral and the literary epic

are all the details of palace-life in the *Odyssey* and feasting and fighting in the *Iliad*, with no development of character and only so much of a hero's past life revealed as is needed to account for his present actions. One consequence of all this, still according to Auerbach, is that there is no concept of peculiarly appropriate language, no 'separation of styles' as he calls it (p. 19); another is that heroes can be described as performing humble and everyday actions because the ideal of sublimity had not been invented.

One cannot help marvelling at the combination of ingenuity and insight that this classic essay in comparative literature reveals. At the same time much of what I have reported is certainly untrue: for example Homer is perfectly prepared to use a sublime style, and can deploy one even in spite of his formular language when he wishes – most obviously of gods, Zeus for example in the *Iliad*, but also of heroes; and there are many contexts from which the ordinary and the everyday are deliberately, as it seems, excluded. It is a nice idea that Homer's gaze sweeps dispassionately over palace, hovel or battlefield and imitates, or gives direct expression to, whatever it sees, but it is nevertheless a mistaken idea. Can it be true that there is nothing hidden, indirect or implicit in Homer, nothing mysterious? I waste no time on the answer; the passage about Odysseus asleep on the Phaeacian ship disproves it totally, and so do the deaths of Sarpedon, Patroclus and Hector in the *Iliad* or Priam's nocturnal journey in the last book of the same poem, to look no further.

The question of speeches provides an opportunity for testing one part of the Auerbach thesis in greater depth, and has the advantage of also bearing on my concern with the oral method and its relation to the abstract, rhetorical and 'grand' styles of Virgil and Milton. First, some facts. Both *Iliad* and *Odyssey* are full of people talking at length. In the sixteenth book of the former, for instance, nearly a third consists of direct speech. Nowhere in either poem are there long stretches of narrative undiversified by speech; it is striking, for example, how much utterance the poet has managed to inject into his version of the folktale adventures of Odysseus in distant lands. Virgil and Milton present a distinctly different picture. In the former, speeches are a relatively unimportant component; they may serve a directly rhetorical purpose (for example of exhortation or persuasion) or make a minimal concession to the realistic narration of human contacts, but the poet is clearly happiest when he is describing events, including personal exchanges, in his own words. In *Paradise Lost*, on the other hand, speech is crucial at particular points; book XI, for example, is for the most part composed of long interchanges between Adam and Eve, Eve and the serpent, Eve and herself, and with Adam again; and the two preceding books formally consist of conversations between Adam and Raphael. Yet elsewhere objective narrative predominates, so that it cannot be said that normal Miltonic practice has much in common with Homer's constant predilection for direct speech.

This predilection is certainly not an innovation by the monumental composer himself – although he may well have accentuated the practice as he probably did with the use and scale of similes. A relatively heavy speech-element must have formed part of the oral epic tradition in Greece for many generations; so much can be asserted for purely linguistic reasons, because of the organic presence of fully developed formulas in contexts exclusive to direct speech. But I would go further than that and suggest that the use of direct speech was probably an extremely ancient characteristic of the epic tradition in Greece. It is already marked in the *Epic of Gilgamesh* and was not inconspicuous in the Mesopotamian poetical style as a whole; and, without asserting direct imitation or many specific details in common, I remain convinced that narrative and poetical trends in second-millennium Greece, like mythological and religious ones, were strongly affected by the ancient Near East and in particular by Mesopotamia.

Yet Homer's use of speeches involves more than the maintenance of a literary tradition or the conventional form of a *genre*. It is through direct speech by the heroes that the poet expresses the heroic *ethos* that is, at the very least, an important part of his epic plan. He does not do so by direct exposition, or even primarily by the contriving of heroic situations in themselves. Moreover he refrains from comment in his own person and keeps subjective judgements virtually out of his poetry. That is one possible result of a long oral tradition, although not a necessary one – the Yugoslav *guslari*, for instance, were not averse from personal comment. Yet in one way it is inevitable that Homer should reflect heroic attitudes through the words of his heroic characters. For much of the Homeric epic is essentially dramatic in conception, and in this respect it differs seriously from most of its successors. It presents the action as drama. That explains something important about the tendency to represent the interplay of persons through their own words, and has its own reasons.

First, most oral singers seem to share the ambition of the *guslari* to 'tell it as it really was'. When Odysseus wishes to praise the Phaeacian singer Demodocus describing the suffering of the Achaeans he does so by saying that Demodocus has sung the events 'in exceptionally good order', λίην...κατὰ κόσμον. What better way to do this than by drawing out of the past the actual words, the threats and boasts and questionings, of the long-dead heroes themselves? Secondly, whereas Virgil is an interpreter, a *vates*, an artist who presents his audience with situations seen and understood through himself, the oral poet conceives himself rather as passively receiving his material from the past by the gift of the gods. He is mainly a receptacle (at least in his own estimation), and if he claims to be 'self-taught'[20] that refers only to the development of his particular repertory and means of embellishment. So Homer's allegiance to this kind of tradition keeps even his ambition relatively concrete: to recreate a real if vanished world rather than to divine the inner meaning of history or the destiny of men. Thirdly, the oral singer may have become temperamentally almost incapable of paraphrasing in his own words what a character was thinking or feeling. His natural method was to elicit the character's own expression of that. The idea of saying things like 'Achilles at this point was rejecting all the usual beliefs about warfare', or more simply 'he realized the whole endeavour was futile' seems not to have occurred, or to have been rejected as inappropriate. Simpler psychological descriptions like '*X* wondered which of two courses to follow' are not uncommon, but when feelings become more complicated than that then *X*'s own statement of those feelings becomes necessary. For the feelings are the man; the poet-reporter describes the man acting, and an important part of the action is the acting out of his thoughts and feelings through speech. It would detract from the realism of the description if the poet interposed himself as interpreter at this point. Acting, thinking, feeling, saying are interconnected aspects of the hero's involvement with his excessively codified environment. Yet to claim like Auerbach that Homer simply externalizes thought through speech, that nothing is held back, is greatly to over-simplify

---

[20] As Phemius does at *Odyssey* 22, 347

the whole situation as well as to ignore the random and complicated elements that enter this heroic environment, whether it be through the unpredictability of the gods, or sudden unheroic impulses, or annoying contradictions in the fundamental heroic concepts of loyalty, honour and fortitude.

Three further points can be made about Homer's use of speeches – which repays a broader study than that of its purely formalistic aspects carried out in Lohmann's work cited in n. 1 above. First, unlike Virgil, Homer only exceptionally uses them for strictly rhetorical and persuasive purposes; when he does so, as in the embassy scene of the ninth book of the *Iliad*, it is still very different from the kind of rhetoric that descended as a blight on subsequent Greek literature from the direction of the citizen-politician and the professional Sophist. Second, from time to time Homer is so carried away by his view of speech as the proper vehicle of heroic values that he pays too little attention to the special demands of context. Pandarus, who treacherously breaks the truce made in *Iliad* 3, is given some fine and conventional utterances before his death in 5, and his special moral ambivalence as blasphemer and oath-breaker is entirely concealed by the normative exuberance of heroic boast and counter-boast. Third, it is in the speeches that rhythm and syntax tend to become most complex, since the speeches represent characters trying to formulate their reactions to fresh circumstances. Moreover the poets are not unaware of the conflict of emotions and expectations, even heroic ones. The heroes are set in a world that is as resistant and implacable as our own, although at different points, and therefore their speeches are full of passionate short utterances, of surprise or moral indignation, of the effort to compress every nuance of pride and proclamation into the interchanges allowed by battle or other approved forms of heroic confrontation. The following passage illustrates almost too clearly the contrast between speech and narrative as Penelope prepares to appear before the suitors:

> Ἡ δ' αὖτ' ἄλλ' ἐνόησε περίφρων Πηνελόπεια,
> μνηστήρεσσι φανῆναι ὑπέρβιον ὕβριν ἔχουσι·   410
> πεύθετο γὰρ οὗ παιδὸς ἐνὶ μεγάροισιν ὄλεθρον·
> κῆρυξ γάρ οἱ ἔειπε Μέδων, ὃς ἐπεύθετο βουλάς.
> βῆ δ' ἴεναι μέγαρόνδε σὺν ἀμφιπόλοισι γυναιξίν.
> ἀλλ' ὅτε δὴ μνηστῆρας ἀφίκετο δῖα γυναικῶν,
> στῆ ῥα παρὰ σταθμὸν τέγεος πύκα ποιητοῖο,   415

ἄντα παρειάων σχομένη λιπαρά κρήδεμνα,
Ἀντίνοον δ' ἐνένιπεν ἔπος τ' ἔφατ' ἔκ τ' ὀνόμαζεν·
''Ἀντίνο', ὕβριν ἔχων, κακομήχανε, καὶ δέ σέ φασιν
ἐν δήμῳ 'Ἰθάκης μεθ' ὁμήλικας ἔμμεν ἄριστον
βουλῇ καὶ μύθοισι· σὺ δ' οὐκ ἄρα τοῖος ἔησθα.   420
μάργε, τίη δὲ σὺ Τηλεμάχῳ θάνατόν τε μόρον τε
ῥάπτεις, οὐδ' ἱκέτας ἐμπάζεαι, οἶσιν ἄρα Ζεὺς
μάρτυρος; οὐδ' ὁσίη κακὰ ῥάπτειν ἀλλήλοισιν.'

(Odyssey 16, 409–23)

Her motives and actions are described in uninterrupted and lightly
enjambed whole verses down to 417, but then when she addresses
Antinous in 418ff. her fear and resentment pour out in short and
passionate bursts that overrun the verse-end to find a temporary but
typical resolution in the proverb-like moralism that occupies most of
423, 'it is unholy to weave evils against each other'.

The speeches in Homer raise two questions with which I was
concerned earlier, of complexity in language and the presentation
of a heroic world-view. They also exemplify the quite different
problem of scale. Some of the conversations, as we have seen, are
arguably drawn out to excess: Agamemnon, Achilles and Odysseus
in *Iliad* 19, Eumaeus and Odysseus in *Odyssey* 14. That is not, of
course, peculiar to the speeches; some of the Iliadic narrative,
especially when it concerns the *minutiae* of battle, is protracted in a
way that can pain or bemuse the modern reader. I admire H. A.
Mason's honesty when he writes that he 'cannot get interested in
long stretches of the epics'.[21] Part of his difficulty may be self-
created, through the idea that one can profitably approach Homer
through the medium of translations; but part of it arises out of the
nature of the poems themselves and especially of the *Iliad* – plainly,
in my own view, the greater of the two, but also plainly lacking the
narrative flow and diversity of the *Odyssey*. Part of the reason for the
enormous scale and detail, with a corresponding slowing of the pace,
may be the *Iliad*'s composite nature, the way in which it has been
agglomerated out of pre-existing materials, perhaps with less drastic
selectivity than in the case of the *Odyssey*. That means that variants
and repetitions are included that any principle of economy – not in
any event a ubiquitous one in oral poetry – woulda utomatically
reject. But often, as in *Iliad* 8 (in which a degree of rhapsodic elaboration may also be detected) there is a clear poetical intention to

---

[21] *From Homer to Pope*, p. 6.

reproduce the inexorable force of battle and the constantly alter-
nating fortunes of the contestants. A still surer instance of artistically
deliberate monumentality of scale is the whole seventeenth book of
the *Iliad*, which for over 700 verses of consistently high quality
pursues the to-and-fro fighting for the corpse of Patroclus. That a
certain suspense is created, whatever Auerbach might say, is undeniable, for during all this time Achilles is known to be still in
ignorance of his friend's death and the loss of his own armour. The
very fate of Troy will depend on his reactions. But there *is* a danger,
none the less, of producing in the hearer a feeling of mild frustration
at the lack of narrative progress. Whether ancient audiences felt
anything similar would depend, clearly, both on the singer's
dramatic power and on the virtuosity of language with which these
themes of struggle are expressed. The great burst of similes with
which the book reaches its formal climax at the end seems to suggest
that the poet himself, at least, was aware of accomplishing a *tour de
force*.

There is an obverse side to the problem of scale, for at many
points the Homeric singer remains concise and allusive, almost
lacunose, where our own literary taste would incline to expansion,
emphasis and explanation. There is rarely anything of Auerbach's
Old Testament mysteriousness (which is in any case partly the
result of a fragmentary tradition) to be seen in these abbreviated
contexts. And yet there may be, here too, a consciously artistic
intention; if so, then it contrasts curiously with the monumental
style as a whole. The Nausicaa scenes in *Odyssey* 6 and 7 have been
much admired for their delicate under-emphasis and brevity, but,
given the obvious subtlety of the poet's insight here, they could have
been developed and deepened somewhat without loss of refinement
or damage to the heroic – or rather the surprisingly *un*heroic – tone.
I suppose this is one reason why the poet keeps his emotional scenes,
at least those involving women, so unemphatically short: that the
traditional hero sleeps with his women, or uses them as servants,
rather than engaging them in delicate conversation. Penelope and
Andromache complicate the issue, but the tendency remains. And
yet Nausicaa is there; the poet has chosen to develop her admiration
for Odysseus although he need not have done so. Did he think, as a
modern critic might argue, that the very insubstantiality of his
reference to her feelings was more effective than a fuller and more

heroic treatment? Or is the reference so tenuous just because the encounter is in itself unheroic and untraditional? One cannot be sure; but it must be admitted that in several other cases of small-scale allusion, and not only those where abbreviation of a longer poem is probable, no specific artistic purpose seems to be served. Again the anomalies and obscurities of oral performance may account for much. Certainly the *literate* epic does not generally exemplify such unevenness of scale. Milton sometimes tries to express what might have been better left unsaid, or remitted to a prose treatise, but he does so in the service of theology rather than of literary art; and something similar is so with Virgil's excursuses into history and aetiology.

Many of the secrets of Homer's art remain inviolate, as they should and must. There *are* techniques and qualities of expression that the critic needs to explore and lay open, if possible, for others; yet in the end the last word should be with Homer himself. Here, then, is the passage describing the dazing and stripping of Patroclus by the god Apollo.[22] The pathetic momentum is already being established, not only in the poet's rare apostrophe to Patroclus in 787 but also, and less directly, in the soiling of the helmet that was really Achilles' and should never have undergone this fate; and in the cumulated reflection that it would now belong for a short while to Hector, yet his own destruction lay close at hand. One may ask oneself yet once again, as one re-reads these words, whether Homer's style is really plain, simple and direct, and whether allusiveness, indirection and a refined symbolism are the contrasting possessions of Virgil; and whether the expression, heavily formular and cumulative but also various and complex in the ways I have outlined, does not contribute in a quite special way to the majestic and relentless actions of the god who brings Patroclus' heroic life to its bitter close:

> Thrice then Patroclus leapt on like swift Ares
> Shouting most terribly, and thrice slew nine men.   785
> But when for the fourth time he charged like a god
> Then for you, Patroclus, appeared the end of your life.
> For Phoebus encountered you in the strong fight,
> And terrible he was; Patroclus did not recognize him as he came
>   through the throng,
> For he was concealed by much mist as he met him.   790

[22] See also the discussion of the wider context on pp. 211f.

And Apollo stood behind him and smote his back and broad
    shoulders
With the flat of his hand so that his eyes whirled round.
From his head Phoebus Apollo cast the helmet,
And it rolled along and clattered beneath the horses' feet,
The socketed helm, and its plume was soiled   795
With blood and dust – before that it was not lawful
For the horsehair cask to be soiled with dust
But it protected the head and graceful forehead of a man divine,
Of Achilles; but then Zeus gave it to Hector
To wear on *his* head, but destruction was close upon him.   800
And there was smashed in Patroclus' hands all the long-shadowed
    spear,
Weighty, great, heavy, armed with bronze; and from his shoulders
The fringed shield together with its strap fell to the ground,
And lord Apollo son of Zeus unloosed his corslet.
Infatuation took hold of his mind, and his glorious limbs were
    paralysed beneath him,   805
And he stood in bewilderment; and from behind in his back with
    sharp spear
A Dardanian man struck him from close by, between the shoulders,
Euphorbus son of Panthous, who excelled all his peers
With spear and horsemanship and his swift feet...

                                        (*Iliad* 16, 784–809)

5

HOMER AND
MODERN ORAL POETRY:
SOME CONFUSIONS

One of the curious things about Homeric studies is the way in which, although opinions in this field fluctuate violently, from time to time certain among them tend to become crystallized for no particular reason and are then accepted as something approaching orthodoxy. It is to try to delay such a crystallization, if it is not already too late, that I direct this brief glance at some current opinions on whether Homer – for the sake of clarity I apply this name in the first instance to the monumental composer of the *Iliad* – used the aid of writing, and in general at the value of comparative inferences based on the heroic poetry of modern Yugoslavia.

There is little point in tracing this question back to Wolf and beyond, partly because it has been done so often before but mainly because, since Milman Parry's demonstration that the Homeric poems bear all the marks of oral composition, the situation has substantially altered. Parry himself assumed that the poems were completely oral, since they so thoroughly exemplify the formular economy and scope of a well-developed oral tradition. This is a very reasonable opinion to which, until a few years ago, most critics who take an interest in such matters seem to have formally subscribed.

In 1952, however, H. T. Wade-Gery in *The Poet of the Iliad* (Cambridge, 1952) argued that the alphabet was adapted to its Greek form for the specific purpose of recording heroic poetry, and that this innovation made the Homeric poems possible; and Sir Maurice Bowra in his valuable book *Heroic Poetry* (London, 1952) proposed that Homer was a brilliant oral poet who subsequently learned the new technique of writing and thus was able to compose a poem of the size and richness of the *Iliad*. Of these two theories the latter is the less vulnerable; but what is common to them both is the assumption that no oral poet could have composed an *Iliad* or *Odyssey* without the aid, somehow employed, of writing. In other words these scholars accepted the theory of a well-developed oral tradition, but combined it with the old belief that such long and complex poems must somehow have been written out, in this case by or at the instance of a singer who lived at the crucial time when the new form of writing was just becoming available.

In the following year Bowra's suggestion was pertinently criticized by Parry's able helper and continuator, A. B. Lord. In his article 'Homer's Originality: Oral Dictated Texts',[1] Lord argued that the comparative study of oral epic, especially in Parry's chosen field of Yugoslavia, made it quite clear that to introduce an oral poet to the art of writing is usually fatal to his art, and at the very least alters the quality of his poetry for the worse and destroys some of its characteristic oral features. He loses spontaneity and his verses become portentous and stilted. Therefore Homer, whose verse was not like this, cannot have taken to writing.

This is a contention that I am prepared to accept, even in spite of the qualifications expressed on p. 130 below. It seems unlikely that Bowra's theory is tenable. For in spite of the huge difference in quality between even the best of the South Slavic bards and Homer – and it is a difference we must never overlook, and one that makes some comparative inferences highly misleading – the essential elements of an adequate oral technique remain common to both. These consist of an exceptional verbal and rhythmic memory and complete familiarity with a large and varied stock of standard or formular phrases and themes. The impact of writing, and as a consequence of deliberate as opposed to spontaneous and semi-automatic verse-making, on any true oral poet, whatever the artistry and complexity of his particular tradition, can be assumed to be highly deleterious to these essential oral qualities; and has proved to be so in the studies made by Parry and Lord in Yugoslavia and by other field-workers elsewhere. Even if a poet trained in the oral technique might exceptionally succeed in transforming his approach so as to be able to write successful poetry, it is virtually certain that what he wrote would show a marked relaxation of the economy of the oral formular system, together with a corresponding increase in non-formular material and in the gratuitous variation of traditional fixed phrases. There is no such relaxation in Homer. For in spite of the extreme subtlety of the uses to which he puts the formular apparatus, the fact remains that in the *Iliad* and *Odyssey* a very large

[1] *TAPA* 84 (1953), 124–34.

number of crystallized formulas are employed with an astonishing economy and lack of unnecessary variation. This suggests strongly, indeed almost imperatively, that the oral technique was used in full and undiminished degree for the main act of composition of each of the two monumental poems.

In place of the theory suggested by Bowra, Lord in the article cited advanced another suggestion that has won rather wide acceptance, at least in the country of its origin. His theory still rests on the assumption common to Wade-Gery and Bowra, that the complexity of the Homeric poems presupposes the aid of writing in some form. The theory is that the monumental composer was a true oral poet, but that he must have gained the advantages of writing, without the unacceptable disadvantages, by *dictating his poetry to a literate accomplice*. That dictation can be successfully carried out by some oral poets is proved by experiments in Yugoslavia. Many of the songs in Parry–Lord, *Serbocroatian Heroic Songs*, vol. 1 (Cambridge, Mass., 1954; hereafter *SCHS*, 1), are dictated. They were dictated to Parry's assistant Nikola Vujnović, who wrote them down and who helped to improve them by pointing out inconsistencies and metrical anomalies as they occurred. Usually although not invariably these dictated texts are more accurate and slightly fuller than the sung versions recorded by phonograph. Yet it must be remembered that the examples in question were written out by an educated and highly intelligent scribe familiar with the principles and practice of oral poetry and often prompted by Parry himself. There is no question, however, of Nikola having put words or ideas into the poet's mouth; and that dictation can be done in less favourable conditions is shown by a remark of the heroic singer Salih Ugljanin, *SCHS*, 1, 383: 'once I saw a man from Plav who had such interest to learn a song when some singer sang it that he wrote it down and took it and read it to them in Plav. He learned it and sang it.' There is also the case of the short (990 lines) and mediocre Cretan song of Daskaloyannes, described most recently by J. A. Notopoulos.[2] This was composed by the illiterate cheese-maker Pantzelió and dictated in 1786 to a simple but literate shepherd called Sephes, who fortunately appended a verse epilogue describing the whole procedure. In cases like these there is of course no means of knowing whether the dictated version is better than the ordinary sung version.

[2] *AJP* 73 (1952), 225ff.

Homer and modern oral poetry

The publication by A. B. Lord of Avdo Međedović's 12,000-line version of 'The wedding of Smailagić Meho', in vol. III of *SCHS*, together with the singer's recorded commentary on his poem, is awaited with eagerness for many reasons. We shall certainly then learn more about the technique of a modern oral poet. We may find out more about the extent to which in dictated texts the material already dictated may be used as a means of controlling what is still to come. Yet it seems doubtful whether this or any other modern experiment will be able to illustrate in any satisfactory and convincing way those deliberate processes of checking, revision, cross-reference, and rearrangement which I suppose to be implied for Homer by scholars like Bowra, Lord, and Wade-Gery. In fact Lord, who was of course already completely familiar with Avdo's *tour de force*, stated on p. 133 of his article that dictation

is an opportunity for the singer to show his best, not as a performer, but as a story-teller and a poet. He can ornament his song as fully as he wishes and is capable; he can develop his tale with completeness, he can dwell lovingly on passages which in normal performance he would often be forced to shorten because of the pressure of time or because of restlessness of the audience. The very length of the Homeric poems is the best proof that they are the products of the moment of dictation rather than that of singing. The leisureliness of their tempo, the fullness of their telling, are also indications of this method. The poetic moments of the tradition, used perhaps sparingly in normal performance, accumulate to provide that richness of poetry which Bowra feels suggests writing.

Lord's opinion on the subject of dictation is of great importance, and his point that the poet who dictates is free from the exigencies of a large audience and a particular occasion is a good one; but the rest of what he says here seems to amount to little more than an expression of the feeling that a long and complex poem implies the aid of writing. There is certainly no intrinsic reason, for example, why 'leisureliness of...tempo' must suggest dictated rather than normal oral poetry. There is little here or elsewhere in Lord's article to support his conjecture that the *Iliad* and *Odyssey* were oral dictated texts. Even though he tells us that in Yugoslavia dictation tends to produce a 'better' poem, yet it does not by any means follow that the same is true for a poet of altogether different calibre, working at a different stage of oral development, and supported by a tradition immeasurably finer and richer, such as Homer was. In short we must beware of an argument that unconsciously runs something like this: 'In Yugoslavia dictated songs are usually superior to those given in ordinary oral performances; therefore all supreme oral epics must be dictated.'

Lord's theory that the *Iliad* and *Odyssey* are oral dictated texts arises from his conviction, first expressed with some suddenness on p. 129 of his article, that although 'Homer...did not need writing to be a creative poet in his tradition', yet 'it must be true that he lived in an age when writing existed and was developed to such a point that the *Iliad* could be written down. It was probably the age of transition from oral to written technique in literature.' This conviction seems, as we have seen, to be based on the length and complexity of the Homeric poems, and not on assumptions about Homer's date and that of the introduction of alphabetic writing. But Lord's hypothesis, which, whether right or wrong, is a useful contribution to the problem, was then used as a premiss by Sterling Dow in an inference about the date of Homer – for Dow the monumental composer of both *Iliad* and *Odyssey*. For in a survey of Homeric studies,[3] Dow accepted the late-eighth-century date for the introduction of alphabetic writing in Greece advanced by Rhys Carpenter,[4] and assumed that, since the *Iliad* and *Odyssey* must have been oral dictated texts, then they must have been composed in the seventh century B.C. This argument rests on two dubious assumptions: first that the alphabet is quite as late as Carpenter thought, and second that the poems were dictated. On the first point, Carpenter's article was a valuable reaction against the tendency to place the introduction of the alphabet back in the tenth or early ninth century; but the discovery of new material, notably the Ischia cup,[5] and the reassessment of some of the older material have confirmed that writing was being used in different parts of the Greek world for quite casual purposes by the last quarter of the eighth century B.C., and was presumably known in places even before this. The second point has already been called into question. Over against both these dubious assumptions there is a not inconsiderable body of evidence to suggest that the *Iliad*, at least, reached something like its present form before the end of the eighth century; one may cite, for example, the extreme improbability of Homer's personality and birthplace

[3] In *Classical Weekly* 49 (1956), 116ff.   [4] In *AJA* 37 (1933), 8ff.
[5] See e.g. *Classical Review* n.s. 6 (1956), 95ff.

having been so thoroughly obscured if he was in fact a near-contemporary of Achilochus.

Confused enough already, the situation is still further complicated by a fact that requires extremely careful evaluation. It is briefly stated by Sterling Dow on p. 117 of the review-article already cited: '*Verbatim* oral transmission of a poem composed orally and not written down is unknown.'[6] This proposition is primarily based on a fuller discussion by Bowra in his *Heroic Poetry*, pp. 368ff., where we read that a heroic poem

> once composed and recited is usually lost, unless by some rare chance someone writes it down. None the less the same story will be told again and again, in slightly different forms, by the same bard and by other bards, and may in these conditions have a life of many centuries. We may therefore speak of the transmission of poems, though it is not actual poems which are transmitted but their substance and technique.

Modern oral poetry confirms that there is much truth in this. Yet it is important to gauge how great, or how small, may be the possible divergence from the original in any attempted repetition of a song either by the same singer or by a different one.

[6] G. L. Huxley has pointed out to me that there are grounds for ascribing a far higher degree of accuracy in oral transmission to the *Rigveda* than to any European poem whose history can be reconstructed. Wackernagel, for example, concluded that despite certain deficiencies 'darf die Überlieferung des RV als einzigartig treu bezeichnet werden' (*Altindische Grammatik* (Göttingen, 1896), pp. xiif.). The situation is complex, and the history of the *Rigveda* before its codification by the diasceuastic schools is in large measure impossible to reconstruct. Even the date of this codification is unknown; it was long after the composition of the earlier hymns, which may provisionally be placed in the sixteenth or fifteenth century B.C., but it was also many centuries before the first written text, the earliest indication of which points to the tenth or eleventh century A.D. The transmission over the intervening period, as in the pre-codification period, was exclusively oral, and an 'extraordinary fidelity', to use Renou's phrase, was guaranteed by special precautions on the part of the original diasceuasts as well as by the religious veneration in which the details of the text were held. On all this one may consult with profit L. Renou and J. Filliozat, *L'Inde classique* (Paris, 1947), vol. I, pp. 270–8 and especially §§515–20, 530–5. Verbal accuracy in the transmission of the *Rigveda* was greatly aided by its sacrosanct character; but this need not diminish its implications for the possibility or impossibility of verbatim oral transmission, to the assessment of which the Vedic poetry is directly relevant. Classical scholars and students of the oral epic require the help of expert Vedists in this extremely difficult field; and in particular one may ask for attention to be given to the distinction between verbal and syntactical accuracy within the verse on the one hand, and accuracy in the preservation of an original order of verses and themes on the other.

It will be easier to judge this question, so far as modern oral poetry is concerned, when the complete Parry–Lord collection has eventually been published. On the evidence provided by the first volume, however, we see clearly that it is the aim of the best singers in the Novi Pazar region to reproduce exactly each song that they hear. Thus Demail Zogić (conversation C, *SCHS*, 1, 239ff.) says that the best thing is for the singer to sing 'as he heard it and as things happen'; of the two vices, omission and elaboration, the former is preferable. At one point Demail admits that exact repetion is impracticable: 'it is impossible to find two singers who can sing a song through clearly from beginning to end, but one will make a mistake, or will add something'; this is explained as due to carelessness or over-ambition. Normally Demail believed that exact repetition by the same singer was possible as well as desirable, as is shown in the following recorded conversation (pp. 240f.):

N: So then, last night you sang a song for us...How many times did you hear it before you were able to sing it all the way through exactly as you do now? *D*: Here's how many times I heard it. One Ramazan I engaged this Suljo Makić...I heard him one night in my coffee house. I wasn't busy. I had a waiter and he waited on my guests, and I sat down beside the singer and in one night I picked up that song. I went home, and the next night I sang it myself...That singer was sick, and I took the gusle and sang the whole song myself, and all the people said 'We would rather listen to you than to that singer whom you pay.' *N*: Was it the same song, word for word, and line for line? *D*: The same song, word for word, line for line. I didn't add a single line, and I didn't make a single mistake.

Slightly later Demail claims that: 'If I were to live for twenty years, I would sing the song which I sang for you here today just the same twenty years from now, word for word.' It was in fact seventeen years later and not twenty when Lord returned to record this same song, 'Alija rescues Alibey's children', from the same singer. Demail did not succeed in justifying his claim. Unfortunately it was impossible to include the translation of this latter version in the first volume of *SCHS*, but on pp. 409ff. Lord summarizes the differences from the version of seventeen years earlier. They seem on the whole to be comparatively minor differences, involving the occasional substitution of one formula or line for another and the addition or subtraction of a number of incidental themes. Lord lists 23 alterations of various degrees of importance in a song of which the later

version was something over 1430 lines long and some 60 lines longer
than the earlier version.

All this may make us more cautious about the kind of conclusion
we draw from Sterling Dow's generalization that '*Verbatim* oral
transmission of a poem composed orally and not written down is
unknown.' Among simple singers like Demail exact repetition is
certainly unknown – although it nevertheless remains their ideal –
partly because they pick up songs so incredibly quickly. Demail
himself could acquire a new song in an evening. Another singer,
Salih Ugljanin, described how he learnt to sing heroic songs when
he was a boy (*SCHS*, 1, 60): 'I began to sing once with the shepherds,
and afterwards I kept on and sang at gatherings.' A third bard,
Sulejman Makić, gave this account (p. 263): 'I heard that Arif
Karalješak was a good singer, and I was small, fifteen years old, and
I brought him to my house and kept him for a year. He sang and
I listened, until I had learned.' The initial learning, in boyhood,
takes longer, but when the singer has built up a repertoire he can
remember a new song sometimes after only one hearing. Thus a later
part of the recorded interview with Sulejman went as follows
pp. 265f.):

N: Listen, you were able to remember songs when you were a boy...could
you still pick up a song today? *S*: I could. *N*: For example, if you heard me
sing a song, let's say, could you pick it up right away? *S*: Yes, I could sing
it for you right away the next day. *N*: If you were to hear it just once?
S: Yes, by Allah, if I were to hear it only once to the gusle.

He then explains that he likes to brood on a song when he has heard
it: 'It has to come to one. One has to think...how it goes, and then
little by little it comes to him, so that he won't leave anything out.'
This almost certainly means that he thinks over the song as he has
heard it, but in terms of his own formular vocabulary which may
differ slightly from that of the other singer. In this way he learns it,
though probably under a slightly different form. In addition his own
form of the song varies somewhat every time he recites it.

It is curious how these Yugoslav singers, under questioning, are
unanimous in saying that the ideal is to 'sing it as it actually
happened', and yet do not seem to make much effort to achieve
uniformity from recitation to recitation. One has to remember that
they are unsophisticated and often rather muddled by anything in
the nature of a complex question about their technique. But it

seems to transpire that they *do* seek to reproduce the songs they have learnt as exactly as possible, although by our literate standards this is not very exactly. They simply do not see, unless it is drawn directly to their attention by someone like Lord or Parry, that it makes a difference whether in a certain context a hero's saddle-bag, for example, is just described as a saddle-bag or whether it becomes the occasion for a short formular digression in which the material and decoration of the saddle-bag are carefully designated. Also there is a very marked thematic similarity between many of the songs they know, so that the temptation to transpose material from one song to another is quite high. When Sulejman Makič was told that Salih Ugljanin claimed to know a hundred songs, this was his reaction (p. 265):

He lies. He doesn't know real songs. Parts of songs perhaps, but not a whole song. *N*: What do you mean by a real song? *S*: Well, it's like this, to sing it all the way through at one time; he confuses them, you know. He leaves things out, and he doesn't finish them. As for a hundred songs, a hundred good songs, he's lying...

There is little doubt that it would not be beyond the phenomenal mnemonic capacity of many of these singers to reproduce a song exactly, or almost exactly, time after time, if they felt that this degree of verbal accuracy were really important and if they realized that their own versions, which they often take as exact reproductions of their model, were subject to considerable variation. It is their professed ideal to achieve verbatim precision, but because of the formular system and the local tradition of hundreds of relatively short songs, many of them thematically similar, they normally do not try very hard to achieve this ideal or indeed perceive that they are falling below it. The small proportion of the Parry–Lord recordings so far published has not yet brought to light a singer who lived in the particular circumstances that I would maintain might produce, even in Yugoslavia, a notably more precise oral transmission. The ideal would be a singer of exceptional *local* preeminence and fame, from whom other singers in the same region learn their craft and virtually the whole of their repertoire without much influence from other quarters. The pupils of this master would thus acquire his formular vocabulary, or at least a part of it, and no other; for different regions tend to produce slightly different formulas for the same thing, so that most singers, who gather songs

from any good singer they may come across, are exposed to considerable formular variation. Further, the special veneration in which the
master would be held would encourage his pupils to keep as closely
as they could to his very words – a motive for accuracy that only
applies within a strictly localized tradition. There would be plenty
of old men in the audience to point out when a younger singer
departed from the version of the master.

If these conditions were to operate, then it seems that we might
find a standard of accuracy in oral transmission that came much
closer to being complete. No such ideal conditions will now be
found, at least in Europe, but it is possible that some districts will
prove better than Novi Pazar in this respect. Unfortunately the
famous singer tends to move around, as did Ćor Huso. He was a bard
who won great repute in the latter part of the nineteenth century and
whose name is revered even now. The most talented of the singers
described in *SCHS*, i, Salih Ugljanin, learned ten songs from him in
a month (p. 61). There may be examples of these songs among those
recorded by Parry, although Salih was old and his memory on this
point erratic; but in any event our ideal conditions are not met,
because Salih learned songs from all and sundry and must have
acquired a very mixed formular vocabulary, while Huso himself did
not stay in one district but travelled even as far as Vienna. In
answer to the question 'What was he, what was his trade, what did
he do?' Salih answered as follows (*loc. cit.*): 'Nothing, he had no
trade, nothing but his horse and his arms, and he went about the
world. He was blind in one eye and his clothes and arms were of the
finest. And he went thus from town to town and sang to everybody
to the gusle.' What we want is a singer with a *local* pre-eminence as
great as Huso's national pre-eminence, in a remote and inbred
region. The later volumes of Parry–Lord may provide an approxi-
mation to such a one; if so, his songs must be studied with special
care to see if they do in fact reveal a greater-than-average verbal
accuracy.

It seems to me that scholars like Bowra, Lord and Dow have made
the mistake of making inferences directly from the details of modern
Yugoslav poetry, or other less carefully studied oral poetry, to the
poetry of Homer. I have pointed out that even in Yugoslavia, where
on the evidence of the poets of Novi Pazar great accuracy of transmission is not generally found, possible conditions could be ima-

gined – and were much likelier to exist a century ago than in the 1930s or today – in which the standard of verbal accuracy would be rather high. Complete verbal accuracy is even now the ideal, and when life was more narrowly regional that ideal was likely to be more successfully achieved. But whatever the truth may here be, the direct equivalence with Homeric poetry is bound to be misleading. The powers of memory of the Greek *aoidos* can have been no less than those of his modern Yugoslav equivalent; but his formular equipment and his imaginative and dramatic capacities must have been far superior. There are three factors in particular that must have favoured a greater standard of verbal accuracy in the transmission of ancient Greek oral poems. The first is the scope, complexity and economy of the formular system – the qualities which Parry himself first conclusively demonstrated. There is no doubt that the traditional language of the Greek oral poets was much more highly organized, as it was much richer, than that of any modern oral poet of whom we know. The Yugoslav singer has a large quantity of standardized thematic material available, and some of this material is expressed in more or less fixed formular language; there are many fixed epithets and repeated lines and half-lines, but there is nothing like the rigid formular structure of the Homeric *aoidos*, by far the greater part of whose phraseology, judging by the *Iliad* and *Odyssey*, was traditional.

The second factor is the much greater metrical rigidity of the Homeric hexameter. The South-Slavic heroic poetry is composed in loose decasyllabic lines sung to an intricate repeated melody from the violin-type instrument called the *gusle*. The musical accompaniment provides rhythmical stability, and allows the rhythm of the words themselves to be treated with considerable flexibility. By contrast the Homeric line has a fixed metrical pattern based on quantity; and, while virtually nothing is known about its musical accompaniment on the *phorminx*, it is highly probable that this was much less complex than that of the *gusle*. Its chief purposes, I would conjecture, were emphasis and diversion and not the regulation of rhythm, which was adequately controlled by the highly formalized rules of the hexameter verse itself. Now both these kinds of rigidity, formular and metric, are likely to increase the degree of verbal accuracy in the reproduction of Greek oral poetry as opposed to Yugoslav. How much they would increase it, it is impossible to say with any degree of certainty, especially in the complete absence of modern comparative material with the fixity of the Homeric poetry. But I would guess that the increase of verbal accuracy would be very marked indeed. The third factor is that the Homeric poems came at the end of the true oral tradition, so that their oral transmission depended for much of its course not on singers but on reciters or rhapsodes. More about these will be found on pp. 126f., but here it is relevant to remark that their abandonment of the *phorminx*, originally an aid to creative composition, shows that their methods and ideals were different from those of *aoidoi* or singers. Greater verbal accuracy may well have been a product of these differences.

In sum it is hard to see any imperative reason why poetry of the Homeric type should not have been transmitted from singer to singer to reciter with only small verbal changes. As for thematic changes – the addition or omission of minor incidents, which forms an important part of the fluidity of the Yugoslav tradition – it may be conjectured that here too the Greek oral tradition, at any rate by the time of Homer, was more highly organized than any modern equivalent. The Trojan theme had presumably gained a pre-eminent position, and judging from the references to other epic subjects within the *Iliad* and *Odyssey* these were relatively restricted in scope and geographical location; thus there was poetry about the wars of Thebes, about local struggles in Elis and Pylos, about the deeds of Heracles, about the Argonautic expedition, and probably about various divine exploits. There must have been many other regional subjects for oral poetry that find no explicit mention in the great monumental poems, but nevertheless I think most scholars would agree that the impression to be gained from the Homeric poems is that the traditional subject-matter of Greek epic was by the ninth or eighth century B.C. more fixed, more compartmentalized, less fluid than that of the Yugoslav singers. If this is so, it would again drastically reduce the amount of expected deviation in the attempted reproduction of oral epics.

The conclusion is that we must withhold credence from generalizations like the following: 'We may therefore speak of the transmission of poems, though it is not actual poems which are transmitted but their substance and technique' (Bowra, *Heroic Poetry*, p. 368). This may be true, up to a point, of the South-Slavic epic, but it is not certainly or even probably true of the Homeric epic. There is no compelling reason from the point of view of transmission why the

Homer and modern oral poetry

Iliad and *Odyssey*, once they gained wide repute, as they presumably did in the lifetime of their monumental composers, should not have been handed down from singer to singer with only comparatively minor deviations. The first official written version of the poems was probably made in Athens in the sixth century B.C. If this is true, and if the *Iliad* was composed, as most of the evidence suggests, in the course of the eighth century, then we are required to accept that the poems survived for about six generations mainly in the oral tradition. I do not see why this should be impossible or improbable: nobody in his senses thinks that the poems did *not* undergo some degree of rearrangement, omission and elaboration during this period, and that is precisely what we should expect from oral transmission even in the comparatively rigid conditions of the Greek tradition. The argument put forward by Lord and enthusiastically accepted by Dow, that the poems must have been written down as soon as they were composed because otherwise they could not have been transmitted, is fallacious and must be absolutely rejected as it stands.

This brings me to an important final point. This is that most Homeric scholars have come to think of the South-Slavic singers as being lesser equivalents of the Homeric *aoidos*. That may be so in some instances, but it is certainly not so in the case of the singers from around Novi Pazar who can be studied in detail in *SCHS*, I. These men are not the equivalent of Homeric *aoidoi*, because the *aoidos* is a creative singer and these men are non-creative reproducers. One must be careful to understand what these terms imply in an oral tradition. I say that the Homeric singer is creative in the sense that Phemius and Demodocus, the bards described in the *Odyssey*, are at times creators of new songs, although doubtless with the aid of the usual traditional stock of words, phrases, lines, short passages and themes. 'Homer' was certainly creative in this sense, although on a far more impressive scale and with a new dramatic purpose. But apart from monumentality and dramatic power, Homer must have been creating almost continuously in the sense of forming new lines out of formular phrases, or new passages to connect traditional passages and to supply fresh or more complex incidents. What he accomplished was creation within the framework of a formalized oral tradition, a process some critics have curiously felt to be derogatory of his powers and his product. Any creative oral poet does this kind of thing, although no other oral poet has ever done it with the brilliance of Homer. From this oral *creativity* we must carefully distinguish the mere *variation* or *contamination* of the poets of Novi Pazar. Enough has been said already to show that in these cases there is considerable interchange of passages between the different songs in the repertoire of any one singer. Each singer thinks that he sings a song exactly as he learnt it and 'exactly as it happened', and he thinks it good and right to do so; but in fact he unconsciously omits a line here and there, or even a minor theme or digression, on some occasions when he sings the song, and he also adds lines or short passages of elaboration which belong more regularly to other songs in his repertoire. This kind of variation is a product of the oral technique, especially of the loose kind of technique that we find in most surviving traditions of oral poetry. It is not creative; the added lines or passages, for example, have not been constructed out of smaller oral components by the singer himself to suit a special purpose, they are lines or passages that he has learnt from another singer, originally in connection with a different song, and they are switched temporarily and unconsciously to a similar context in the song he now sings.

It is obvious that there is a certain overlapping of terms in this assessment of oral originality. It could be argued that there is a small element of creativity in this kind of transposition, just as there is an element of predetermination in the Homeric creativity; but I think that in its broad lines the distinction I have outlined is real and significant. The fact is that the Novi Pazar singers have learnt their songs from older singers, and they muddle them up a bit; only one of them claims to have invented a song of his own, and in general they make it perfectly clear that they can only extend their repertoire by committing to memory a song learned from another singer. The quality of the exception confirms the validity of the general rule; for the short song about the war against the Greeks that Salih Ugljanin admitted, rather reluctantly, to having composed, is of extremely poor quality and only comes to life when it incorporates traditional themes, which it does at the slightest opportunity.[7]

The Novi Pazar singers are in most respects not like Homeric *aoidoi*, they are like post-Homeric *rhapsōdoi* or rhapsodes. In the Greek context it seems justified to draw a distinction between the creative oral poetry of the Homeric *aoidoi* and the reproductive oral

[7] See *SCHS*, I, 119–21 and 370.

poetry of the later *rhapsōdoi* who recited well-known songs, chiefly the *Iliad* and *Odyssey*. The *aoidos* accompanies himself on the *phorminx*, a lyre-like instrument whose purpose I suppose to have been to provide emphasis and conceal gaps or hesitations rather than to set a rhythmical pattern; the rhapsode's appurtenance is the staff, an aid to rhetorical emphasis in recitation. In Greece there are reasons for believing that the *Iliad* and *Odyssey* came very near the end of the creative oral tradition. The introduction of writing, and the supremacy of the monumental poems themselves, no doubt hastened the decline of creative oral poetry. The first we hear of rhapsodes places them in the post-Homeric, literate era, and they are particularly associated with the recitation of the Homeric poems; Pindar called the Homeridae, somewhat ambiguously, ῥαπτῶν ἐπέων...ἀοιδοί, 'singers of stitched lays [*or* words]' (*Nem.* 2, 1f.). I have suggested earlier that the greater complexity and formalization of the Homeric tradition may have given the rhapsodes, prone to expansion as some were, greater verbal accuracy than their modern Yugoslav counterparts.

I believe that the close study of a modern oral tradition is, as Parry thought, a valuable aid to our understanding of the conditions in which the Homeric poems were composed. The Yugoslav oral tradition is a fruitful one, and it has already helped to establish many of Parry's initial inductions as credible and indeed certain. It can tell us, therefore, much about the methods and tendencies of the Homeric *aoidos*. But it probably will not show us precisely how the *aoidos* created oral poetry, as opposed to rearranging it, partly because most if not all of the modern Yugoslav singers appear to be non-creative. Avdo Međedović may turn out to be an exception. When his monumental poem is published it will be of great importance to see whether he was simply throwing in reserves, as it were, from a large repertoire of other songs, so as to expand the familiar themes of the wedding of Smailagić Meho; or whether he was rearranging and combining traditional features to such an extent, and with such a completely new result, that he could be called creative in the sense in which many *aoidoi* of the Homeric tradition must have been. Again one is aware of the limitations of the distinction between 'creative' and 'reproductive' in an oral tradition; there is a continuous line from one to the other, and in any event I should expect Avdo to be further along that line than Salih Ugljanin and the other singers from Novi Pazar. But it seems to have been completely overlooked so far, and is essential to recognize for the future, that a substantial part at least of the Yugoslav poetry is closer to what was recited by the Greek rhapsodes than to what was sung by the creators of the *Iliad* and *Odyssey*. Obviously the two situations, ancient and modern, do not exactly match: the rhapsodes, who had abandoned a musical accompaniment, were further away from the creative tradition, in quality but not in time, than the Yugoslav guslars of Novi Pazar. The Greek tradition passed with astonishing and probably unique rapidity from its highest point to complete decline. The Yugoslav tradition, as seen in the Novi Pazar singers, is at a stage that cannot be exactly paralleled in what we know of Greek poetry, although it is an invaluable guide to what might have happened at a certain period – a stage in which the oral tradition is still 'alive', in that poetry is learned by bards who make use of the formular technique of memory, but is moribund to the extent that the creative stage lies in the past. Some new poetry may be made on modern subjects, but in a debased style only distantly related to that developed in the old heroic tradition. On this and other questions there is much fresh evidence to be published. In the meantime it will be prudent for Homeric scholars to remember that inferences based on modern oral traditions must be founded on a more careful assessment of the true nature of those traditions than has been made up to now; and in particular that the difference in sheer excellence between Homer and any modern oral poet whatever may imply technical distinctions not of corresponding but at least of significant magnitude.

6

HOMER'S *ILIAD* AND OURS

Adam Parry's article 'Have We Homer's *Iliad*?' is one of the most readable of recent discussions of Homer.[1] As it happens, I disagree with much of it – but that is not surprising, since much of it is taken up with disagreeing with me. In the pages that follow I shall be primarily concerned to question the validity of some of the author's detailed arguments and to probe some of his underlying assumptions.

First we should note the general position that Adam Parry, by the end of his study, occupies. It is the apparently old-fashioned one that Homer wrote down, or had someone else write down, virtually every word of the *Iliad* (and presumably also the *Odyssey*) as we have it. Yet it differs from extreme Unitarianism, and takes account of Milman Parry, by accepting that Homer belonged to an oral tradition and composed his poetry, at least at the detailed level, by traditional means. He did not construct his verses like a fully literate poet, but used the new technique of alphabetic writing for the development of traditional, unlettered poetry into the extended form and complex texture of an *Iliad*.

This position differs from that of most contemporary Homerists not only in the idea that Homer might have written out his poetry in person (a suggestion previously made by Wade-Gery, Bowra, Lesky and others), but also in the argument that the poems as we have them are, with minimal exceptions, completely as he wrote them (although there are others, like W. B. Stanford, who are inclined to defend even the ending of the *Odyssey* as completely Homeric). Many learned readers of Homer evidently have little patience for inevitably arid surveys of the formular language and schematic structure of the great poems; they will gratefully accept the simple picture of Homeric composition that Adam Parry has unfashionably and even daringly revived. Yet simple explanations of complex phenomena are not always correct.

Of the two principles he assigns to A. B. Lord, that poems suffer

[1] *Yale Classical Studies* 20 (1966), 177–216.

fundamenta change in the course of oral transmission and that contact with literacy always destroys oral techniques of composition, Adam Parry accepts the first and challenges the second. I had questioned the first and accepted the second.[2] Lord has recently come to the defence of his second principle,[3] but in spite of some long arguments on his part and an insistence that what he said was that a literate oral singer had not been, rather than could not be, discovered in modern Yugoslavia, I now concede that Adam Parry is right to maintain that the effects of literacy on singers in Yugoslavia are likely to be distinct from those on singers in ancient Greece. This is because literacy in the former instance implies urban culture, and therefore a whole set of values antipathetic to the leisurely circumstances of the oral epic and the traditional ideology of heroic poetry. In ancient Greece, on the other hand, the new writing system of the eighth century B.C. did not carry with it, at least at first, any widely altered system of values or the implication of a radically different way of life. In theory a singer might have acquired or approved of the new method of recording without basically revising his traditional approach to poetry or his adherence to the inherited language of the oral epic.

There are still difficulties in the idea that the heroic singer, of all people, would have seized so eagerly upon the alphabet as Adam Parry or Wade-Gery (in his *The Poet of the Iliad* (Cambridge, 1952)) has implied. The agents of traditional culture are normally the last, not the first, to make use of radically new techniques. A natural antipathy may be thought to subsist between an oral tradition and the spread of writing. Adam Parry thinks it is a reasonable guess that a singer of about 725 B.C. 'would, if he had learned how to manipulate the magical σήματα which had come to him from the Phoenicians, not be inclined to change his thoughts or modes of expression at all' (p. 215). Yet it is the initial decision to learn about writing, and not any particular subsequent effect, that is hardest to accept for an unlettered bard. Homer, it is true, was no ordinary singer – and it is that consideration, and not generalising about *aoidoi* or *guslars*, that keeps alive the possibility of his having made some use of writing.

Other difficulties in the hypothesis have not been diminished by Adam Parry's astute disposal of part, at least, of the contact-with-

---

[2] See e.g. *The Songs of Homer* (Cambridge, 1962), pp. 99f. and 87f.
[3] *HSCP* 72 (1967), 3ff.

literacy argument. Against the objection that the making of a very
large book is improbable so soon after the first introduction of the
alphabet, and at just about the time of the earliest surviving (and
very rough-and-ready) alphabetic inscriptions on pots, he can do no
more than reply that 'there is no evidence whatever that the act of
writing on so large a scale would not have been possible at that date.
It would, of course, have been a remarkable event. And so was the
composition of the *Iliad*' (p. 184). But in reality there is plenty of
contrary *a priori* evidence – and nothing more direct than that, for
this period, can reasonably be expected: for example the evident
limitations of book-production even in the full classical period, the
apparent lack of early fixed texts of the Hesiodic *Works and Days* and
the ending, at least, of the *Theogony*, and the indications of a progressive emergence of small-scale written poetry from about the
middle of the seventh century B.C. Moreover the production of a
complete written *Iliad* late in the eighth century would indeed, and
contrary to what Adam Parry asserts, be more remarkable in its way
than either the hellenizing of the alphabet or the notion of an *Iliad*
itself. The alphabet had been around in the Near East from at least
the thirteenth century B.C., and was bound to reach Greece once
trade with Cyprus and the Levant was fully restored in the ninth;
and the *Iliad* had surely had lesser precursors, many on the subject
of the Trojan *geste*, that were ripe for monumental development if a
poet of special genius and vision were to appear.

A different kind of difficulty in the concept of an autograph *Iliad*
and *Odyssey*, or any fixed and directly authorized copy in the years
immediately after Homer, is the existence in our texts of passages,
some of considerable length, that appear to have been accreted later
than the main process of monumental composition. Adam Parry
seems content to accept our texts as completely authentic apart from
'scribal errors and interpolations' (p. 182), by the last of which he
seems to mean very minor additions of a verse or two in length.
Obviously I cannot go fully here into the complex question of the
status of large sections like the Doloneia in the *Iliad* or the ending of
the *Odyssey*, or into those other anomalies that no amount of
sympathetic interpretation seems quite to remove; reference may
perhaps be made to the discussion of such matters in my *The Songs
of Homer* (Cambridge, 1962), especially chapters 10 and 11. No severe
analyst, I yet share the feeling of many careful students of the poems

that, although several apparent inconsistencies can be accounted for either by a properly sympathetic understanding of their context or in relation to the complexity of the inherited tradition and the difficulty of integrating different pre-Homeric versions, there remain certain anomalies, both stylistic and structural, which, like the ending of the *Odyssey*, are more probably due to post-Homeric elaboration and expansion. That poem cannot, to be sure, have ended exactly at 23, 296 – but modern critics as well as ancient have obviously found it hard to justify all that follows in our vulgate text down to its final and bizarre conclusion. Adam Parry himself, as I suspect, is far from happy about this, although in his article he simply observes that there are scholars who defend both this and every other questionable episode.

Be that as it may, no one who doubts the pristine quality of any substantial passage of either poem can accept the theory of a Homeric autograph or quasi-autograph text without serious misgivings – unless perchance that text was instantly lost (in which case we are back with oral transmission); or unless it bore no authority sufficient to prevent further substantial changes, which, although possible, seems eminently improbable. It is hard to conceive that an *Iliad*, in this case identical with the poem we know, would not have been quickly recognized as a great masterpiece, quite distinct in quality and aims from its predecessors. And Homer's own copy of the *Iliad*, a portent of book-production as well as of literature, must have seemed in the circumstances little short of miraculous. Adam Parry asks whether 'the lack of any record of the...act of putting such long poems into writing' is any stranger 'than our virtually complete lack of any record of the person of Homer himself, on any theory' (p. 185). But the two phenomena are not independent of each other. The lack of information about Homer is in any case surprising, but becomes less so if we are dealing with a singer in an age before written texts and records. A full-scale autograph copy, if we are to imagine such a thing, quite apart from the possibility of titles and the addition of biographical material about the author, would make Homer's personal anonymity even harder to explain.

Against this inherently difficult theory of an autograph copy can be set, too, the ancient tradition that by the sixth century B.C. the sequence of the poems was so loose, so subject to personal and individual preferences, that an official text had to be promulgated in order to control rhapsodic recitations in the competition at the Panathenaea. All Adam Parry does about this is to refer to J. A. Davison's comments on the old and exaggerated idea of a 'Panathenaic recension'.[4] Davison was justifiably sceptical about the critical processes involved; and yet even his questionable opinion that in the sixth century B.C. the Panathenaea 'was a festival of very little importance' did not prevent him from observing that 'This is the first point at which we have any direct justification for assuming the existence of a written text of the Homeric poems' (p. 219). It may be added that the tradition about the Homeridae of Chios can be traced back at least to the time of Acusilaus in this same century, and that it is almost incredible that their fame should have survived at all if there were a Homeric autograph copy which they did *not* own; and hard to believe that their reputation would be so vague and equivocal if they actually possessed such a version.

Let us turn for a moment from the difficulties surrounding a literate Homer to those of the alternative as I have framed it elsewhere: the idea that the *Iliad* (to concentrate for the sake of simplicity, as Adam Parry does, on the greater and probably the earlier of the two monumental poems) survived in a still oral tradition after Homer's death, for at least two and possibly more generations, until the time of the earliest and presumably selective rhapsodic texts and in some degree until a more or less complete Panathenaic version in the sixth century. Adam Parry's main objection to this idea is Lord's first principle (also stated by Bowra and others, after Milman Parry), that poems suffer 'fundamental change' in the course of oral transmission. I have already questioned this principle at some length, arguing that the changes made over the years even by some of the Yugoslav singers are not 'fundamental' at all.[5] Adam Parry suggests that I misrepresented the implications of Demail Zogić's reply to certain pertinent questions, put to him on behalf of Milman Parry, about the guslars' accuracy of reproduction (p. 188). He also repeats a judgement of Lord's that certainly contains some truth, that non-literate singers are incapable of sharing our own conception of verbatim accuracy. And yet Zogić's statement is not, after all, totally confused. He distinguishes quite clearly between the ability of a single singer to retain a song accu-

[4] A. J. B. Wace and F. H. Stubbings (eds.), *A Companion to Homer* (London, 1962), pp. 237f.   [5] E.g. *The Songs of Homer*, pp. 99ff.; cf. pp. 118–21 above.

rately over a long period and the ability of two singers to copy precisely a song they have acquired from a third.[6] The single singer, he thought, can reproduce a song exactly even after many years. His own performance after a seventeen-year interval shows that he somewhat overestimated his powers; but the changes in his late version were nevertheless comparatively minor ones. On the other hand his feeling that no two singers would accurately reproduce a substantially unfamiliar song belonging to a third is interesting and probably sound – for what a singer seems to do in acquiring a new song is to assimilate it as far as possible in terms of phrases, motifs and episodes that he already possesses. This inevitably involves an intermittent and personal adjustment of what he hears; and each individual will tend to adjust somewhat differently, taking the song as a whole. Yet in the case of a great poem acquired by many different singers these adjustments are presumably liable to be neutralized by subsequent comparison, both by the singers themselves and by their audiences; so that something closer to the archetype, and relatively well agreed, is finally achieved.

There must nevertheless have been a considerable number of changes in an enormously long poem transmitted orally over say two or three generations. Here Adam Parry suggests a quantification of the rate of change that can only be described as seriously misleading (pp. 188f.). It is based on the assumption that any change is always a novelty, that is, a departure from everything that preceded it. On the contrary: the changes made by heroic singers are usually changes within the limits of the tradition – the substitution for a particular episode or description of an equally traditional alternative that happens to be more familiar to the assimilating singer. The Yugoslav heroic tradition included a store of major plots, minor episodes, typical actions, typical scenes; and it is probable that in this respect the Greek hexameter tradition was closely similar. Each singer acquired a portion of this whole store as his personal repertoire. Variation comes either from the partial adjustment of new material to his pre-existing resources, or from the decision to elaborate or shorten it, on a particular occasion, through his own exuberance or fatigue or the special needs of his audience. In either case it is obvious that the process of change, either from performance to performance or from singer (and generation) to singer, is unlikely

---

[6] See his remarks quoted on p. 119 above.

to be cumulative in either arithmetical or geometrical progression. The description omitted on one occasion tends to be restored on the next; the alternative typical scene preferred by one singer, when he acquires a song from another, may be replaced once again from within the limited tradition when he in turn hands on the song to a third. And the model of isolated singers passing on an 'original' is itself, of course, a misleading one. Even the Yugoslav circumstances suggest that singers in the same general region tend to have roughly similar repertoires – although the more able singers naturally have the larger ones – and so exercise a considerable degree of mutual control. This is not less but perhaps even more so when songs are acquired from a singer recognized as exceptional – and even Salih Ugljanin, the best of the Novi Pazar singers but no genius, can be seen in the conversations reproduced in Parry–Lord, *Serbocroatian Heroic Songs*, 1 (Cambridge, Mass., 1954), to have gained a certain status as one whose versions deserved to be emulated. In a tradition more closely knit than the South Slavic, which for many causes the Ionian tradition is likely to have been, there is no reason why changes made to a song in the course of two or three generations should greatly exceed those made within a single lifetime.

The argument so far primarily revolves around relatively short songs capable of being given at a single sitting, the stock-in-trade of the typical oral heroic poet. Yet it is important, as I believe (although the contention has up to now made little impact on Adam Parry, A. B. Lord and others), to remember that the *Iliad* was *not* a typical and normal song of this kind, and therefore that it is likely to have behaved somewhat differently in the process of transmission. It was a very special poem, one that must rapidly have achieved exceptional fame and overshadowed its far shorter predecessors. This circumstance alone completely alters the probabilities of accurate reproduction. A. B. Lord has emphasized that what is dangerous to an oral tradition is not literacy, in particular, so much as the general concept of a fixed text. Our opinion of the effects of writing must be adjusted in the light of what Adam Parry has shown in the case of modern urban literacy; but Lord's main point remains. And yet, apart from literacy, what was more likely to lead to that concept of a fixed text than the creation of a phenomenal poem like the *Iliad*? With the ordinary heroic song it did not matter if a singer diverged from his model, which was usually anonymous and could in most cases be improved without too much difficulty. With Homer's monumental *Iliad* the situation was altered. The process of creative assimilation might now become one of conscious and imitative reproduction – something as fatal to the vitality of the poetical tradition as a whole as it was preservative of the *Iliad* itself and its complement the *Odyssey*. Therefore a motive for accurate reproduction presented itself in ancient Ionia as it never has done in modern Yugoslavia, at least until literacy and scholarship made their insidious impact there.

To a difference of end may be added a difference of means; for it is here that the greater complexity and tighter organization of the Greek oral tradition make their effect. Given the wish to reproduce a long poem, it was presumably easier to do so within the much stricter metrical and verbal system of Greek hexameter poetry than in the loose and fluid medium of the guslars – since the most important factor here is not the range or scope of material so much as its economy of expression and its careful lack of genuine alternatives. Adam Parry tries to invalidate this argument, but his logical objections, beside being formally debatable in themselves (e.g. on pp. 186f. and 202f. of his article), overlook this crucial point: that the unique systematization of the language of Greek heroic poetry merely provides the opportunity, and not the motive, for a kind of reproduction that could greatly surpass that of the guslars in respect of accuracy. The motive, on the contrary, would arise out of the special position of the *Iliad*, its untraditional monumentality, and the stimulus it would naturally provide for that 'concept of the fixed text' on which Lord has focused attention.

That *all* oral singers and story-tellers are incapable of close reproduction is in any event an inference drawn primarily from the Yugoslav conditions and material, and is logically indefensible unless we believe that all oral traditions are closely similar in all respects. D. C. C. Young in his entertaining piece 'Never blotted a line?' includes, among a certain amount that is less convincing, some highly relevant information about the remarkable capacity for exact memorization possessed by certain non-literate Celtic poets and story-tellers.[7] Quite what stimulated them to accurate reproduction is irrelevant. It may have been the rivalry of printed books rather than the desire to recreate a masterpiece, or it may have been some-

---

[7] *Arion* 6 (1967), 279–324, especially 295ff.

thing in themselves quite independent of the concept of a fixed text. What is important is their actual ability to be accurate, even in an unformulated tradition. This is not clutching at straws; I freely concede that Homer's immediate successors are likely to have borne a greater resemblance, in most respects, to Salih Ugljanin of Novi Pazar than to Duncan Macdonald of South Uist; but the resemblance was in any case far from complete, even leaving aside the question of quality – and in the capacity for accurate reproduction, at least, the Gaelic crofter may provide a more relevant comparison than the Slavic butcher.

The antithesis to memorizing, which it is fashionable to play down as an element in heroic poetry, is improvising, which since the time of Milman Parry has usually been correspondingly overrated. Once again we are indebted to D. C. C. Young for correcting (perhaps even over-correcting) the imbalance, most clearly in the article already cited. Certainly there runs through Adam Parry's treatment a persistent implication that what confronts us in the Greek oral tradition is 'improvising poetry' – an idea derived, of course, primarily from Milman Parry, who would surely have altered his views on this question had his study of the Yugoslav singers not been prematurely terminated. There is an element of improvising, as there is an element of memorizing, in the performance of any oral heroic song in a non-literate tradition. Yet there can be little doubt that the composer of a large-scale song would build it up gradually and deliberately. He would repeatedly practise it to himself, and he would progressively elaborate and develop it in public performances; the improvisation on any one occasion would in all probability be relatively slight. This is an important consideration that renders the whole process of composing or learning a vast epic like the *Iliad*, on the assumption that writing was not used, much less formidable and chaotic than is implied by Adam Parry with his imaginary target of an essentially improvising Homer surrounded by disciples entirely devoid of the faculty of memory.

Several pages of Parry's study are devoted to my schematization of the possible phases of an oral tradition, from originative to full creative stage, from creative to primarily reproductive, and from reproductive to degenerate and quasi-literate. He believes that the idea of a reproductive phase was devised to explain how the Homeric poems might have survived for a time in an oral tradition, and on the grounds that the Yugoslav songs collected by Parry and Lord are so obviously inferior to Homer that they must belong to some lower and reproductive category. That was not my argument at all. The reproductive stage in Yugoslavia thrust itself on my attention not because the songs there are relatively jejune and unimaginative (which they certainly are) but because 'If you ask these singers [*sc.* from the Novi Pazar region] where a song comes from they answer that they learned it from someone else.'[8] In an oral poetical tradition, so long as it retains any vitality whatever, there will always be some overlap between creation and reproduction. Even the creative singer, if he is working against the background of a tradition, is reproducing a great deal from that tradition; even a predominantly reproductive singer tends to alter what he receives, to merge it with other material from his repertory, in a manner that has some (not very important) contact with what we mean by creation. Yet it still seems both legitimate and useful to distinguish a tradition which, at a particular phase of its existence, seems to be mainly concerned with reproducing songs that must have been substantially developed in some earlier generation, from one that is definitely expanding, that uses older poetry and inherited techniques to create substantially new songs with the help of an individual observation and imagination. The appearance of neologisms like 'kolega' and 'niform' in Yugoslav songs of the recent past no more proves that these poets were still creative in any real sense than do the pathetic attempts at original composition that were laboriously extracted from a few singers known to Parry and Lord – the 'Song of Milman Parry' and the like.[9] On the other hand the composition of the *Iliad*, untypical though it must have been, in all probability presupposes a contemporary tradition that was still vitally creative.

The main conclusion to be elicited from such a distinction should be that direct analogies between the Homeric and Yugoslav singers, and between their methods, are apt to be precarious. In implying that we should necessarily be able to trace a reproductive stage in the development and decline of the Greek oral tradition I was certainly going too far, as Adam Parry observed; in particular the phrase 'the life-cycle of an oral tradition' contains an illegitimate implication of almost biological generality. It is theoretically conceivable, I

[8] *The Songs of Homer*, p. 97.
[9] A. B. Lord, *The Singer of Tales* (Cambridge, Mass., 1960), pp. 272ff.

suppose, that the monumental poems and the spread of writing between them killed off the ancient oral tradition with startling suddenness – that the Greek singers never reached that stage of slavish dependence on the pre-existing tradition that is so clearly represented among the *guslars* of Novi Pazar. And yet the *possibility* of a Greek reproductive phase is surely an important factor in the total situation (especially since it would accord with the evident fluidity of the early text) – a phase that would not in any even be exactly parallel to the Yugoslav, not only because the traditions were themselves so different in scale and form but also because of the special situation created by the monumental poems. Such a reproductive phase, or anything like it, would completely alter the chances of successfully transmitting a great oral poem. The chief value of the Yugoslav analogy is to *raise possibilities* about the methods, capacities and limitations of the unknown Homeric singers. No 'principles' can be securely founded on it, neither (as I implied with the 'life-cycle' terminology) that all traditions necessarily go through a reproductive stage, although they may still do so, nor (as Lord stated and Adam Parry accepts) that reproduction, when it takes place, is always totally inaccurate – that, in Sir Maurice Bowra's words, 'it is not actual poems which are transmitted but their substance and their technique'.[10]

Undismayed by the *a priori* difficulties of Homer writing or dictating the *Iliad* in person, Adam Parry very naturally concentrates on difficulties inherent in the alternative. He finds it hard to imagine when the poem reached its definitive form if it were not at the time of its complete committal to writing. 'Had Homer, Kirk can be asked, often sung the *Iliad* all the way through?' (p. 185). I am not sure that this kind of question is, after all, legitimate; but in this instance I do not mind replying, Presumably yes. Insinuations of physical difficulties based on Avdo Međedović's need for frequent cups of Turkish coffee are really better left aside. A more serious quandary concerns not the singer's physique but the circumstances in which he might have performed such a poem. I have argued that neither the nobleman's court nor the religious festival – the main traditional candidates – provide as likely an occasion as informal popular gatherings like weddings or horse-fairs;[11] but once again the

---

[10] *Heroic Poetry* (London, 1952), p. 368.
[11] E.g. p. 36 above; also *The Songs of Homer*, pp. 274–81.

most important factor is the exceptional fame of a particular singer and a particular song, even an unwieldy one, that could produce an audience quite apart from normal occasions. The feats of endurance demanded of audiences at Bayreuth or in the theatre of Dionysus at Athens provide some analogy, although here the formality and quasi-religious quality of the occasion are an added factor. Against these necessary uncertainties it must be admitted that the availability of writing might at least provide a definite motive for undertaking a monumental poem, and one that we happen to understand.

Adam Parry also asks 'Did he [*sc.* Homer] say on some occasion: "I'll never do better than that: reproduce *that* version!"?' Again I am not sure that the implication of the need for a definitive text within the author's lifetime is justified in the case of oral poetry; and in any case one could frame equally amusing and awkward questions about the alternative theory, of writing out or dictating. However, since Parry suggests that I cannot imagine how the great poems were passed on to other singers, it is worth replying that there is no great difficulty here, given the powers of assimilation possessed by many known singers and given the assumption of tremendous personal authority for Homer and an unusual audience-response to his *Iliad*. An outstanding singer attracts disciples and imitators, even to some extent in the limited circumstances of the Yugoslav guslars; and Adam Parry is surely wrong in saying that 'It is hard to imagine why...singers would hand down to each other a poem of that length' (p. 201). Once the *Iliad* had been developed, there would be no lack of singers to acquire it in a form as close as possible to that which Homer, with some variation no doubt from performance to performance, had given it. Whether those singers were for the most part independent, or in some sense pupils and apprentices, must remain uncertain; yet the group of testimonies concerning the Homeridae, the 'Descendants of Homer', has its possible application here. When Pindar mentioned the Homeridae at *Nemeans* 2, 1 he was probably thinking of rhapsodes in general. The scholiast asserted that they had originally been actual descendants of the poet who performed his poems. That looks like conjecture. Yet the core of the tradition, that there were people who called themselves Homer's 'descendants', who considered themselves his offspring in blood or in spirit, and who had special claims on his poetry, looks like an ancient one that goes back even beyond the sixth century B.C. It

conveys some suggestion that the singers who first acquired the *Iliad*
may have been, or tried to become, an exclusive group, and may
have enjoyed some kind of patronage or support from Homer while
he lived.

The unreal question about precisely which version would be
chosen for assimilation is of interest mainly because of an underlying attitude it reflects: that the idea of a (slightly) fluid *Iliad* is
repellent and indeed meaningless, and that the poem we read in a
modern printed text must be *the* Iliad. Perhaps I might be allowed
to make one more quotation from my *The Songs of Homer* (pp. 100f.),
with some added emphasis at the end:

the curious thing is that precision of transmission through these centuries
[*sc.* down to the sixth] should ever be envisaged as necessary or probable.
The text of the Homeric poems, as it has come down to us, suggests imperatively that at many points the transmission through this period was *not*
exact – that many post-Homeric locutions and variants, implicating
complete episodes, intruded themselves at this time into the 'original'
poetry of the monumental poets. *At the root of this form of the oral-dictated-text
argument lies the sentimental and irrational feeling that our version of Homer must
be the 8th-century version itself.*

Adam Parry beautifully exemplifies this attitude, to which his slight
variation of the dictated-text theory makes little difference. Admittedly he tries to offer some justification for his opinion – but that
the feeling preceded any ratiocination is clearly suggested by
language like the following: 'The whole Homeric Question...is,
after all, a function of one thing: the overwhelming and universally
acknowledged greatness of the Homeric poems *as we have them*'
(p. 190; original italics); 'More important to our concept of what
we have in the text of the *Iliad*, the application of Lord's first
principle [which, it should be remembered, Parry accepts] gives us
the comforting sense that our *Iliad* is in its essentials a faithful
transcript of the song the great poet sang' (p. 182).

Adam Parry's rationalization of this feeling depends on a long and
rather fascinating argument to the effect that the *Iliad* we know is so
tightly structured and so closely textured that any change beyond
the minimal would destroy its entire essence. Therefore, since what
we possess is something unified and admirable, it cannot differ from
what Homer composed and sang (on one particular occasion) by so
much as would be entailed by two or three generations of oral
transmission.

Admittedly Adam Parry and I differ, for reasons explained above, about the probable degree of change during such a period of transmission – and it should be emphasized once again that there may be no valid grounds for considering our *Iliad* to be very seriously different from the versions that Homer sang. Even apart from that, Parry's argument about closeness of texture seems rather misleading. What he does is to take two or three well-known scenes and argue that they are so subtle in structure and expression, as they stand, that they must exactly reproduce the great artist's intention and cannot have been altered by any subsequent process of transmission. His main example comes from the Teichoscopia in the third book of the *Iliad* (pp. 197–201). I would not dream of disputing that the carefully contrived and brilliantly effective vignette concerning Helen and her two absent brothers, the Dioscuri, reproduces pretty exactly the words of Homer himself; and so no doubt do most, perhaps all, of the great *tours-de-force* of the two poems. Achilles' remarkable language in his rejection of the Embassy in *Iliad* 9 is another of Adam Parry's examples. Here the possibility of some flexibility of expression is greater, but I would not wish to deny that this is a speech that bears many marks of the great composer's *ipsissima verba*. The whole Nausicaa episode in the *Odyssey* would be another obvious instance, and on a still larger scale. Even so, Parry's statement of his case is curious. This is what he writes about the Teichoscopia scene: 'change the order of statements, add a bit here, subtract a bit there, develop the thoughts in some other manner, and we no longer have the great scene we know' (p. 200) – again the emphasis on *what we know*, our surviving texts, as providing an immutable standard in itself. But now he continues with a crucial and even more debatable generalization: 'But the *Iliad* is made up of a succession of such scenes, arranged in a fairly exact order.' Does he mean a *continuous* succession? Apparently he does; and in any event this is what his argument requires. But that is obviously not the case. What about the masses of much less tightly organized material in between – a large part, for instance, of the battle-poetry of the *Iliad*, of which elements and incidents can be switched to and fro, or even on occasion omitted, without distorting the essence of the poem as a whole or even noticeably altering the character of their immediate context?

I do not believe that even Adam Parry, with his enviable sense of

literary *nuance*, could make a convincing case on internal grounds for
the necessary preservation of the exact wording and order of many
relatively inconspicuous sections of the *Iliad*. My argument is not,
of course, that each of those sections has in fact been seriously altered
in the course of transmission – I am sure most of them have not – but
that *some* of them may have been *somewhat* altered. Let Adam Parry
apply his kind of analysis to much of the eighth book of the *Iliad*, for
instance, and he will find it harder to persuade his readers that the
preservation of the essence of the whole vast poem depends on the
assumption of immutability for every detail, than he will by selecting
some of the brilliant highlights. He admits that some scenes are
'more moving, or more highly charged, than others' (p. 201). Why
must all these others have survived unchanged? Because 'they must
all be such as to create the impression they now create, or we shall
not have our *Iliad*'! I cannot help feeling that Parry's argument, for
all its appearance of subtlety and sensitivity, boils down to something like this: 'Our *Iliad* is an extraordinary poem, and all we have;
therefore it is by Homer. Homer's version cannot have been different – if it had been, it would not be the extraordinary poem we
have.'

Even his analysis of the Teichoscopia scene requires Adam Parry
to presuppose this dubious 'If we changed it, it wouldn't be the
Iliad' argument. In emphasizing that its purpose is as much to
introduce the audience to Helen as to describe the leaders of the
Achaean army, he plays down the surprising characteristic discussed
on pp. 82–4 above, the dismissal of Ajax in a single verse, in order to
argue that the description of Idomeneus, a relatively minor figure, is
particularly timely and well-placed (p. 198). But can one really
accept that making the Ajax description harmonize in length with
those of Agamemnon and Odysseus – with whom Ajax is formally
grouped by the τὸ τρίτον of 225 – would have seriously disrupted the
texture of the whole poem? On the contrary, a case could easily be
made to show that it might actually improve it, especially since a
proper account of Ajax would in no way infringe Adam Parry's
attractive interpretation of the succeeding emphasis on Idomeneus.
Or consider his earlier contention that 'the encounter between
Achilles and Hector [*sc.* in *Iliad* 22] gains immeasurably from other
encounters elsewhere in the poem, for example from the chivalrous
encounter of Glaucus and Diomede in VI, which presents a different

and strongly contrasting view of the heroic code and heroic feelings'. Are we really to believe that this particular 'gain', if it exists, would have been different if the Glaucus–Diomedes scene had occurred not in the sixth book but in the seventh or eighth? Admittedly Parry feels that the significance of this scene is partly determined by the preceding *aristeia* of Diomedes in 5 – but then similar arguments for special significance could no doubt be found had the scene occurred elsewhere in the poem. Even for the major set-pieces, therefore, I should tend to place the theoretical dividing line between deliberate planning and incidental effect somewhat differently from Adam Parry. That is a largely subjective matter, and therefore of restricted value for the assessment of general theories. And yet Parry himself is essentially trying to establish such a theory – that our text almost exactly reproduces Homer's – on the basis of such subjective impressions as that the *Iliad* is in essence 'a long poem dealing critically with the heroic conception of life' (p. 192). Like much of his argument, this overlooks the mass of detailed and potentially fluid poetry, often concerned with fighting, that separates the most prominent, memorable and potentially stable scenes. And even some of these are less stable in actuality than one might expect – scenes that are crucial to the plot, like much of the first book of the *Iliad*, and yet are dotted with probably post-Homeric forms, perhaps as a result of constant and special attention from the rhapsodes.

At the end of his article Adam Parry draws attention once more to the curious fact that the composition of the monumental poems seems to have occurred quite soon after the introduction into Greece of a viable writing system. Is this not likely to be a case of *post hoc ergo propter hoc*? Obviously one denies the possibility at one's peril. But before succumbing to the apparent logic of sequence, a logic that has proved fallible at many other points of cultural history, it is prudent to recall the following probabilities: that the introduction of the alphabet into Greece, perhaps not long before 800 B.C., was itself the result of widening commercial and cultural contacts, and that it is these that were the fundamental cause of other specific innovations – the monumental funerary vases of the later Dipylon style, monumental temple buildings like the eighth-century temple of Hera in Samos, and the beginnings of Daedalic sculpture at roughly the same period. Such innovations, which roughly coincide with but in no way depend on writing, may provide a loose but real parallel to the development of large-scale heroic poetry. It is a mistake to press literary and visual analogies too hard, but I believe that the climate of the eighth century B.C. in Greece was one of innovation and, literally, expansion.[12] To this the Homeric poems may well have been one kind of response, quite independently of the development of the alphabet.

The evidence is still too slight for anyone, however judicious, to settle once and for all these detailed problems of how the poems were composed and transmitted. I have my own opinion, Adam Parry has his, and there are several other possible variants. Provided one primarily confines oneself to exploring and testing particular arguments and approaches while keeping the emotive urging of personal convictions within reasonable human limits, the continuation of the debate remains worthwhile. Yet I am bound to admit that when one considers the utterly *a priori* nature of most of our evidence for these matters; when one remembers the depth of our ignorance of the other conditions of cultural and social life in the Greek world in the eighth and earlier seventh century B.C.; when one reflects on the arbitrary, emotional and often juvenile responses that lie at the heart of some of one's most cherished scholarly convictions – then, indeed, the blood runs (or should run) cold.

[12] See Chester G. Starr, *The Origins of Greek Civilization* (New York, 1961), chapter 7.

7

VERSE-STRUCTURE AND
SENTENCE-STRUCTURE IN HOMER

Milman Parry was aware that the oral style of Homer depended not only on the use of formular phrases but also on the distribution of those phrases, and the sentences they composed, from verse to verse. In particular he devoted a brilliant article to 'The distinctive character of enjambment in Homeric verse'.[1] This was supplemented by 'Whole formulaic verses in Greek and Southslavic heroic song';[2] and the use of enjambement in the ancient Greek and modern Yugoslav traditions was further compared by A. B. Lord in 'Homer and Huso III: Enjambement in Greek and Southslavic song'.[3] These studies have not been often cited, nor have they given rise to kindred studies of much importance. Yet they are in a sense preliminary; and Parry's first article, which is the basic one, reports in only broad terms the statistics on which his (and some of Lord's) conclusions rest.

It is the purpose of the present study to re-examine the different types of enjambment and see if further analysis is possible on the lines indicated by Parry; and to carry on the inquiry into the effects of sentence-structure, in relation to the hexameter verse, on the style of the *Iliad* and *Odyssey*. I have made a detailed schematization of the 867 verses of book 16 of the *Iliad*, showing the occurrence of enjambment, internal stops, cumulation and associated phenomena; this analysis, with the explanation of the symbols used, appears in the appendix as Table A, while Table B gives a summary of totals by 50-verse sections. The purpose of such an analysis is to widen the basis of statistical knowledge about enjambment and so on on the one hand, and to present this knowledge in visually accessible form on the other. There is no additional advantage in such a schematic summarization of results, and reference to the Greek text should be made for confirmation of apparently significant sequences and concentrations of structural phenomena which show up from the

---

[1] *TAPA* 60 (1929), 200–20.
[2] *TAPA* 64 (1933), 179–97.   [3] *TAPA* 79 (1948), 113–24.

schematization. No startling or particularly concrete results can be expected from this kind of inquiry; rather, at best, a heightened understanding of the complexity of Homeric style, of its relation to oral procedures and of the interaction between rhythm and meaning. Parry wrote of his own inquiry that 'a study in style like the present one fulfills its aim as it goes ahead, forming for us bit by bit a clearer sense of the way in which a poet has fitted his thought to the pattern of his verses'.[4]

Enjambment is the carrying over of the sentence from one verse into the next, involving an overrunning of the verse-end. In the simpler forms of oral poetry (like the South Slavic) almost every verse contains a sentence, almost every sentence fills out a verse. There the style is simple, progressive, unperiodic: 'paratactic' in a sense, since the thought is divided into parcels, as it were, which are delivered up successively and separately. More developed and accomplished singers, like those of the Homeric tradition, carry the thought in varying degrees from one verse into the next, and so produce much subtler and more complex effects both for rhythm and for meaning. Even in the *Iliad* and *Odyssey* such 'enjambed' verses are barely in the majority (although that depends on how precisely one defines the sentence); in the literate hexameter epic of Virgil and Apollonius, on the other hand, the status of the verse-end as a semantic limit decreases significantly, and the strongest kinds of enjambment become far commoner than in any oral tradition.

There are different kinds and degrees of enjambment. Parry's main division was into 'unperiodic' and 'necessary'. He applied the former to cases in which the sentence *could* have ended with the verse, but in fact is carried on into the succeeding verse by the addition of further descriptive matter (adverbial or epithetical) or of 'a word or phrase or clause of the same grammatical structure as one in the foregoing verse'.[5] This kind of progressive extension of the sentence is typical of what Parry called the 'adding style' used by singers. Parry's term for it, 'unperiodic', is derived from Dionysius of Halicarnassus. Its negative form makes it confusing, and I propose to use 'progressive' instead. By 'necessary' enjambment, on the other hand, Parry referred to cases where the sentence could not be considered complete by the end of the verse and *must* be carried on into the following verse. He rightly subdivided this category into two

---

[4] *TAPA* 60 (1929), 229f. [5] *Ibid.*, p. 207.

types. The first consists of cases in which a subordinate clause, for example, fills one verse, and is succeeded by the main clause in the next. In these cases we should normally expect to find weak punctuation, marking some degree of pause, at the point of enjambment. The second type consists of cases in which the sense runs straight on from the end of one verse to the beginning of the next; the former verse cannot be said to contain a whole thought (even of the kind 'when he had gone') or to describe a completed action; rather it is of the 'when he | had gone' type, in which 'had gone' comes in the succeeding verse. In this second subdivision of 'necessary' enjambment no punctuation of any kind can be envisaged at the end of the enjambed verse. Of these two subdivisions I propose to term the former (for which Parry gave no special name) 'periodic', since it is involved in that kind of sentence; the latter 'integral'. In nearly all Homeric cases of integral enjambment the verse-end intervenes at a point of natural articulation in the sentence, even though not at a point where pause or punctuation would occur. Very rarely it intervenes more drastically between words which belong closely together; for example between a preposition or preceding epithet and its noun. Such rare cases I shall term 'violent'. This terminology is summarized in the table below which also gives the crude 'pragmatic' test, in terms of possible or conceivable punctuation, for each kind of enjambment.

Number	Term used here	M. Parry's term	Possible punctuation
0	(No enjambment)	(No enjambment)	Strong stop (actual)
1	Progressive	Unperiodic	Strong stop (conceivable), comma (actual)
2	Periodic	Necessary (type 1)	Comma
3	Integral	Necessary (type 2)	None
4	Violent		None

The *numbers* shown in the table have some relevance, since they are used to indicate kinds of enjambment in the schematic analysis of book 16 (appendix, pp. 172ff.). I shall also use them at times, for brevity, in the main text. They have the advantage of symbolizing the *degree* of enjambment – of involvement of one verse with the next – from none (0) to violent (4). It will be seen later that the concept of degree can be misleading, or rather that it needs to be controlled by the concept of kind. I emphasize that the main divisions are into 'unenjambed' and 'enjambed' on the one hand (o contrasted with 1, 2, 3, 4); and into 'progressive' and stronger types (Parry's 'necessary'; 1 contrasted with 2, 3, 4) on the other.

Some examples will illustrate the distinctions and uncover further problems of differentiation.

> "Ὣς οἱ μὲν περὶ νηὸς ἐϋσσέλμοιο μάχοντο·
> Πάτροκλος δ' 'Αχιλῆϊ παρίστατο, ποιμένι λαῶν,
> δάκρυα θερμὰ χέων ὥς τε κρήνη μελάνυδρος,
> ἥ τε κατ' αἰγίλιπος πέτρης δνοφερὸν χέει ὕδωρ.

(16, 1–4)

0: *no enjambment.* (The symbol actually used in the analysis is 0, underlined, since underlining marks all strong stops – see the explanation of symbols used in Table A, pp. 172f. Thus 0̄ means a whole-sentence verse, since there is a strong stop at the end of the preceding verse also.) 16, 4 above is unenjambed, an example of 0; it completes a (longer) sentence that ends with the verse. It is in a sense enjambed with its predecessor, but the term 'enjambed' is normally restricted to verse-end qualities only. On the other hand 16, 1 is a possible example of a whole-sentence, independent verse, 0̄. It is not the strongest example, since its μὲν leads on to the δ' of the next verse; it could be punctuated by a comma, not a strong stop as in e.g. Monro and Allen's Oxford Classical Text.

1: *progressive enjambment.* For example 16, 2 and 3 quoted above: each could terminate the sentence, which actually continues by the addition first of a participial clause describing the main subject, then of a relative clause expanding a simile applied to the main subject.

2: *periodic enjambment.* For example 16, 36, εἰ δέ τινα φρεσὶ σῇσι θεοπροπίην ἀλεείνεις, or 16, 21, ὦ 'Αχιλεῦ, Πηλῆος υἱέ, μέγα φέρτατ' 'Αχαιῶν, must clearly be continued in the succeeding verse by a main clause to which they are preliminary. Nevertheless each verse ends with a pause, which marks the conclusion of a subordinate (or in other cases correlative or antithetical) clause or phrase; the pause could always be indicated by a comma.

3: *integral enjambment.* For example 16, 81f.,

> ἔμπεσ' ἐπικρατέως, μὴ δὴ πυρὸς αἰθομένοιο
> νῆας ἐνιπρήσωσι...

Here the end of 81 does not coincide with the end of a separate phrase or clause, and no comma is possible; the semantic impulse continues more or less uninterrupted into the next verse. Of course the end of the verse-unit itself probably implies, here and everywhere, *some* interruption by pause or emphasis, and this interruption might be accentuated by the normal sentence-end associations of a verse-end formula like πυρὸς αἰθομένοιο. In 16, 46, for example, this second factor is lacking:

ὣς φάτο λισσόμενος μέγα νήπιος· ἦ γὰρ ἔμελλεν
οἷ αὐτῷ θάνατόν τε κακὸν καὶ κῆρα λιτέσθαι.

4: *violent enjambment*. There are three plausible cases in book 16:

<table>
<tr><td align="right">ἀλλ' ὁπότ' ἂν δὴ
νῆας ἐμὰς ἀφίκηται ἀϋτή</td><td>(62f.)</td></tr>
<tr><td align="right">δεινὴν δὲ περὶ κροτάφοισι φαεινὴ
πήληξ βαλλομένη καναχὴν ἔχε</td><td>(104f.)</td></tr>
<tr><td align="right">ἀλλὰ μεσηγὺ
νηῶν καὶ ποταμοῦ</td><td>(396f.)</td></tr>
</table>

Of these 62f. is the least striking. 104f. is odd since normal formular usage (probably as in 13, 805, ἀμφὶ δέ οἱ κροτάφοισι φαεινὴ σείετο πήληξ) has been disrupted. This might reflect literate intervention: see pp. 197ff., on Archilochus' drastic remodelling of Homeric formulas. In the third case 397 might be an elaboration that converts μεσηγύ from adverb to preposition and so creates the excess.

Clearly the distinction of 4-type from 3-type enjambment is to some extent subjective, and in the totals in Table B I have counted them together. In any case 4 is so rare as to be statistically unimportant. Another difficulty arises from the distinction, in one type of sentence, between 3 and 2. For example 16, 433f.:

ὤ μοι ἐγών, ὅ τέ μοι Σαρπηδόνα, φίλτατον ἀνδρῶν,
μοῖρ' ὑπὸ Πατρόκλοιο Μενοιτιάδαο δαμῆναι.

On the one hand there is a distinct pause (marked here by a comma) at the end of 433, produced by the parenthetical description φίλτατον ἀνδρῶν. On the other the main sentence continues straight over the verse-end (ὅ τέ...Σαρπηδόνα... | μοῖρ'...δαμῆναι); that is, the verse-end does not coincide with a major structural break in the sentence, and if it were not for the structurally unimportant parenthesis the sentence would run across the verse-end without syntactical interruption or possible punctuation. In grammatical terms the enjambment is integral, type 3; in phonetic or auditory terms it is akin to periodic, type 2 enjambment. In the analysis it is counted as 2 but distinguished as 2 −. Such cases are not numerous, but they call attention to an important duality in the concept of enjambment as a whole.

This duality is that of continuity of sense and continuity of sound. The term 'enjambment' implies, primarily, the first of these; and, since a grammatical definition of the sentence (for example) is more accurate than any possible definition of the pause at the end of different types of verse, there is much to be said for restricting the classification, like Parry, to what can be assessed grammatically. At the same time our own reading of a Homeric sentence may well give an approximate but valuable indication of the *total* interruption, as a compound of pause and emphasis, between one verse and the next; and this because our (Indo-European) language and many of our speech-habits are not basically distinct from those of the Greeks. This total interruption has its own range of stylistic implications.

The effects of enjambment on style can, indeed, be divided into two main classes corresponding with the distinction between sense-enjambment and sound-enjambment: (*a*) the effects of continuing sense beyond a certain range of words or syllables (i.e. beyond the verse considered as a unit of length merely); and (*b*) the effects of varying the rhythmical structure of the poetry by differences of interval and intonation at the ends of verses. Class (*b*) is parallel to the effects of rhythmical variation, and the interactions of rhythm and sense, *within* the verse, as discussed by H. Fränkel.[6] That parallel reminds us that the interplay between rhythmical and semantic units is relevant outside the verse-unit (that is, in the relations of one verse to another) as well as inside it, and that the dichotomy between the sound aspects of enjambment and its sense aspects is potentially misleading as well as possibly useful. The actual stylistic effects of enjambment are the product both of the continuation of sense in various ways and of particular phonetic effects at the intervals between verses; that should not be forgotten.

Now (*a*) raises the question of complexity; style is affected by the length and complexity of propositions, whether in verse or in prose. The oral style in its simpler manifestations avoids long and complex

---

[6] See *YCS* 20 (1966), 76ff. and pp. 101f. above.

sentences, for obvious reasons. Sense-enjambment entails a departure, in the direction of greater complexity, from that simple style: either deliberately (so as to produce a particular effect, or to encompass a thought which could not easily be reduced to a short sentence or a series of such) or accidentally. Enjambment-complexity needs to be treated together with other types: complex sentence-structure within the verse, special rhythmical complexity within the verse, complex uses of formular phraseology, or sheer length of sentence. Long sentences of four verses or more are indicated in the analysis of book 16 in the appendix, and these instances of sheer length – in which both the singer and his audience have to retain an uncompleted thought for an unusually long period – have their own stylistic implications for the technique of oral poetry. Again, class (*b*) – the phonetic effects of enjambment – can be either accidental or deliberate (or rather, instinctive). They may be by-products of (*a*), length and complexity, or they may be consciously or unconsciously sought by singers as appropriate to their subject-matter of the moment. The analysis of book 16 suggests that sound-enjambment is sometimes unrelated to subject; and we must remind ourselves that certain rhythmical or phonetic effects may be preferred, in poetry, for their own sake, without reference to the special content and supposedly appropriate style of a particular verse or passage. Singers may have liked the variety of enjambment, and more or less unconsciously introduced it on many occasions for that reason alone. Yet there are certainly many passages of book 16, as will be shown on pp. 160ff. in which enjambment has a special relation to the subject-matter, and there can be little doubt that it was an important element in the *choice* of styles within the embracing category of the oral hexameter style in general.

A further difficulty in the classification of enjambment can be caused by what I term 'cumulation', a special aspect of the adding style. It will be necessary, before describing the difficulty, to give a provisional indication of what cumulation entails. A kind of cumulation occurs whenever progressive enjambment takes place: the singer sings a verse potentially complete in itself, then he qualifies or adds to it in a succeeding verse connected by progressive enjambment. In the broadest sense, indeed, any simple and paratactic narrative is cumulative; each new piece of information, as the story proceeds, can be envisaged as being heaped upon its predecessor.

It is important to remember, then, that in its narrower and most typically Homeric aspect cumulation (on which see also pp. 78–81) is simply a special application of a general principle of linear narrative.

In this narrower aspect cumulation can be regarded in the first instance as a means of elaboration. The elaboration can be purely *decorative*, in that it enriches a concept already outlined and semantically adequate in itself; or it can be *explanatory*, in that it adds a qualification necessary in the whole context to a statement which in itself is formally complete. Clearly it is sometimes impossible to draw a sharp line between these two uses. Now a further theoretical distinction can be made between purely *supplementary* cumulation, whose purpose is solely to supplement (either by decoration or by explanation) what has already been stated in a preceding verse, and *transitional* or *prospective* cumulation, which provides some further description of what has preceded but the main purpose of which seems to be to lead into a new thought and a fresh accession of meaning. Furthermore cumulation can either take place in a whole verse (in which case it is one aspect of progressive enjambment) or in the first part of a verse: either by the addition of a single cumulative word at the beginning of the succeeding verse (this I call 'runover-word cumulation', abbreviated in the analysis as rc), or by the addition of a clause or phrase which continues to the main caesura (this I call 'half-verse cumulation', abbreviated as hc).

These distinctions may be illustrated from two similes in the sample:

Πάτροκλος δ' Ἀχιλῆϊ παρίστατο, ποιμένι λαῶν,
δάκρυα θερμὰ χέων ὥς τε κρήνη μελάνυδρος,
ἥ τε κατ' αἰγίλιπος πέτρης δνοφερὸν χέει ὕδωρ.   (16, 2–4)
αὐτίκα δὲ σφήκεσσιν ἐοικότες ἐξεχέοντο,
εἰνοδίοις, οὓς παῖδες ἐριδμαίνουσιν ἔθοντες,
αἰεὶ κερτομέοντες, ὁδῷ ἔπι οἰκί' ἔχοντας,
νηπίαχοι· ξυνὸν δὲ κακὸν πολέεσσι τιθεῖσι.   (16, 259–62)

Here 16, 3 is an elaboration, explanatory rather than decorative: it is germane to the whole scene that Patroclus is weeping, is deeply moved. The next verse, on the other hand, is purely decorative – it enriches the picture of the spring, but is not essential to it. It is a good example of whole-verse cumulation; while part-verse cumulation is well exemplified in the second passage. εἰνοδίοις in 260 is an instance of runover-word cumulation, and it is transitional or prospective as well as supplementary: it introduces a new description of the wasps directly related to, and leading on to, the information that boys annoy them, and that they then retaliate on the public. Verse 261 is an example of half-verse cumulation which is elaborative in an explanatory sense: the boys make the wasps angry *because they repeatedly provoke them.* Here the cumulation is supplementary and not prospective; the further progress of the narrative is achieved by a further runover-word cumulation, νηπίαχοι in 262. This is an elaborative word, supplementary in a sense, but its main function is to lead into the new information contained in the rest of the verse: that as a consequence of the boys' folly many people suffer. In this case the material introduced by a prospective cumulation, while it is fresh, merely completes a particular scene. Sometimes a cumulation will lead on, directly or indirectly, to an important new accession of meaning; so for example in the well-known runover-word cumulation (the participle being a common type) of *Iliad* 1, 2, οὐλομένην, ἣ μυρί'...

Clearly cumulation is an important factor in the relation of verse-structure to sentence-structure; and its assessment, which cannot be reduced to precise rules, affects the interpretation of certain cases of enjambment. Cumulation at the beginning of a verse presupposes a special pause or interruption at the end of the preceding verse; the enjambment at that point is not integral, and, even if a cumulative runover-word is an epithet qualifying a noun at the end of the preceding verse, it is natural to regard it as a kind of afterthought, an attribute dropped into place once the main idea is outlined in its essentials. On occasion, however, one cannot be sure how a singer would have treated the semantic – and therefore rhythmical – flow from verse to verse; in other words, whether the sequence is cumulative or not. In 16, 17f.

ἦε σύ γ' 'Αργείων ὀλοφύρεαι ὡς ὀλέκονται
νηυσὶν ἔπι γλαφυρῇσιν ὑπερβασίης ἕνεκα σφῆς;

it is impossible to be sure that 18 should be treated as an instance of half-verse cumulation. It consists of two elaborative and inorganic phrases, each filling about half the verse. But supposing, like Allen in OCT, we print a comma after ὀλοφύρεαι. Then the sentence runs on more smoothly, the enjambment becomes integral not progressive, and 'by the hollow ships' becomes a more pointed qualification of 'they are being destroyed'. In my analysis I have counted such ambiguous cases as being, indeed, cumulations; and that entails assessing the enjambment of the preceding verse as progressive and not integral. Thus, in concentrating attention on the cumulative nature of the style as a whole, I have probably understated the total number of integral enjambments – a total that can never be precisely determined, since the singers themselves might vary from performance to performance in the treatment of such ambiguous connexions.

THE NATURE OF XVI AS A SAMPLE

Book 16, the fourth longest book in either Homeric poem, contains a crucial sequence of the monumental plot in the intervention and death of Patroclus, and many different types of description: arming and preparation for battle, divine scenes, speeches both calm and excited, exhortations and taunts, fighting scenes of all kinds (generic scenes, rapid incidents, major duels, fighting round a corpse), many developed similes. The book does not contain any long section untypical of the *Iliad* as a whole – like the Prologue in book 1, the Embassy in book 9, the Dolon episode in book 10, the Beguiling of Zeus in books 14 and 15, the Funeral Games in book 23, Priam's visit to Achilles in book 24. Its one unusual aspect, indeed, is its very lack of action off the battlefield and outside Troy and the Achaean camp; it is untypical of the style of the *Iliad* only in that it is too typical of it. Yet in sum it is no worse as a sample, and probably better, than most other complete books. It is somewhat more extensive, with its 867 verses, than Milman Parry's 600-verse sample, composed of the first hundred verses each of books 1, 5, 9, 13, 17, 21 (i.e. every fourth book after the first).

THE LIMITS OF PRECISION IN STYLISTIC ANALYSIS

It has been seen that classification difficulties arise in the analysis of enjambment and cumulation. The very fact that the inquiry involves style as well as syntax shows that high precision should not be expected. Moreover the present investigation concerns not literary but oral style, in which additional intangibles like the rhythmical and declamatory habits of ancient singers enter the discussion. Obviously the estimation of oral style, founded as it must be solely on the evidence of later written texts, on the comparative study of oral poets of other cultures, and on a precarious use of *a priori* suppositions, cannot be reduced to fully precise terms.

One of the dangers of presenting any kind of detailed analysis in this kind of inquiry is that of giving a misleading impression of precision, either achieved or at least intended. Thus the analysis in Table A and the list of totals in Table B look complicated and vaguely scientific. The effort to reduce a set of observations on 867 different units to concise form is apt to produce these effects, and numerals and abbreviations can hardly be avoided. But enough has been said here about the difficulty of establishing precise criteria, and about the irreducible remainder of equivocal instances, to counteract that merely superficial impression. The important question arises whether, if subjective interpretations cannot be excluded, one should attempt a detailed analysis at all. The dangers of trying to subject general phenomena to specific analysis have been known since Aristotle; are we trying to be too specific here?

Obviously I believe not; the phenomena under investigation are among the most concrete aspects of style and are to a large extent, at least, determined and categorized by precise criteria like the length of a hexameter verse. More debatable questions like 'What constitutes a sentence?' or 'When is an addition an afterthought?' affect our judgement of only a relatively small minority of verses. It seems to me beyond dispute that there are differences of sentence- and verse-structure in different passages of the *Iliad* and the *Odyssey*, and that the establishment of these differences, in as accurate terms as are possible, is a worthwhile critical activity. That means, not only presenting broad totals in the form of percentages for random samples, as Parry did, but also undertaking the detailed analysis, with full presentation of workings, of major continuous sections of the poems. If the indefinite limits of certain categories call attention to the ambiguous structure of certain types of Homeric sentence, and the ambiguous effects of different emphases and pauses, that is all to the good. There are bound to be differences of opinion over the classification, in certain respects, of a small minority of verses. These differences scarcely affect the preliminary and general stylistic observations that follow; and they do not concern at all those parts of the analysis, like the occurrence of the simple runover word or the positioning of many internal stops, which are hardly subject to variety of interpretation.

Verse-structure and sentence-structure

THE DISTRIBUTION OF STRUCTURAL CHARACTERISTICS IN THE SAMPLE

A. Whole-sentence verses

(i) *Actually complete, independent verses* ($\overline{0}$'s *in the analysis*). In the first instance unusual occurrence of this and other characteristics will be deduced from the totals for each sequence of 50 verses, as given in Table B. These 50-verse sections possess no more than an arbitrary statistical unity, and provide a mere initial indication that must be checked against the analysis and then against the text. The analysis may show, for example, that occurrences in a section are in fact concentrated in its latter part, and spread into the beginning of the following section. Needless to say the constitution of the section in terms of subject-matter is important.

$\overline{0}$'s vary considerably in the course of the 50-verse sections: two sections have 10 instances each, while another has 1 and a third none at all. The high frequencies come in 601–50, or more particularly (as reference to the analysis shows) in 608–32; and in 701–50 (particularly 720–50, with 9 occurrences). In the first of these passages Aeneas attacks Meriones and taunts are exchanged, then Patroclus exhorts Meriones to action not words. There are three concise speeches, each with a whole-sentence introduction like 616, Αἰνείας δ' ἄρα θυμὸν ἐχώσατο φώνησέν τε. Such introductory verses are a relatively common source of $\overline{0}$'s, and sometimes there is also a whole-verse resumption of the 'thus he spoke' type. Patroclus' speech ends with two *gnomai*, each of which fills a verse; this again is apt to occur in some types of battlefield speech, and we may note the tendency of moralisms to fill a complete verse. There is also a series of 3 $\overline{0}$'s at 608–10, in battle-narrative. The action at this point is fairly rapid, but the sequence appears accidental, except in so far as singers seem to have had a tendency to create short sequences of verses of similar type (p. 166 below). Turning to 720–50, we find Apollo urging on Hector and Cebriones and panicking the Achaeans; Patroclus and Hector meet, and the former kills Cebriones and exults over him. Of these 31 verses 11 are speech; there is a sequence of 4 $\overline{0}$'s at 720–3, composed of an introductory 'Apollo spoke' verse and an abrupt series of question, wish, and comment. Similarly 3 other whole-verse sentences are accounted for by the introduction

157

(744) to a short boast by Patroclus and by the laconic first and last verses (745, 750) of the speech itself, which are carefully interrelated and enclose a more leisurely simile-like conceit. The other 2 $\bar{0}$'s occur together in a concise description of Hector's movements at 731f.

The sections low in $\bar{0}$'s are 51–100 (only 1 instance) and 151–200, or rather, as the analysis shows, 140–208; in these 69 verses there is no single whole-sentence verse. The former span consists entirely of Achilles' long and impassioned speech to Patroclus (which begins at 49 with a whole-verse exclamation immediately after a 'thus spoke' verse). Column G of Table B shows that this speech has a very high proportion – 26 instances – of periodically and integrally enjambed verses; this naturally reduces the possible number of whole-sentence verses, which are in any case out of place in this kind of disordered utterance. The second long run of $\bar{0}$-less verses, 140–208, begins in the course of the arming of Patroclus; then come the preparation of horses for him, the marshalling of the Myrmidons and catalogue of their leaders, and Achilles' exhortation. $\bar{0}$'s re-establish themselves with the last verse of that speech, a concise closing instruction, and the 'thus speaking' verse (210) that follows. Yet only 9 verses of the 69-verse sequence are speech; this scotches any feeling that excesses or deficiencies of whole-verse sentences tend to occur in speeches. In fact the passage, unlike the previous one, is not high in periodic or integral enjambment; rather, whole-sentence verses are prejudiced by a high degree of progressive enjambment, and that is associated with heavy cumulation. Verses 145–54 strike the eye in this respect in the analysis, and in the text the description of the horses and of Automedon is heavy with whole-verse cumulation, the leisurely adding of one detail after another: 'And he bade Automedon swiftly to yoke the horses / – him whom he honoured most after Achilles breaker of men / – and was most faithful to await his call in battle' (145–7). This kind of description of a minor figure is closely paralleled in the list of Myrmidon leaders, where again there is a heavy concentration of cumulation, this time part-verse cumulation (170ff.). Arming scenes and those describing minor figures are ripe for elaboration and tend to be strongly cumulative, and this excludes whole-sentence verses; such scenes compose the bulk of our passage.

Finally, the analysis shows up a remarkable sequence of 5 $\bar{0}$'s outside the sections dealt with: 126–30 consists of 4 urgent verses of instruction from Achilles to Patroclus, followed by a brief 'thus spoke' and a concise statement of Patroclus' reaction:

> 'ὄρσεο, διογενὲς Πατρόκλεες, ἱπποκέλευθε·
> λεύσσω δὴ παρὰ νηυσὶ πυρὸς δηΐοιο ἰωήν·
> μὴ δὴ νῆας ἕλωσι καὶ οὐκέτι φυκτὰ πέλωνται·
> δύσεο τεύχεα θᾶσσον, ἐγὼ δέ κε λαὸν ἀγείρω.'
> ὣς φάτο, Πάτροκλος δὲ κορύσσετο νώροπι χαλκῷ.

We may contrast this urgent style with that which makes use of heavy enjambment and broken verses (pp. 163–6); it gives an impression of businesslike and urgent conciseness, rather than disordered thought or action or ideas too complex for the ordinary bounds of speech. It may be noticed that the urgency does not deprive Patroclus of his epithets, although the verses that follow are spare enough.

(ii) *Potentially complete verses ·$\underline{0}$'s, ·1's)*. Column B in Table B gives the total of verses which could formally be regarded as complete in themselves but in their extant use are connected with a neighbouring verse, usually in progressive enjambment. The total is 129, about 1 verse in 7; of these only 8 are ·$\underline{0}$'s (for the exact reference of this and other symbols see pp. 172ff.). The distribution varies from 16 instances in section 1–50 (actually 1–40) to only 1 instance each in 301–50 (actually 300–71) and 601–50.

To take the high rate first: 1–50 is high in verse-end, low in internal strong stops, and also low in integral enjambment (cols. O, N, F). This implies, in plain language, that in this conversation between Achilles and Patroclus the sentences are fairly numerous and tend to begin with the verse; progressive enjambment and whole-verse cumulation are fairly common. The result conveys much information in a moderate and unhurried style. In the low sections, on the other hand, progressive cumulation is rare; in 301–50 most of the sentences begin with a verse in integral enjambment with its successor – some 3 out of 4, indeed, a remarkable proportion. That is incompatible with potential whole-sentence verses, and the numerous internal stops and integral enjambments, too, are quite out of keeping with whole-verse cumulation or potential or actual whole-sentence verses. What, then, is this passage about? It is almost entirely a rapid and impetuous description of fighting of the 'man took man' variety (306, ἔνθα δ' ἀνὴρ ἕλεν ἄνδρα), in which the effect of disordered or complex action is quite different from the systematic and somewhat leisurely impression conveyed by many potentially whole-sentence verses. The total of 225 actually and potentially self-contained verses, over the whole sample of 867, is suggestive: more than a quarter of the verses in this book consist of statements (usually simple, but with a few instances of strong internal stop) which exactly match the verse in length.[7]

B. Enjambed verses

(i) *Progressive enjambment (type 1)*. The totals of 1's (col. D) vary considerably, between 22 instances and a mere 6 or 7. The highest incidence is in 151–200; but if this section is widened to 131–206 the proportion rises to 37 occurrences in 76 verses, or 48%. Verse 131 comes exactly at the beginning of the arming of Patroclus, and the passage then covers the list of horses and of Myrmidons and Achilles' exhortation; comment has already been made on the lack of $\overline{0}$'s in all this (pp. 158f.). There is a leisurely but systematic advance of the narrative, with a loving development of details. Cumulation, and especially whole-verse cumulation, is part of this style, especially in lists of minor figures (p. 158); and that relies on progressive enjambment too.

Other concentrations of 1's or ·1's stand out from the analysis: e.g. 2–10, Patroclus weeps and Achilles questions him (straight-forward narrative with some internal pause; but the last 3½ verses are a simile, heavily cumulative as similes tend to be); 530–7, Glaucus exhorts the Trojans (leisurely, no marked character; 2 or perhaps 3 cumulative verses); 733–9, Patroclus kills Cebriones (inevitability, not urgency or leisureliness, is the main impression conveyed by this straightforward narrative, with all its verses in progressive enjambment).

Of sections low in progressive enjambment 301–50, with but 7 instances, consists (except for the first 5 verses) of the confused fighting discussed just above. The passage is notable for its frequent integral enjambment and internal stops, especially at the

---

[7] This proportion must be kept distinct from 38.3 % of unenjambed or potentially unenjambed verses, which could or do end with the sentence but do not necessarily begin with it, i.e. are not necessarily complete in themselves.

bucolic caesura; and is correspondingly low in whole-sentence verses. Progressive enjambment, cumulation, leisureliness, system and inevitability are quite out of place in this deliberately disordered and hurried style. Verses 601–50 are again low in progressive enjambment with only 7 instances, of which 3 come in similes. The rest, mainly fighting and taunts, is in a moderate style with no marked formal characteristics.

(ii) *Periodic and integral enjambment* (*types* 2 *and* 3). Integral enjambment is more common than periodic, by my criteria, in the proportion of 181 to 106 occurrences over the whole sample. There is an important distinction between the two types from the point of view of the history and development of oral poetry. Integral enjambment is exceedingly rare in the Yugoslav singers: of 2400 lines of poetry examined by A. B. Lord less than 1% had this type of strong enjambment, and all except one instance came in the songs of a single unusually sophisticated singer, Avdo Međedović.[8] On the other hand it is extremely frequent – much more so than in Homer – in the literary epics of Virgil and Apollonius. According to Parry it occurs in every second or third verse in Virgil and Apollonius, against about every fifth verse in Homer.[9] Moreover Parry observed that the literary epic is addicted to what I have classed as violent (type 4) enjambment.[10] There is no doubt that in the post-oral period the integrity of the essential rhythmical unit, the verse, was infringed more and more; and in the oral period the Yugoslav comparison suggests that the simpler and less sophisticated singers were, the more conscious they were of the verse-end as a limit of meaning. Unfortunately the development of the Greek oral epic is too obscure for us to conclude that heavily or integrally enjambed verses are relatively late in the tradition. Integral enjambment may have occurred even in the formative stages of stories about Troy,

[8] *TAPA* 79 (1948), 119, cf. *The Singer of Tales* (Cambridge, Mass., 1960), pp. 54 and 284 n. 17.

[9] *TAPA* 60 (1929), 217.

[10] Apollonius has a preceding adjective at the verse-end of about every twentieth, Virgil about every tenth, verse (Parry, *TAPA* 60 (1929), 219). In some circumstances, of course (for example where the following noun is at the end, not the beginning, of the next verse; e.g. *Argonautica* 1, 686), the enjambment is much less violent than in cases like φαεινή | πήληξ (*Il.* 16, 104) or ἀρίστην | βουλὴν (*Il.* 9, 74). Parry also noted that πᾶς, πολύς, ἄλλος are more commonly separated from their noun in this way in Homer and seem to form a special case.

although we may feel that the earliest narrative poetry of all consisted largely of independent and unenjambed verses. It may be significant that the most conspicuous typical passages in Homer (the preparation of a meal, the beaching or departure of a ship; cf. e.g. 2, 421–31; 9, 206–21; 1, 432–7, 475–87) are relatively low in integral enjambment, though internal stops and part-verse cumulation do occur. Indeed, if the hexameter verse developed as a unit and not as an agglomeration of shorter units then it is possible that integral enjambment and strong internal stops entered the poetical tradition at a comparatively early stage; for A. B. Lord has well pointed out that the longer dactylic hexameter has greater opportunities for the completion of a thought before the verse-end than has, for example, the shorter decasyllable of the South Slavic tradition.[11]

Periodic (type 2) enjambment is prominent in the sample in 401–50 (11 instances), or rather 415–65 (15 instances in 51 verses). The passage begins with a list of Trojan victims of Patroclus, then Sarpedon rallies the Lycians and faces him. Zeus wonders whether to save his son and is dissuaded by Hera; he sends bloody rain, and the fighting continues. Seven of the 2's occur in the exchange of speeches between Zeus and Hera. Like many of the shorter Iliadic speeches, these debate alternative courses of action and different contingencies, and therefore contain disjunctions and conditional clauses; and whole-verse protases and alternatives tend to give rise to 2's.[12] Similarly there is a notable concentration of periodic enjambment in verses 10–40, again mainly owing to alternatives, conditions and the like. That is mainly why, in 1–50, periodic enjambment is, exceptionally, commoner than integral. On the other hand 2's are low in 501–50 (only 2 instances), a passage full of incident: Sarpedon dies, Glaucus is wounded, relieved by Apollo after a prayer, and rallies Hector. There are two speeches, but the first is a prayer and the second an exhortation; in neither type are conditions or alternatives to be expected, and periodic enjambment is absent. In the remainder of the passage a rapid but simple style

[11] E.g. *TAPA* 79 (1948), 123.

[12] 'Tend to', because this depends on whether the protasis, for example, precedes or follows the apodosis. If the former, the enjambment is periodic; if the latter, it is progressive. The distinction is not so arbitrary and mechanical as it looks: in the former case the singer has formed a complex and periodic sentence in his mind before he starts the first verse; in the second the condition is framed as an afterthought, and the mode of conception may well be different.

with many verse-end stops inhibits the stronger forms of enjambment in general.

Integral enjambment is a more conspicuous stylistic characteristic than periodic enjambment, both in its number of occurrences and in its whole effect on the sound and rhythm of the poetry. The two sections highest in 3's are 301–50, the man-took-man fighting, and 51–100, Achilles' impassioned speech to Patroclus; both are rapid, urgent, and heavily broken up by internal stops (cols. M and N). Strong overrunning of the verse-end is often caused by stops at the bucolic caesura (which account for no less than 70 of the total of 182 instances of integral enjambment in book 16); this is so in the former passage, which is high in s·'s, although not in the latter (col. T). There is, however, a conspicuous sequence of such enjambments at 60–3:

> ἀλλὰ τὰ μὲν προτετύχθαι ἐάσομεν· οὐδ' ἄρα πως ἦν
> ἀσπερχὲς κεχολῶσθαι ἐνὶ φρεσίν· ἤτοι ἔφην γε
> οὐ πρὶν μηνιθμὸν καταπαυσέμεν, ἀλλ' ὁπότ' ἂν δὴ
> νῆας ἐμὰς ἀφίκηται ἀϋτή τε πτόλεμός τε.

Here it is as though whole-sentence verses were being systematically displaced so as to straddle the verse-end; the sequence of displacements causes a mounting tension that is relieved, with a sense of completion, in the undistorted whole verse at the end. This is an effective piece of rhetoric, in which the transgressing of the verse-units helps to reproduce Achilles' indignation and excitement, his spilling over of thought after thought, until the closing verse, with its inevitable restoration of the rhythmical norm, reinforces the simple basic idea 'not until the fighting reaches my ships'.

A less regular sequence, making a more disordered and less rhetorical effect, is seen a little later in the same speech at 70–3; and a similar irregularity in the placing of the internal stop makes an analogous impression in the description of chaotic battle at 373–6:

> Τρωσὶ κακὰ φρονέων· οἱ δὲ ἰαχῇ τε φόβῳ τε
> πάσας πλῆσαν ὁδούς, ἐπεὶ ἄρ τμάγεν· ὕψι δ' ἄελλη
> σκίδναθ' ὑπὸ νεφέων, τανύοντο δὲ μώνυχες ἵπποι
> ἄψορρον προτὶ ἄστυ νεῶν ἄπο καὶ κλισιάων.

Again the closing verse, uninterrupted by internal stop in contrast with its predecessors, has a marked effect and seems to embody in its smoother rhythmical flow the idea of the long and swift retreat of the chariots once they had extricated themselves from the rout. Yet often these effects are purely rhythmical and can have no intended relation to the meaning. A distinction in the flow of a concluding verse, in a long sentence or stylistically unified passage, often seems to have been sought by singers; either as in this type or in its converse, an interrupted verse after a sequence of uninterrupted ones, such as 389–92, 462–5, 487–91. Other sequences of integral enjambment occur at 727–9, 833–5; the former conveys a salutary warning because it seems to have no special motive and produces no special effect, being part of a description of fighting and divine intervention which, although full of incident, is not particularly wild or hurried. The latter comes in Hector's boast over the dying Patroclus; he seems to become excited, flushed with arrogance, at this point, after a quiet beginning in 830–2. Among concentrations (not sequences) of 3's that show up in the analysis but not in the 50-verse totals the most conspicuous is 103–25, which contains 11 cases of integral enjambment (including one violent) in 23 verses, 6 of them after a stop at the bucolic caesura. This passage, generally high in internal stops, describes the rapid and critical fighting during which fire is set to one of the Achaean ships; it is as urgent and broken-up as the man-took-man section at 306–50, but is disguised in Table B because it is immediately followed by the arming of Patroclus, with little strong enjambment and a marked change in style.

Sections notably low in integral enjambment are 1–50, 551–600, 751–800; in each of these periodic enjambment is relatively high. The first passage (Achilles and Patroclus) has already been discussed; the others are almost entirely narrative, not speeches, and describe mixed fighting. Verses 551ff. are interesting, since a large part of the passage (especially 569–607) describes violent fighting with a fairly swift transition from one encounter to another. Yet the effect is subtly different from that of the other notable confused-fighting passage at 306–50; here there is a good deal of cumulation and a number of pauses at the main caesura, but (from 562 on) almost no stop at the bucolic caesura with its usual consequence of obtrusive enjambment. The effect is of steady, almost interminable fighting rather than of great passion and confusion. On 751–800 see pp.165 and 170

C. *Internal stops, short sentences*

Internal stops, since they diminish the unity of the verse as a rhythmical continuum, are more obtrusive and often have a more marked stylistic effect than verse-end stops. The man-took-man fighting of 306ff. has already been remarked on several counts; it is notably high in internal stops both weak and strong (cols. M, N); the broken effect suits the broken fighting, but it is wise to remember that a similar effect might be due simply to a singer's concentrating a great deal of incident in a small space. Incidentally this section does not have many double internal stops (ss's); these give the most staccato effect of all, but are uncommon. They are most prominent, and then only 5 in total, in 1–50. Of the 5 instances, 4 occur in the interchange between Patroclus and Achilles at 7–21, since they are most frequently caused by the use of a simple vocative within the verse. The repeated use of the vocative does, of course, have a distinctly emotional effect.[13]

No 50-verse section is outstandingly low in total internal stops (which include, of course, those produced by part-verse cumulation and simple runover words); but it may be useful to consider 751–800, which is lowest with 21 instances. As it happens, half-verse cumulative stops are high within this total, other types exceptionally low (cols. J, Q–T). This, with the high frequency of progressive enjambment, suggests a strongly cumulative passage. It describes the fight for Cebriones' body, then the stunning of Patroclus by Apollo, and it includes three similes (which tend to be cumulative) accounting, without their 'apodoses', for 10 verses. It is revealing that at this dramatically crucial point the poet avoids a staccato style; rather the deliberate, cumulative effect (which is notable, as often with armour, in the verses on the helmet as it falls to the ground, 793–800) conveys a certain sense of inevitability.

In many other places, however, the more obvious device of using short sentences is chosen for the representation of violent action. The following passages stand out from the analysis as being particularly high in all stops, especially strong ones, and the brief description of their content tells its own tale:

---

[13] Sometimes the vocative may not cause a very marked break in the stream of sound; e.g. verse 29 is not counted as having double internal stop:

ἕλκε' ἀκειόμενοι· σὺ δ' ἀμήχανος ἔπλευ, Ἀχιλλεῦ.

19–22   urgent conversation
67–73   part of Achilles' impassioned speech
102–107   missiles rain on Ajax
122–129   ship fired, Achilles excited
289–296   Patroclus routs Trojans
315–325   man-took-man fighting
330–341   man-took-man fighting
400–406   Patroclus kills Thestor
550–555   Trojans react strongly to Sarpedon's death
625–632   Patroclus rebukes Meriones
656–662   Trojans panic
787–792   Apollo strikes Patroclus
833–846   mostly Hector's angry boast over Patroclus.

Only the last two of these passages need further comment. The former is part of a description that has already been assessed as generally deliberate and not staccato; but these few verses describe the actual blow. In the latter Hector's angry speech is succeeded by a more fluid reply from the dying Patroclus (844–54), which reflects, intentionally or not, his weakness and resignation as death approaches.

Finally, we may observe from the analysis certain sequences of stops in the same position in the verse, which exemplify the sporadic tendency of singers to repeat a rhythmical pattern – perhaps because they just stuck in a rhythmical groove, as it were, perhaps because they liked the repetition (as they certainly liked anaphora and alliteration, for example) from time to time. A sequence of four weak stops at the main caesura in 79–82 illustrates the tendency:

> πᾶν πεδίον κατέχουσι, μάχῃ νικῶντες Ἀχαιούς.
> ἀλλὰ καὶ ὣς, Πάτροκλε, νεῶν ἀπὸ λοιγὸν ἀμύνων
> ἔμπεσ᾽ ἐπικρατέως, μὴ δὴ πυρὸς αἰθομένοιο
> νῆας ἐνιπρήσωσι, φίλον δ᾽ ἀπὸ νόστον ἕλωνται.

The masculine caesura of 81, in contrast with the feminine caesuras of the other verses, slightly reduces the effect, which is more marked in 743–5 with a sequence of hephthemimeral stops (ṣ's), partly because of the comparative rarity of this position anyway (col. S):

> κάππεσ᾽ ἀπ᾽ εὐεργέος δίφρου, λίπε δ᾽ ὀστέα θυμός.
> τὸν δ᾽ ἐπικερτομέων προσέφης, Πατρόκλεες ἱππεῦ ·
> ‘ὢ πόποι, ἦ μάλ᾽ ἐλαφρὸς ἀνήρ, ὡς ῥεῖα κυβιστᾷ.’[14]

---

[14] For other examples see 71–3, 347–9, 584–7, 626–8. Particularly noticeable are the sequences of stops at the bucolic caesura followed by integral enjambment;

D. Cumulation

(i) *General remarks.* Much has already been said about cumulation, which implies a state of mind and a whole technique of poetical assimilation rather than a particular structural device leading to a particular stylistic effect. For this reason I shall not attempt to detect concentrations of whole-verse cumulation, except where they may be suggested by the more specific indications provided by runover words and, to a lesser extent, half-verse cumulations. The criteria for determining whole-verse cumulation (for example, among ·1 verses not first verses in their sentence) are far too vague, and it may prove difficult to sharpen the criteria even after the much fuller investigation that cumulation and the adding style, in general, deserve.

In its more 'decorative' uses (p. 153) cumulation probably varied from performance to performance, in response to the energy and imaginativeness of the singer and the reaction of his audience. Some cumulations will appear particularly successful, and will gradually be worked into the permanent texture of an individual song, to be assimilated, perhaps, by younger singers. Others will be discarded, reverting to the singer's general repertory or to the context from which he originally acquired them. The fact that cumulation is often inorganic means that it may sometimes be due to post-Homeric efforts at elaboration, whether by subsequent oral singers and reciters or by copyists and glossators. Yet, because of the essentially cumulative nature of the oral style as a whole, it is almost always impossible to be sure that a doubtful-looking cumulation is non-Homeric; in a sense the poems were always in a process of elaboration from the formation of Homer's shorter prototypes to the gradual making of the monumental poems, and probably, also, during the period of subsequent oral performances of those poems whether by Homer or by his successors.

(ii) *Cumulation within the sentence.* The particular problem presents itself whether, if the adding style is a fundamental mode of oral composition and re-creation, passages that are not overtly in the adding style can have been oral. There is a particularly good test-

in addition to 60–3, quoted earlier, cf. 109f., 168f., 353f., 395f., 517f., 552f., 834f. More complex patterns, too, can be traced through the analysis.

case in book 16, namely the man-took-man fighting from 306 to 350. This passage, in which internal stops and integral enjambments and the overrunning of the verse-end are rife, in which the simplicity of the verse as the primary rhythmical unit is suppressed or transcended (however one happens to look at it), lies at the opposite extreme from heavily cumulative passages in which one verse leads to the next either with a new sentence or with progressive enjambment. Was it not very difficult, perhaps impossible, for an oral and illiterate poet to develop or to assimilate such a long and complex sequence, in which there is little opportunity for leisurely aggregation and in which many of the verses are strongly interwoven with their successor, so as to confront the singer with a confusing tension between units of rhythm and of meaning?

First, I think it must be admitted that this exceedingly complicated kind of passage is likely to have been within the grasp only of the most proficient singers. If there is a serious case for supposing some help from writing in the composition of our *Iliad*, then in relation to the detailed deployment of language it must rest largely on passages like the one under consideration. Yet the complexity of this passage *from the point of view of the singer* should neither be exaggerated nor exactly equated with the undoubted complexity of its effect on the reader or, probably, the hearer. Closer examination shows that the cumulative principle *is* at work, within the sentence rather than in the accretion of verse on verse. Consider the first 11 verses, 306–16:

> Ἔνθα δ' ἀνὴρ ἕλεν ἄνδρα κεδασθείσης ὑσμίνης   306
> ἡγεμόνων. πρῶτος δὲ Μενοιτίου ἄλκιμος υἱὸς
> αὐτίκ' ἄρα στρεφθέντος 'Αρηϊλύκου βάλε μηρὸν
> ἔγχεϊ ὀξυόεντι, διαπρὸ δὲ χαλκὸν ἔλασσε·
> ῥῆξεν δ' ὀστέον ἔγχος, ὁ δὲ πρηνὴς ἐπὶ γαίῃ   310
> κάππεσ'. ἀτὰρ Μενέλαος ἀρήϊος οὖτα Θόαντα
> στέρνον γυμνωθέντα παρ' ἀσπίδα, λῦσε δὲ γυῖα.
> Φυλεΐδης δ' Ἄμφικλον ἐφορμηθέντα δοκεύσας
> ἔφθη ὀρεξάμενος πρυμνὸν σκέλος, ἔνθα πάχιστος
> μυὼν ἀνθρώπου πέλεται· περὶ δ' ἔγχεος αἰχμῇ   315
> νεῦρα διεσχίσθη· τὸν δὲ σκότος ὄσσε κάλυψε.

There is obvious cumulation, in part-verse form, only at 307 and 309; 312 is cumulative, too, in a form that happens not to be recorded in our limited analysis. There is, then, a certain amount of ordinary progressive composition even in this apparently uncumulative passage. Moreover the 5 integral enjambments do not give rise to long or complex sentences in themselves: less than 3 verses in the longest instances. We notice once more the important function of the four positions in the verse where internal pause occurs; they are in fact the caesuras that mark off the cola identified by Fränkel, but here they are used as the limits of sentences – secondary limits, admittedly, but not purely random ones once the verse-end is abandoned as primary limit. Often it can be seen that short sentences which cross the verse-end in integral enjambment are composed of brief phrase-units dropped successively, as it were, into these colon slots. That process is itself cumulative in a valid sense as can be seen in 313f., where ἔφθη ὀρεξάμενος provides a possible completion of sense but is supplemented by a more detailed specification which fills the next slot, and so on. Now these phrases are often standardized units or adaptations of them – formulas, in fact. Here metrical, structural and formular analyses coincide; and here we see most clearly how the proficient singer could have handled a passage as apparently complex and irregular as the present one by oral means alone. Whether such a passage could have been easily passed down for long in the tradition is more doubtful; it is probable that passages like these were the work of Homer or a close predecessor; but that is another question.

(iii) *Runover-word cumulation.* This is not very frequent over the whole sample, with some 48 occurrences in 867 verses (col. K). The cumulated runover word is a conspicuous element in the Homeric style, but its scope tends to be exaggerated. So does that of the simple, uncumulated, strongly enjambed runover word, which occurs only 27 times in the book. These 27 instances are not exactly after-thoughts,[15] they are an integral and necessary completion of the sentence. At the same time the singer could undoubtedly have fitted his meaning into a complete verse, and that he did not do so suggests that he favoured the runover word as a stylistic device for its own sake. It follows that runover-word cumulation, also, may sometimes have been practised for the sake of the runover effect as much as for the cumulative effect. Neither rc's nor r's are common enough to have a significant distribution over the 50-verse sections;

---

[15] Except, possibly, in a limited sense and in a small minority of instances: Bassett, *TAPA* 57 (1926), 116ff.

but, taking the totals for both together, 151–200 (actually 157–94) has a relatively high frequency with 9 instances. Of these 3 occur in a single simile, 156–63, and a fourth in its 'apodosis'; the rest (4 rc's, 1 r) come in catalogue-summaries of minor characters (Myrmidon leaders in this case), which are notably cumulative. Might this provide a significant connection between the style of these brief sketches and that of the developed similes?

(iv) *Half-verse cumulation.* This is high in 751–800, with 9 instances; the passage is also noticeable for its dearth of other internal stops and integral enjambment. Only 4 verses in it can be regarded as whole-verse cumulations, and it only has a single runover-word cumulation. The half-verse cumulations are most concentrated in the descriptions of Patroclus' last rushes at the enemy and of his stunning by Apollo (781–800). I have already remarked that the impression given is of inevitability or inexorability rather than of urgency and rapidity; but an equivalent concentration at 575–600, with 7 instances, is a scene of mixed fighting where the narrative is rather leisurely, devoid equally of great urgency and any special sense of inevitability. It is worth noting that 3 of the former 9 instances are organic to the general context in that the latter half of their verse leads into the next verse in integral enjambment; the other 6 verses are complete in sense by their close, and are inorganic. Thus only a minority over this section fulfil the function that runover-word cumulation often performs, of leading into a fresh topic, of providing a transition, more subtle and variegated than that of ordinary progressive enjambment, between one chain of thought and the next. The total of 83 instances of half-verse cumulation (against e.g. 48 of runover-word cumulation) in the 867 verses of the sample shows that this is an important structural type that deserves special categorization. Other part-verse cumulations – for example, those extending to the bucolic caesura – are negligible by comparison.

(v) *Other cumulative passages.* Other passages that stand out from the analysis as cumulative are as follows:

131–154	arming of Patroclus
172–186	catalogue of Myrmidons
190–195	(ditto)
60–262	simile

Arming scenes, descriptions of pieces of armour, developed similes, the description of minor figures and their genealogy whether or not in a catalogue – these are the typical *loci* for cumulation; but it is a mode of composition that can make itself felt even in some passages of fighting.

CONCLUSION

One danger of this kind of stylistic analysis is tautology. The mere identification, totalling and setting down of characteristics like enjambment and cumulation – if done with reasonable *general* accuracy, which is difficult in itself – do not reveal much more about the style of a passage than that it is, precisely, cumulative or not, heavy or light in enjambment. Sometimes the listing of formal, structural characteristics simply reproduces the obverse side of other listed characteristics, and it is important not to be misled here. Nevertheless, certain general conclusions *have* emerged – far fewer, I am sure, than could be elicited by a fuller study based upon more sophisticated criteria by someone with the classificatory genius of a Milman Parry. The total usage and detailed distribution of whole-sentence verses, both actual and potential, of progressively, periodically, and integrally enjambed verses, of probably cumulated beginnings of verses, of verses interrupted by internal pause in various positions, reveal something important about the complexity and variety of the Homeric style in its structural aspects. Moreover the relation between structure and meaning becomes clearer. Certain structural properties tend to be accompanied by certain stylistic effects and to be associated with certain sorts of subject-matter; but there is no rigid correspondence between structure and style, and in many cases a quite different effect can be produced, according to context, by similar structural means, or conversely different structural means can produce a closely similar effect. There is nothing remarkable in the conclusion that short sentences with broken verses and heavy enjambment give an effect of rapidity and urgency in speech or action. That is obvious enough, although it helps to have a degree of quantitative documentation. But the observation that an apparently similar effect is sometimes attained by quite distinct means (so far as rhythm is concerned, at least) – namely by a sequence of whole-sentence verses – may not be so obvious, and raises a series of possibly fruitful questions.

Obviously such investigations must be carried beyond the range of a single part of the *Iliad*. I would like to see them extended to sizeable portions, not less than about 250 verses in length, of other books of both poems; for test purposes, indeed, to particular passages with an apparently individual style as well as to passages apparently composed relatively late in the tradition – to Nestor's reminiscences and the Phaeacian scenes as well as to the Doloneia, Priam and Achilles, and Odysseus' false tales. Much of Homer, in any case, is probably in a style that does not exceed in any one direction, but contains a more or less harmonious mixture of the various structural, rhythmical and formular elements. Even in book 16 it is noticeable that many stretches have lain low during our analysis: yet 201–300, 651–700 and 801–50 (which contains, indeed, the wounding and death of Patroclus) are stylistically as effective, to use general terms, as the passages that show an obvious excess or deficiency in certain characteristics. Yet the study of those characteristics in their more extreme uses can help to illuminate their less dramatic function in the frequent stretches of more 'normal' poetry. That is part of the justification of the present type of investigation.

APPENDIX

The schematic analysis, in terms of enjambment, stops, sentence-length, cumulation, of *Iliad* 16.

EXPLANATION OF SYMBOLS USED IN TABLE A, THE VERSE-BY-VERSE ANALYSIS[1]

Strong stops

Underlining of a symbol marks a strong stop (colon or full stop), either at the verse-end (when an enjambment-number is underlined) or internally (when s, r, hc or rc is underlined).

---

[1] The analysis sometimes presupposes a punctuation different from that of e.g. OCT.

Verse-structure and sentence-structure

Enjambment

<u>0</u>   indicates no enjambment (and, of course, a strong stop at the verse-end).

·<u>0</u>   (see ·1).

$\underset{=}{\underline{0}}$ indicates a whole-sentence unenjambed verse.

1   indicates *progressive* enjambment.

·1   indicates 1-type verses which either do or could begin a sentence; that is, they are potentially complete in sense. Similarly with ·<u>0</u>.

2   indicates *periodic* enjambment.

2−   indicates verses in which the main sentence is interrupted by verse-end as in 3, but a weak stop at the verse-end is induced by e.g. a parenthetical phrase (see pp. 150f.).

3   indicates *integral* enjambment.

3−   indicates integrally enjambed verses in which the over-running sentence or clause begins at the bucolic caesura.

4   indicates *violent* enjambment (counted with 3 in Table B).

Internal stops

s marks an internal weak stop (possible comma) ⎤ position in verse
<u>s</u> marks an internal strong stop   ⎬ indicated by
                                            ⎦ dot, as below.

·s = stop at position 3, 2 or $1\frac{1}{2}$, rarely 1.[2]

ṡ = stop at main caesura, position 5 or $5\frac{1}{2}$.

ş = stop at position 7.

s· = stop at bucolic caesura, position 8.

ss marks two internal stops in the verse, position and strength as further indicated: e.g. ·<u>ss</u>.

[2] Positions as follows: 1 $1\frac{1}{2}$ 2 3 $3\frac{1}{2}$ 4 5 $5\frac{1}{2}$ 6 7 $7\frac{1}{2}$ 8 9 $9\frac{1}{2}$ 10 11 12

                        − ∪∪ −   ∪∪ − ∪∪ − ∪∪ − ∪∪ − ∪

Cumulation

hc   indicates the special cases of cumulated clauses or phrases ending with a stop (<u>hc</u> if strong) at the main caesura, position 5 or $5\frac{1}{2}$.

rc   indicates runover-word cumulation: a single word is cumulated at the beginning of the verse, followed by a weak or strong stop and a fresh impulse of meaning.

Runover word

r   indicates the simple (uncumulated) runover-word, completing the meaning of the preceding verse (which is in integral enjambment).

Sentence-length

| marks sentences of 4 verses or more.

Verse-structure and sentence-structure

Table A. *A verse-by-verse analysis of* Iliad *16 in terms of enjambment and other structural features*

No.			No.			No.		
1		0̄	40		·1		ṡ	0
	s·	·1			3	80	ṡ	2–
		1		r	1		ṡ	3
		·0		rc	0		ṡ	0
5		·1			3			·1
		·0	45		0			1
	ṡṡ·	·1		s·	3–	85	hc	3
	rc	1			0		ṡ	0
	hc	1			0		s·	3–
10		·0		·ss·	0			2
	·sṡ	0	50	s·	2			3
	s·	2			0	90	ṡ	0
		0			2			2–
	s·	·1			1		ṡ	1
15		·1		hc	0			3
		0	55	ṡ	0		r	0
		·1			2	95	r / ṡ	3
	hc	0		hc	2–			0
	·ss	0			1		·s	2–
20	ṣ	0		rc	0		s·	2
	·sṣ	2	60	s·	3–		ṡ	2
	·s	·0		s·	3–	100		0
	ṩ	2–		s·	4–			0
		0			0		ṡ	0
25		2			·1			·1
		·1	65		·1			4
		·0			3	105	rc	3–
		·1		ṡ	3		s·	1
	hc	0		r	1		ṡ	3–
30	s·	·1		rc	1		s·	0
	rc	2	70	rc	3	110	s·	3–
		0		ṡ	3		s·	3–
	·s	·1		ṡ	3		·s	0
	ṡ	1		ṡ	0			2
35	hc	0			3			3
		2	75		0	115	ṡ	1
		2			·1		ṡ	3
	ṡ	1		hc	3		s·	3–
	rc	0		s·	3–			

Table A (*cont.*)

			0				1		rc		0
		s·	2−		rc	s·	3−	205			·1
120		·s	3			·ṡ	0		rc		0
		ṡ	0				3			s·	3−
		ṣ	3	165			2			ṣ	0
		·ṣ	0		r		1				0
		ṣ·	3−				0	210			0
125			0			s·	3−				0
			0			s·	·3−				2
			0	170			0		hc		2
			0				·1				0
130		ṡ	0		rc		0	215		ṡṣ·	0
		·s	0				·1				·1
			·1		hc		0		rc		0
	rc		0	175			·1				·1
			·1		hc		1			ṣ	1
135			0			ṣ	1	220		s·	3−
			·1		hc		0			·ṣ	1
	rc		0				·1				3
			·1	180	rc		1		hc		1
	rc		0		hc		3			ṡ	1
			0		r		1				0
140			·1				0	225		s·	3−
	hc		3				·1				2
	r		1	185	hc		1				0
	hc		1		rc		0				·1
	hc		0				3		rc		1
145			·1				2	230		ṡ	·0
			1				3			s·	·1
			0	190		ṡ	1		hc		0
			·1				·1			ṡṣ·	2
	hc		1				0			s·	3−
150			1				·1	235			0
			0		rc		1				2
			·1	195			0		hc		2
			1				·1				0
			0			ṡ	0				2
155			·1				3	240			1
		s·	2			ṡ	0		rc	s·	1
	rc		2	200		·s	·1			s·	3−
			3				1				3
	r		0		hc		0			ṡ	3
160			·1			ṡ	·1	245	r		0
											2

TABLE A (*cont.*)

Line			Val
			1
			0
		ś	0
250		ṣ	0
			3
	r		0
			3
		ś	1
255		ṣ	3
			0
			3
	r		0
			·1
260	rc		1
	hc		1
	rc		0
			3
		ś	3
265			0
			3
		ś	0
			0
			2
270		ś	·1
		s·	3–
			1
			3
		·s	0
275			0
		s·	3–
			0
			2
	hc		2
280		ś	1
			3
		ṣ	0
			0
			·1
285	hc		1
			1
		ś	3
			0
		ś	3

Line			Val
290		ś	1
	rc		1
	hc		0
		ś	0
		s·	3–
295		ṣ	3
	hc		0
			3
			2
			·1
300	rc		1
			2–
		ś	0
			2–
			1
305		ś	0
			·1
	rc		3
			1
	hc		0
310		ś	3
	r		1
		s·	0
			3
		s·	3–
315		ṣ	3
		ṣ́	0
			2
	rc		0
		ś	3
320	hc		1
			3
		s·	2–
		·s	3
		ṣ́	0
325		ś	0
			3
		ś	1
		s·	3–
		ś	0
330			3
		s·	3–
			0

Line			Val
		s·	3–
			0
335		s·	3–
		ś	0
		s·	3–
		s·	3–
		ś	1
340	rc	s·	3–
	r	ṣ	0
			3
			0
		ś	0
345			3
	r		3
	hc		0
		ś	3
		ś	3
350		·ṣ	0
			0
			2
	rc	·s·	3–
		s·	3–
355			0
		s·	3–
		ś	0
			3
		ś	2
360			2
			0
			0
		ś	0
			2
365	hc		1
			1
		s·	3–
		s·	1
	rc		0
370			3
			1
			·1
	hc		3
		ṣ́s·	3–
375		ś	3

TABLE A (*cont.*)

		0			3			2
		2	420		2			2–
	ṡ	1			0			2
	hc	0		ṡs·	0	465	s·	0
380		·1		s·	3–			·1
	rc	1			1		hc	1
	ṡ	0	425	rc	0		hc	1
	ṡ	0			0		ṣ	0
		2		ṡs·	0	470	ṡs·	3–
385	hc	3			3		r	0
	r	2			2			0
		1	430		0			2
		·0			·1			0
		·1			·0	475	ṡ	0
390		·1		s·	2–			0
		1			0			·1
	ṡ	0	435		·1			·1
		0			3		rc ṡ	1
		2–			2	480	rc	1
395	s·	3–			0			0
	s·	4–			0			·1
		3	440	ṡ	0		hc	3
	ṡ	0		ṡ	2–			0
		·1			0	485	rc	·1
400	s·	0		·ṡ	0			0
	ṡ́s·	2–		ṡ	0			2
	ṡ́	3	445		2		hc	2
	·ss·	3–			3			·1
	ṡ	1			0	490		3
405	hc	1			3		ṡ	0
	s·	3–		ṡ	0		·ss·	3–
		1	450	ṡ	2		s·	0
		0			2–			2–
		·1			0	495	ṡ	0
410	ṡ	0			2			0
		·1			·1			3
	hc	1	455		1		s·	3–
	hc	3			1	500		0
	r	0		hc	0			0
415		2		·s	0			·1
		2			·1		hc	3
		2	460	hc	3		ṡ	0
		0		s·	0			

TABLE A (*cont.*)

505		0			·s	·1			2
		·1		rc	ṡ	3	590		2
	hc	0	550		ṣ	3		ṡ	2
		0			ṣ	3		ṣ	0
		0			·s	0		ṡ	2–
510	s·	3–			s·	3–		r	1
	r	1			s·	3–	595	hc	3
	hc	0				0			0
		0	555			0			·1
	·s	3			·s	·1		hc	0
515	ṡ	1				0		ṡ	·1
	hc	0				·1	600	hc	1
	s·	3–			·s	1		s·	3–
	s·	3–	560		s·	3–		ṡ	0
	ṡ	0				0			·1
520		·1			·s	0		·ss·	3–
	hc	1				2–	605		0
	hc	0				2		s·	3–
	ṡ	·1				1		ṡ	0
	ṡs·	3–	565			0			0
525		1		hc		0			0
		0				·1	610		0
	ṡ	0				0		ṡ	3
	ṡ	3				0		ṡ	1
	ṡ	0	570			2		rc	0
530		·1			s·	1			3
		0				1	615	r	0
		2		rc		2			0
	ṡ	0				0		·s	3
		·1	575			·1		s·	0
535		1		hc		0			0
		·1				·1	620	·s	3
		0		hc		1		s·	3–
	·s	·1		hc		3		ṡ	0
		2–	580	r		0			2
540	ṡ	0				·1			2–
	ṡ	·1				·1	625		0
		0		rc		0		·s	0
		0			ṡ	2–		·s	0
	ṡ	·1	585		ṡ	0		·s	3
545		1			ṡ	·1		ṡ	0
	rc	1		hc		0	630	ṣ	0
		0				0			0

Table A (*cont.*)

	ṡ	0		·s	0	720		0
		2–			·1		·ss·	0
	hc	2			2–		ṡ	0
635		1			1			0
		1	680	ṡ	0		·s	·1
		0			·1	725	ṡ	0
		3		s·	3–			·1
	r	3			0			3
640		0			2–		s·	3–
	s·	3–	685	s·	1		ṡ	3
		1		rc	2	730	·s	0
	hc	0			0			0
	s·	3–			0			0
645		1			·1			·1
		2	690	rc	0		hc	1
		2			0	735	hc	1
		3		ṡ	2		ṡ	1
		3		·s	0		ṡ	·1
650		1			·1		rc	1
		0	695		1		hc	0
		·1			0	740	s·	3–
		3		·s	0		r	1
		3			·1		hc	3
655	ṡ	0		hc	1		ṣ	0
		0	700		3		ṣ	0
	s·	3–		r ṣ	0	745	·sṣ	0
	ṡ	0			3			2
	s·	·1		r	1			1
660	rc	1			0		hc	1
	ṣ	3	705		2			0
	r	0			0	750		0
		·1		·ss·	3–			·1
	hc	3			1		hc	3
665		0		hc	0		ṡ	0
		0	710	·s	·1		ṡs·	0
	ṡ	3			0	755		0
	s·	3–			0			·1
		1			2			2–
670	ṡ	0			0		ṡ	0
		·1	715		·1			2
	s·	3–			1	760		2
		1		rc	1			0
		1			1			0
675	hc	0			0		s·	3–

TABLE A (*cont.*)

No.				No.				No.			
			0				1	850	hc		0
765			2–		hc		3			ṡ	0
			1				0			s·	3–
			1	810			·1				1
			·1		hc		0				0
	hc		1			ṣ	·1	855			0
770			2–			·s	1				·1
	r		0			s·	3–		hc		0
			·1	815			0				0
			1				2–			·s	0
			·1				0	860		ṡ	2
775	hc		3				3				0
			0			ṡ	2				3
			2	820			1			ṡ	0
		s·	0		hc		0				·1
			2			ṡ	0	865			0
780			0				2			ṣ	·1
			·1				·1		rc		0
	hc		1	825	hc		1				
			0				0				
			·1				3				
785	hc		0				1				
			2				·0				
		·sṡ	0	830		·s	·1				
			·1				2–				
	rc		0				0				
790			0			·s	3				
		·s	·1			ṣ·	3–				
	hc		0	835		s·	3–				
			0			ṣ	0				
			·1			·s	·1				
795	hc		1				0				
	hc		3			ṡ	2				
			1	840		ṡ	3				
			3				0				
		ṡ	1			ṡ	0				
800	hc		0			ṣ	0				
			·1			ṡṣ·	3–				
		s·	3–	845		s·	1				
			0		rc		0				
			0				2				
805		ṡ	·1				0				
		·s	3				·1				

Table B. Tabulation of the phenomena listed in Table A, by 50-verse sections with totals
(For key to symbols see pp. 172ff.)

Verses	0̄	·0̄+·1	0̄+·0̄+·1	1 (inc. ·1)	2	3	2+3	s (inc. s̲)	ss (inc. s̲s̲ etc.)	hc	rc	r	All internal stops (i.e. H, J, K, L, +2×I)	Internal strong stops	Verse-end strong stops	All strong stops	·s, ·s[s] (inc. r, rc)	ṡ, š[s] (inc. hc)	ṣ	s·
1–50	6	15	21	17	8	3	11	12	5	4	4	1	31	5	22	27	11	8	2	8
51–100	1	4	5	10	9	17	26	21	0	4	2	3	30	10	14	24	7	19	0	6
101–150	8	8	16	15	2	12	14	18	0	4	4	1	27	10	21	31	9	11	0	7
151–200	0	12	12	22	4	9	13	10	0	5	6	3	24	7	15	22	10	9	1	4
201–250	6	7	13	14	8	8	16	16	2	5	5	1	31	4	20	24	6	14	2	9
251–300	4	4	8	14	4	16	20	17	0	5	4	2	28	8	16	24	7	14	3	3
301–350	2	1	3	7	4	22	26	27	0	3	3	3	36	15	17	32	8	17	2	10
351–400	5	6	11	13	8	13	21	18	1	4	3	1	28	7	16	23	4	13	0	10
401–450	7	5	12	9	11	10	21	12	4	3	1	1	25	9	20	29	4	14	0	7
451–500	6	8	14	14	9	7	16	10	2	6	3	1	24	4	20	24	6	11	1	4
501–550	7	11	18	18	2	9	11	20	1	6	2	1	31	7	21	28	6	19	1	4
551–600	4	10	14	17	9	5	14	15	0	8	2	2	27	9	19	28	8	14	1	4
601–650	10	1	11	7	6	15	21	19	1	2	1	2	26	5	22	27	9	9	1	7
651–700	5	9	11	17	4	10	14	16	0	3	3	1	23	5	19	24	7	9	1	6
701–750	10	6	16	18	3	7	10	13	3	6	2	3	30	5	22	27	11	11	4	4
751–800	6	10	16	20	8	5	13	6	2	9	1	0	21	5	19	24	2	13	0	3
801–850	5	9	14	14	6	11	17	19	1	5	1	0	27	9	19	28	6	13	2	6
851–867	4	3	7	4	1	2	3	6	0	1	1	0	8	1	10	9	2	5	0	1
Column	A	B	C	D	E	F	G	H	I	J	K	L	M	N	O	P	Q	R	S	T
Totals	96	129	225	248	106	181	287	275	22	83	48	27	477	125	332	455	125	222	21	103

8

FORMULAR LANGUAGE AND ORAL QUALITY

J. A. Notopoulos has maintained at length that the practice of oral poetry in Greece extended beyond the bounds of the Homeric tradition in Ionia. In *Hesperia* 29 (1960), 177ff., he argued in favour of the probability that there was a long-standing mainland tradition, exemplified in the Hesiodic poetry and also, no doubt, in some of the north-mainland subject-matter of the *Iliad*. Subsequently Notopoulos extended his examination to the Homeric Hymns and the fragments of the Cyclic epics.[1] In these contributions there gradually becomes obtrusive an underlying assumption that requires detailed reconsideration both for its own sake and because of its crucial position in Notopoulos' general argument.

The assumption can be put very briefly: it is that any hexameter poetry which contains a high proportion of Homeric (or Hesiodic) formular phraseology (both in verbatim repetitions and in the use of so-called formula-patterns) must be, like the *Iliad* and the *Odyssey*, oral. In other words, the heavy employment of the traditional phraseology of the Ionian epic – without regard, I think it would be fair to add, to possible differences of skill in the articulation of that phraseology – is in itself a total and adequate proof of oral composition.[2]

This is, of course, a very remarkable contention, of which the effect would be to demonstrate that virtually the whole corpus of the Homeric Hymns – to take the most conspicuous case – was orally composed by singers of pure Homeric type. That would indeed be, as Notopoulos himself claims, a 'sudden, major breakthrough'.[3] Now there are notable stylistic differences, detectable through and in spite of the plethora of Homeric phraseology, between different hymns of the 'Homeric' collection: between the long hymns and the

---

[1] *AJP* 83 (1962), 337–68 (Hymns); *HSCP* 68 (1964), especially pp. 18–45 (Cycle).
[2] Thus 'solidly formulaic character' is described by Notopoulos as constituting the '*sine qua non* test' of the oral character of early epics (*HSCP* 68 (1964), 30f.). Indeed the presence of *one* key phrase is implied (pp. 33f.) to reveal the oral character of frag. 1 of the *Cypria*.   [3] *HSCP* 68 (1964), 62.

shorter ones, between different parts of the long hymns themselves, and between various shorter hymns. Notopoulos is not concerned with such differences. Because both the Delian and the Delphic part of the composite Hymn to Apollo contain a high proportion of formular language, they are according to him both fully oral.[4] He allows, of course, that there are likely to be differences in date of composition for different parts of the corpus, within the range of the period extending from the eighth century B.C. down to the sixth.[5] The situation with regard to the Cyclic poems is similar, and so too with the whole Hesiodic corpus including the *Scutum*: they are all seen as fully oral (and so, almost by definition, the work of illiterate singers), and all come from within this period.

Before this viewpoint becomes widely accepted it should be examined more closely.[6] There is little point in holding back my own judgement that the viewpoint is wrong: not necessarily wrong in effect (although usually so, as I believe) but certainly wrong, or at least imperfect and misleading, in method. In short, Notopoulos has attacked a subtle and complex problem with an excessively blunt instrument – the idea that, because all oral poetry is formular, all formular poetry must be oral.

There is, of course, more to it than that; Notopoulos is too skilled to be deceived by a mere false conversion; but his real reasons for making that kind of assumption (in whatever logical form one likes to put it) seem tenuous and indeed unexamined. In essence he poses an extreme disjunction: either this post-Homeric hexameter poetry is the product of conscious and deliberate literary imitation, or it must be oral poetry similar in method to the poetry of the *Iliad* and *Odyssey*. In fact, as I shall show later, there are intermediate stages which also deserve serious consideration.

[4] Roughly 87 % of the verses of the Delian part contain one or more formulas, roughly 93 % of the verses of the Delphic part do so according to the analysis given by Notopoulos at *AJP* 83 (1962), 358. The corresponding figures for the *Iliad* and the *Odyssey* are 88 % and 93 % (p. 359). This is, in fact, a very rough-and-ready kind of analysis even when regarded as a merely quantitative type: Homeric verses containing only one formula (especially by Notopoulos' wide definition of 'formula', including formula-types) are in fact rare. Some method of indicating the amount of formular material within the verse is necessary if even this very limited quantitative comparison is to have much value.

[5] *AJP* 83 (1962), 353.

[6] Surprisingly little comment appears to have been made; but see now A. Hoekstra, *Homeric Modifications of Formulaic Prototypes* (Amsterdam, 1965), esp. p. 17.

Formular language and oral quality

First, however, let us consider what Notopoulos terms literary *mimesis*. In the nineteenth century, at least, it was widely supposed that the Homeric Hymns, for example, were due to precisely that kind of imitation – they are school works, as it were, and the result of a conscious effort on the part of literate composers to imitate, with some adaptation to the special requirements of a hymn, the language and style of Homer. Now this is a one-sided view, certainly; but Notopoulos rejects it as a totally impossible one. He consigns it to the limbo of obsolete absurdities by a single broad contention: that the 'oral theory' developed by Parry and further elaborated by Lord proves that 'literary mimesis' with this degree of formular content is impossible. I do not believe that in the articles cited, or anywhere else, Notopoulos ever says substantially more on this subject than he does here: 'Lord's decisive chapter on the way formulae work in oral composition should bury the ghost of literary mimesis for ever'.[7] As a preliminary I should like to suggest that the implied argument is formally defective, since *no* description of 'the way formulae work in oral composition' can of itself rigorously define the way in which formulae might be used in literate composition. Second, the truth is that Lord's chapter, valuable as it is, has nothing whatever to say about literary mimesis.

What Notopoulos has in mind, presumably, is that the extreme functionalism of a formular system such as we find in Homer (or rather, of *the* system we find in Homer; for that system, *pace* Lord, is unique in its degree of functionalism) entails that the system was developed for oral use. As Lord puts it, 'Without this usefulness the style, and, more important, the whole practice [*sc.* of formular composition] would collapse or would never have been born.'[8] That was argued by Milman Parry and is certainly true. But is it a corollary that literary imitation can never achieve the same degree of usefulness or functionalism *or anything resembling it*?

The answer to this question surely depends on the *kind* of imitation. Imitation so slavish as to consist in simply rearranging whole verses and passages from the Homeric tradition might, as it happens, retain close to 100% of the potential and apparent functionalism of the formular vocabulary of those particular verses and passages.

[7] *AJP* 83 (1962), 360; the reference is to Lord's third chapter, 'The Formula', in *The Singer of Tales* (Cambridge, Mass., 1960).
[8] *Singer of Tales*, p. 65.

Now the literate imitation of oral poetry is without doubt an impure form of literature, but it can happen (and has happened, certainly, in more recent times and with other traditions); and, if it were to be slavish in the sense above, that would not in itself destroy the natural qualities of the original oral poetry – or at least those qualities which pertain to its formular phraseology. In practice the mere rearrangement of Homeric verses and verse-sequences was not carried on, or, if it was, examples have not survived. But consider a somewhat less slavish and less exact degree of imitation, in which half-lines derived from the *Iliad* or the *Odyssey* are recombined, or other formulas that fill substantial and useful portions of the verse are deployed in fresh combinations. This would be a sort of mechanical reproduction of the instinctive oral process of composition; we know it can be done, since most of us who are interested in Homer as oral poetry have probably done it at some time or another for our own amusement. This is literate pastiche; we operate from our exact knowledge of the text and assemble our formulas from the printed page. A low activity, indeed; and in fact nearly all literary imitation of oral epic produces results greatly inferior to the model. Yet that does not of itself prove Notopoulos' point. On the contrary, most of the Homeric Hymns, like the pseudo-Hesiodic *Scutum* or the exiguous fragments of the Cyclic poems, are vastly inferior to the Homeric exemplar. They are inferior precisely in this respect, that they take the Homeric language of formulas and redeploy it mechanically, woodenly and with faulty or obtrusive articulation; and, where they attempt to develop or elaborate it, they often overstep the traditional boundaries of interest, taste, factual realism or linguistic naturalness.[9]

The last sentence concedes what is obviously true, that the post-Homeric hexameter poetry with which we are concerned is both less and more than the slavish imitation that was posited to prove that literate imitation and full formular structure are not necessarily incompatible in theory. Even the lesser Hymns do more than merely

[9] Against the possible objection (e.g. by Lord, *AJP* 85 (1964), 85) that we cannot tell clearly what was 'traditional' since 'we have two poems from ancient Greece and nothing more', I reply that these two immensely long poems present a corpus of oral style and oral elaboration from which, with care, we can learn a great deal about the probable progress of the tradition and the probable limitations of its capacity for extension and development. Naturally we would like to have evidence which was more explicit and more complete.

rearrange established formular phrases. There is some new vocabulary,[10] a few new themes and ideas. These could certainly be the
result of literate intervention, but they could also be due to regional
variation or other special developments in an oral tradition. We
know that adaptation and extension of the traditional language go on
constantly within any living oral tradition: new words, for example,
are not necessarily a sign of non-oral origin, provided that they serve
some useful purpose. But, if it is true that not all formular extension
is non-oral, it is equally true that not all of it need be oral. There are
indeed two kinds of formular extension, and some sort of criterion is
needed by which they may be distinguished. I do not mean to
imply that it necessarily exists or is available. But my own view is
that a loose and tenuous criterion *is* available, and that it is associated
with ease of handling, consonance with the general lines of the
previous tradition, preservation at least of oral economy. In other
words, and not to put too grand an appearance on a simple thought,
oral extensions of the oral tradition are likely to maintain the main
qualities of that tradition. If fluent handling of the formular vocabulary was a characteristic of the preceding tradition (as it presumably
was with the Homeric singers), then we should expect that fluency to
be continued, with at most a steady but slight decline. Only if the
practice of oral poetry suffered some significant interruption would
that cease to be probable. Nothing in the known history of the
seventh or sixth centuries B.C. is likely to have caused such an
interruption – except, of course, the spread of literacy itself. The
intervention of literate techniques of composition and literate tastes
and ambitions would certainly reduce the clarity, ease and simplicity
of the old use of formulas. It is my belief that they *are* reduced, in
part at least of the poetry we are considering, and that literate
intervention, in one form or another, is the probable cause.

No one can doubt that literate imitation of the *Iliad* and *Odyssey*
was possible in the sixth century as in the fifth and fourth. By literate
imitation in this context I mean an imitation, with some degree of
extension, which is committed to writing, which owes some of its
detailed working-out to the aid of writing, but which might be
founded upon a close *memorization* of the Homeric poems. These were
known by heart by many Greeks of the fifth and fourth centuries and,

---

[10] Some of it is curiously Attic: see O. Zumbach, *Neuerungen in der Sprache der
homerischen Hymnen* (Winterthur, 1955), pp. 57–63.

presumably, of the sixth as well. Their vocabulary influenced all the non-dactylic poets who were the successors of the *aoidoi*, some of them profoundly. Many Greeks, whether or not they were poets by profession, would have found it easy enough to write more or less in the Homeric style, using the Homeric formular vocabulary in a way that would be artificial – since they were not working as true oral singers – and would show many signs of strain, but that would achieve that merely quantitative resemblance which Notopoulos has roughly distinguished.

They could have so composed – but did they in fact do so? Were some of the Hymns, some parts of the Hesiodea, some of the Cyclic epics actually due to this kind of imitative technique? Unfortunately we have no direct evidence on this subject, and are unlikely to be able to find even indirect evidence which would be compelling one way or the other. There is no simple answer to this kind of question, and certainly no simple criterion like the greater or lesser incidence of formulas derived from the Ionic tradition. But at least one piece of later evidence proves absolutely, despite Notopoulos' insistence to the contrary, that literate pastiche was sometimes practiced. When one considers the learning, ingenuity and love of *paegnia* manifested by poets of the Hellenistic age, it is not surprising that the Homeric poems became the models for pastiche; and it is to that intellectual and poetical milieu (rather than to the full classical period to which Pigres is assigned in parts of our tradition) that the *Batrachomyomachia*, the Battle of the Frogs and Mice, must probably be assigned.[11] This laboured jest, consciously mock-heroic, naturally makes much use of Iliadic language and Iliadic formulas. Many of these formulas are adapted or extended to fit the circumstances of pond life, and that is part of the joke. No one could seriously suggest that this is an oral poem, or indeed that it closely resembles the Hymns, the Hesiodea or the Cyclic fragments. Its literacy, declared in the opening verses with their mention of the poet composing with his tablets on his knee, is manifest and undeniable; but so, in patches at least, is its formular quality – if 'formular' here can be taken to include a purely artificial and superficial use. This quality deserves a brief survey.

---

[11] Hoekstra, *Homeric Modifications*, p. 17, observes that the *Posthomerica* of Quintus of Smyrna is a good example of close literary imitation, formular style and all. Its lateness is irrelevant.

Apart from the repetition of complete Homeric verses (like 152 τοίγαρ ἐγὼν ἐρέω ὥς μοι δοκεῖ εἶναι ἄριστα or 205 δούπησεν δὲ πεσών, ἀράβησε δὲ τεύχε᾽ ἐπ᾽ αὐτῷ) and many half-line or other formulas (like 168 εἰς οὐρανὸν ἀστερόεντα or 170 ἔγχεα μακρὰ ∪ – ∪ |), there are many instances of formular adaptation. For example the first half of 168, Ζεὺς δὲ θεοὺς καλέσας: this is not taken directly from the *Iliad* or the *Odyssey* or any other known source, but | Ζεὺς δὲ (e.g. *Il.* 8, 2), | νεῦσ᾽ ἐπὶ οἷ καλέσας (*Od.* 17, 330), and θεοὺς ἀγορήνδε καλέσσας | (e.g. *Il.* 20, 16), show clearly enough how the wording of the later poem is compounded. Two verses later, at 170, ἔγχεα μακρά is Homeric enough, as already noted, but the whole verse is strictly speaking 'new': πολλοὺς καὶ μεγάλους ἠδ᾽ ἔγχεα μακρὰ φέροντας. Yet its parts are all Homeric: compare e.g. *Il.* 12, 57, | πυκνοὺς καὶ μεγάλους, while φέρονται -ες -ας comes frequently at the verse-end as does ἠδ᾽ as a connective after the main caesura. This whole verse could conceivably have occurred in some lost part of the epic tradition, although the total effect is not very happy; so it is not proved that the literate poet of the *Batracho-myomachia* could achieve this degree of formular recombination. Yet his powers *can* be proved by referring to his replacement of Iliadic proper names by the comic names of frogs and mice, or by his adaptation of the formulas of Homeric battle-scenes to the mock-heroic warfare of his animals: for example 17f.,

> εἰμὶ δ᾽ ἐγὼ βασιλεὺς Φυσίγναθος, ὃς κατὰ λίμνην
> τιμῶμαι βατράχων ἡγούμενος ἤματα πάντα,

or 226ff.,

> Λιτραῖον δ᾽ ἄρ᾽ ἔπεφνεν ἀμύμων Βορβοροκοίτης
> χερμαδίῳ πλήξας κατὰ βρέγματος · ἐγκέφαλος δὲ
> ἐκ ῥινῶν ἔσταξε, παλάσσετο δ᾽ αἵματι γαῖα.

The sharp and experienced observer (or, more to the point perhaps, the careful and assiduous concordance-user) easily detects in this sort of thing much that is foreign to the Homeric tradition, even apart from the mock-heroic conversions. Yet there is a good deal, too, that *is* traditional and that has been deployed in a manner other than utterly slavish. The fact is that this poet, whom we tend to regard as a mere hack and whose popularity in later antiquity and in the later middle ages is no tribute to the literary judgement of those periods, can imitate Homer quite well when he wishes, not only by verbatim repetition but also by the recombination and adaptation of formulas:

> "Ὣς ἄρ' ἔφη· καὶ τῇ γε θεοὶ ἐπεπείθοντ' ἄλλοι,
> πάντες δ' αὖτ' εἰσῆλθον ἀολλέες εἰς ἕνα χῶρον.
> καὶ τότε κώνωπες μεγάλας σάλπιγγας ἔχοντες
> δεινὸν ἐσάλπιγξαν πολέμου κτύπον· οὐρανόθεν δὲ
> Ζεὺς Κρονίδης βρόντησε, τέρας πολέμοιο κακοῖο.   (197ff.)

All this from a professedly literate poet of mean ability and a period when the oral tradition was utterly dead.

If we started marking up the last passage, for example, with those solid or broken underlinings that Notopoulos (following Parry and Lord) uses to distinguish formula-repetitions or formula-patterns respectively, we should end up with just as impressive-looking a network as anything he produces. And on his principles we ought therefore to claim that this passage must be oral poetry. We know in fact that it is not, and in addition we can recognize by careful (and not just superficial) examination that it has certain characteristics which reveal that its composer is not a natural oral singer. Of course this is in part an unfair argument: the *Batrachomyomachia* as a whole would not possess the quantity of formular language that occurs in the passages I have selected, and thus would not share the total formular characteristics of many of the Hymns, for example. But it does suffice to invalidate, utterly and completely as I believe, the contention that 'literary mimesis of the *Iliad* and *Odyssey*' is impossible; and the Homeric pastiche of Quintus of Smyrna, several centuries later, does the same.[12]

Formular *quantity*, then, proves to be an imperfect test of orality. It raises the possibility, certainly; but the *Batrachomyomachia* proves, if proof be needed, that literary imitation can result in as heavy a concentration of formulas as can be found in the oral exemplar. It does not achieve this degree of concentration consistently, in more than patches, but that may be due to its author's special intention of parodying, rather than more or less exactly reproducing, a style. The Hymns, Hesiodea and Cyclic fragments are for the most part consistent in their predominant employment of formular language;

---

[12] A. B. Lord disagrees with much of this, and of the pages that follow, in *HSCP* 72 (1968), 26–33. His discussion does not persuade me to alter what I have written.

the difference may be due to earlier date, greater reverence for the Homeric model, and so on, rather than to a truly oral kind of composition.[13]

If a poem on the Homeric model is oral, then it will certainly possess formular *quantity*, but it will also possess a natural style (and of course a traditional economy in vocabulary) of which an important part is concerned with the deployment, adaptation and articulation of formulas and may be crudely termed formular *quality*. Literate imitations will be unlikely to achieve this natural quality, which is a more subtle, less tangible and less easily imitable aspect of oral style. It is to this, then, that one will look for a criterion that is theoretically more reliable but also, unfortunately, more subjective in practice than the merely quantitative assessment of formular characteristics.

Thus a short Hymn like xxvii, to Artemis, is stuffed with Homeric phraseology, but gives a forced, redundant or plethoric, and artificial impression. When one examines the poem closely one notices that a verse like 12, εὐφρήνῃ δὲ νόον χαλάσασ' εὐκαμπέα τόξα, contributes to this impression of strain by some new uses of what at first sight appears to be traditional formular language. Phrases like εὐφρήνῃ δὲ νόον are reserved in Homer for the idea of pleasing another person (e.g. *Od.* 20, 82, μηδέ τι χείρονος ἀνδρὸς ἐϋφραίνοιμι νόημα); the part of oneself that one gives pleasure or pain to is the φρήν, in phrases like φρένα τερπόμενον (*Il.* 9, 186). As it happens τερφθῇ has already occurred in the preceding verse, of which 12 is an expansion or repetition. Perhaps that accounts for the apparently new adaptation; though it is worth noting that, whereas the repetition of an idea in a separate verse is not uncommon in the oral tradition, it does not normally entail the use of unfamiliar or untraditional language; the singer is prepared to create, but presumably not often in this kind of small-scale, normally automatic elaboration. εὐκαμπέα, too, is not otherwise applied to the bow (it is not found in the *Iliad* but appears twice in the *Odyssey*, once of a key and once of a sickle). A frequent

---

[13] I do not of course mean to suggest that the Hymns and the other works are necessarily *not* oral; rather that Notopoulos' quantitative criterion is indecisive, and must be supplemented by other criteria. Even then a definite decision may be impossible for the bulk of this poetry. My own impression is that the longer Hymns are for the most part oral, but that many of the shorter ones are literate; that the Cyclic fragments are in part literate; that much of the poetry associated with Hesiod is oral, but that the *Scutum* shows signs of skilled literary intervention.

formula is καμπύλα τόξα; I suppose there is no reason why εὐκαμπέα τόξα should not also be an oral formula, used when the extra syllable was required, since the space from the hephthemimeral word-break to the end of the verse was one that sometimes needed to be filled by a single formula. Yet it remains curious that no such formula occurs in the *Iliad* or the *Odyssey*, where τόξον or τόξα recurs nearly eighty times and where καμπύλα, ἀγκύλα and παλίντονον, -α in various positions in the verse seem to form an adequately flexible mainstay of the system. But the really odd word in our verse is χαλάσασ'. This verb does not occur in the Homeric poems; that does not of itself worry me – what does so is that its uses in post-Homeric literature show that when applied to a bow it regularly means 'loose' in the sense of 'unstring', while the context here suggests that it means 'loose' in the sense of 'discharge, release, shoot'.[14] The former meaning is clear in the only other occurrence of the verb in the Hymns (*Hy. Ap.* 6). Here a non-Homeric verb is used in a sense that is surprising even by the standards of its post-Homeric application. That in itself may not argue decisively against its oral quality: what aggravates the situation is that it is an un-economical variant for a well-developed and traditional formular expression of this kind of concept, namely that of stringing, un-stringing or, more specifically, discharging a bow: τιταίνουσ' ἀγκύλα τόξα is an obvious and fully traditional phrase that would have avoided some of the strains of the verse with which we are presented. That it is a (short) syllable shorter presents no real problem.

Four verses later in the same Hymn another verse, also concerned with the bow, points in the same direction. Here the language seems more exactly Homeric: ἔνθα κατακρεμάσασα παλίντονα τόξα καὶ ἰούς (16). Yet παλίντονα τόξα καὶ ἰούς gives a weak and anti-climactic effect, mainly because of the last two words (contrast *Il.* 15, 472); moreover hanging up *arrows* is a slightly odd idea in itself. It makes sense only if the arrows were in a quiver, which must have been the case; but the traditional formular language has a perfectly good word for that, namely φαρέτρη: τόξον δ' ἀγκρεμά-σασα παλίντονον ἠδὲ φαρέτρην (cf. *Il.* 1, 440, 15, 443) would have

---

14 That is, the participle χαλάσασ' must surely depend on εὐφρήνη δὲ νόον. The only alternative would be to attach it to verse 13: 'having unstrung her bow she comes into the hall...'; but that leaves εὐφρήνη δὲ νόον intolerably in the air.

been a far more satisfactory, and fully traditional, way of expressing the poet's thought.[15]

Verse-sequences like these may look very Homeric by the crude criterion of vocabulary or sheer quantity of formulas; they look very un-Homeric, very untraditional, in certain other important respects. It is not my purpose here to argue that they *must* therefore be non-oral; that certainly could not be proved. But they do raise a distinct possibility – perhaps more – of non-oral, imitative composition, and that should not be disguised by sweeping generalizations or excessive enthusiasm for the idea of oral poetry as such.

I have already noted that, as a whole, the short Hymns present more untraditional characteristics of style than the longer ones. In contrast with Hymn XXVII, the Hymn to Delian Apollo, for example, seems fluent and traditional in its handling of the oral language. All of it, that is, except for its first eighteen verses, a prologue that has been generally recognized as a later attachment to the hymn. Unfortunately it is just this passage that is chosen by Notopoulos as typical, and subjected to a detailed examination.[16] Those who wish to analyse sample passages of hexameter poetry might do well to avoid prologues and opening passages altogether, as they are particularly prone to reworking. Yet Notopoulos' use of this passage helps my case, although not his own, by emphasizing once again the contrast between the quantitative occurrence of Homeric formulas and the qualitative use and articulation of those formulas. Notopoulos' underlinings, whether broken or continuous, make an impressive ocular demonstration of 'Homeric' style; but once the subtler criterion of articulation and use is brought to bear, the 'Homeric' style becomes much less certain – in fact a careful reading of the passage reveals that beneath the surface it is strikingly un-

---

[15] ἀγκρεμάσασ' is vastly preferable to κατακρεμάσασα, which stresses hanging *down* (from a peg in its only Homeric use, *Od.* 8, 67) and is inappropriate here – unless the extraordinary suggestion in LSJ *s.v.* κατακρέμαμαι is correct, that the meaning in this passage is 'having hung the bow on herself'. I take it that she hangs the bow and quiver on a wall or pillar, as normally in Homer with bows, quivers and lyres.

There is another difficulty at the beginning of the following verse, 17, where καλὸν χορόν from 15 has to be understood, with some strain, as object of ἡγεῖται, with ἐξάρχουσα χορούς in 18 as resumptive and elaborative. Alternatively χορούς in 18 is intended to be the object of ἡγεῖται, with the rest of 17 strictly parenthetical – but in that case ἐξάρχουσα is strange. Whichever is correct, the sentence-structure is clumsy and unnatural.

[16] *AJP* 83 (1962), 354ff.

traditional. Consider what this prologue tells us: that the gods in Zeus' house tremble and leap to their feet when Apollo approaches, stretching his bow (1–4); that Leto looses his bow (i.e. unstrings it, ἐχάλασσε; compare what was said on this verb on p. 192 above) and closes his quiver, takes his bow from his shoulders and hangs it up 'against the pillar of his father', πρὸς κίονα πατρὸς ἑοῖο (8), where one would expect – and the formular language of the tradition would most naturally supply – 'of his father's *house*' or some similar phrase; then Zeus himself offers Apollo nectar (10), and finally the birth of Apollo in Delos is referred to, with Leto 'leaning against tall mountain and Cynthian hill', κεκλιμένη πρὸς μακρὸν ὄρος καὶ Κύνθιον ὄχθον (17), a clause in which the linking of generic and then more specific description is only superficially similar to Homeric repetitions of the κατὰ φρένα καὶ κατὰ θυμόν kind (and in which ὄχθος, for what it is worth, is unknown to the hexameter tradition). The last verse, 18, of this prologue further describes Leto as leaning 'closest to the palm-tree, under the streams of Inopus', ἀγχοτάτω φοίνικος ὑπ' Ἰνωποῖο ῥεέθροις, in which ἀγχοτάτω is an *Atticism* (and a grossly uneconomical departure from the tradition, in place of the traditional and metrically equivalent ἄγχιστον) and ὑπ' with the dative, of water, is bizarre.[17]

There are three particular peculiarities in this passage: the ethos of the description of Apollo – his fierce arrival and the respect shown him by the other gods, including Zeus; the description of his bow and quiver and what happens to them (here we may fruitfully compare the uncertain language of the bow-passage in Hymn XXVII considered above); and the description of the birth of Apollo in Delos. In the last two cases it is the manner of using and varying formular language, as much as the underlying thought, that seems strikingly untraditional. (There are, of course, other points at which this prologue diverges from Homeric practice or belief, but they can be paralleled from other Hymns and are a perfectly possible development carrying no implications for the treatment of the traditional epic language). The peculiarities raise a legitimate doubt about the method and date of composition of this prologue: a doubt which will be felt more or less strongly by different judges, but which there is no advantage in concealing by the misleadingly one-sided quantita-

---

[17] Reiz's ἐπ' for ὑπ' looks an obvious improvement; but why should the tradition have stuck so firmly to the *lectio difficilior*?

tive type of analysis. That analysis does, of course, have its positive lesson: that even poetry very dissimilar from the Homeric in ethos and idiom may contain a high proportion of Homeric vocabulary and phraseology. The same lesson was learned from the consideration of certain passages of the *Batrachomyomachia*.

The dangers of the *qualitative* criterion, on the other hand, are obvious enough. Its application involves a personal opinion about what may or may not be acceptable oral practice in the way of analogy and oral extension. Not all singers were in the class of a Homer – probably he had no equal. Even a good singer would have his less adept days. Normally the process of tradition would eradicate the weaker songs, but some might survive. The examples from the Hymns considered above may be violent and concentrated enough to cause serious doubt about a completely oral origin. In the fragments of the Cyclic poems, by contrast, the departures from a smooth and traditional application of the formular language are rarer and more ambiguous. Fr. II (Allen, 2 Kinkel) of the *Thebais*, for example, contains in its ten verses one conspicuous departure from the economy of an epithet-system and one rather strained combination of two uses of a traditional phrase. In verse 3, ἀργυρέην Κάδμοιο θεόφρονος· αὐτὰρ ἔπειτα, the choice of θεόφρονος – a compound unique in the epic tradition – is a clear departure from the thrift of the oral epic. The standard laudatory epithet for this position in the verse is δαΐφρονος (28 × in Homer, 2 × in *Hy. Dem.*); compare for example *Il.* 11, 197 (cf. 9, 651) εὗρ' υἱὸν Πριάμοιο δαΐφρονος, Ἕκτορα δῖον.[18] There may be some reason for emphasizing Cadmus' piety or godlike qualities at this point, but it is hardly enough to justify, by the normal standards of the oral tradition, the obtrusive departure from accepted phraseology. This sort of thing smacks of the literate poet.

Then at verse 6, when Oedipus perceived his father's valuable gifts set beside him, 'great evil fell upon his spirit', μέγα οἱ κακὸν ἔμπεσε θυμῷ, and he cursed his two sons. Notopoulos simply underlines these words as a Homeric formula, and refers in a note to *Il.* 17, 625 and *Od.* 12, 266.[19] Yet neither these verses nor others that he might have cited explain the oddness of the *Thebais* phrase.

[18] On the use of δαΐφρονος see M. Parry, *L'Épithète traditionnelle dans Homère* (Paris, 1928), pp. 159ff.
[19] *HSCP* 68 (1964), 29 and 72.

ἔμπεσε θυμῷ is evidently a well-established formula; it is used five times in the *Iliad*, once in the *Odyssey*. What 'falls upon the spirit' is a kind of emotion: usually anger, χόλος ἔμπεσε θυμῷ, once fear. In the Odyssean occurrence an extension takes place, and a word or saying falls upon, or rather 'into', Telemachus' spirit (12, 266), meaning that Telemachus remembered that saying. In the *Thebais* fragment the application is different again; the author is probably now thinking of another kind of formula involving ἔμπεσε, represented by *Od.* 2, 45 and 15, 375, ∪ – κακὸν ἔμπεσεν οἴκῳ. An evil can come upon a household; can it come upon the spirit? And if so, in what sense? The exact sense is surely ambiguous in the fragment: what falls upon Oedipus' spirit might be an evil emotion, namely rage, or a bad (undesirable) emotion, namely grief, or it might be a great evil for the future. Yet in the first and second case the exact emotion should and would be named in normal traditional language: for example by the words δριμὺς χόλος ἔμπεσε θυμῷ (cf. *Il.* 16, 206, 18, 322; δριμύς here rather than κακός, to establish a metrically equivalent phrase). The verse would probably have been cast somewhat differently if ἄχος, grief, had been involved – had been clearly in the composer's mind, that is; but any true oral poet could have expressed the idea 'grief came upon him' after the masculine caesura in several different ways, all clear, unambiguous and fluent. In the third case, if μέγα οἱ κακόν in the *Thebais* fragment implies 'great evil' in more general terms, as in the μέγα...κακόν (in a similar rhythmical context) of *Il.* 11, 404 and *Od.* 9, 423, then its application to Oedipus' spirit is strained indeed; to avoid an almost meaningless vagueness we should have to understand κακόν to mean ἄτη. No precise reconstruction of the author's state of mind at this moment of composition is possible, but it looks as though he is simply conflating two distinct formular applications of ἔμπεσε: an emotion 'falls upon' the spirit, an evil 'falls upon' a house. Our author, for no apparent reason, has made an evil 'fall upon' the spirit of Oedipus, with consequent detriment to clarity and sense.

The question is whether a fully oral poet, completely and instinctively familiar with the traditional language of formulas, would have committed this kind of mild *gaffe*. Again, obviously, no certain answer is possible: I merely observe that a difficulty of this kind is relevant to the oral or literate status of this passage, and that unfamiliarity with the traditional uses and possible extensions of a traditional phrase must be balanced against sheer quantity of formular phraseology. In the present case, I confess, my own feeling is that the superficial combination of formular uses, together with the underlying semantic confusion, is more appropriate to the literate *pasticheur* than to the illiterate, instinctive and usually logical singer.

The use of epic phraseology in the post-Homeric era extended, of course, beyond hexameter poetry. Callinus, Tyrtaeus, Solon, Alcman and Alcaeus all use epic words and phrases to a noticeable degree. Recently D. L. Page has shown that the surviving fragments of Archilochus are replete with epic language – much more so than had been suspected.[20] This language occurs not only in the dactylic poems but also in the iambic elements of the mixed poems and even in the purely iambic or trochaic poems. In these non-dactylic, epodic poems the dactylic formulas of the epic have to undergo some re-arrangement or adaptation. Page argues that cretic types of verse may be quite old, and certainly go back beyond the introduction of alphabetic writing into Greece *ca.* 800/750 B.C. He thinks, too, that the adaptation of dactylic formulas into cretic shapes may be a traditional occupation, carried out orally, and that in the majority of his poems Archilochus too was composing as an oral poet. Now the argument for the antiquity of epodic poetry is interesting, but it seems to me that no more than a possibility can be regarded as established. Moreover Page seems to accept the essence of that other argument, presented in its clearest form by Notopoulos, which I have been trying to question: that the frequent use of Homeric (or at least Ionic-epic) phraseology is a sure sign that the poetry in which it occurs was composed orally, that is, in the way in which the *Iliad* and the *Odyssey* were composed. He adduces as supporting evidence the relative newness of alphabetic writing even around the middle of the seventh century, when much of Archilochus' composition was probably done. This particular point seems to me (as it seemed to some of the members of the *Entretien*) to be uncompelling. The written composition of an *Iliad* before 700 B.C. may well be difficult to envisage, but the writing of short poems some two generations later is a very different matter.

Archilochus is, of course, in a different category from that of the

---

[20] *Entretiens Hardt*, x (Vandœuvres–Genève, 1965), 119ff.

composers of the Hymns and the Cyclic poems; the amount of exact verbal repetition of epic phraseology is not so large (surprisingly large though it may be), even in the purely dactylic poems. What is chiefly of interest is the conversion of dactylic formulas into cretic variants. Here, in my opinion, probability is against Page's hypothesis of oral composition, since oral poetry is by its nature conservative and functional. Semantic and rhythmical needs overlap to produce a system of language whose units are only rarely susceptible of radical variation. A formular phrase has a particular association for the singer, a single function which it, and it alone, performs whenever semantic and rhythmical needs conspire to demand it. That any true oral singer would take such formulas and deliberately apply them to different rhythmical functions, in a different type of verse, seems *a priori* unlikely (although here we must remember that rare singers in the modern Balkans have been, or become, bilingual, and have succeeded – although usually, it seems, under difficulties – in converting songs from one language to another).

Using Page's analysis one can see that there are two degrees of formular adaptation in Archilochus:

(1) Simple alterations of word order, number or case: e.g. fr. 31, 2 West, ὤμους κατεσκίαζε καὶ μετάφρενα. Compare (as Page observes, p. 150) *Il.* 2, 265, *Od.* 8, 528, μετάφρενον ἠδὲ καὶ ὤμους; similarly fr. 19, 2–3 West, οὐδ' ἀγαίομαι | θεῶν ἔργα, on which Page (*ibid.*) cites *Od.* 20, 16, ἀγαιομένου κακὰ ἔργα, and *Il.* 16, 120, ἔργα θεῶν.

(2) The reworking of a complex formula, with changes not only in word order and word form but also in some terms (this occurs especially in the trochaic tetrameters): e.g. fr. 134 West, οὐ γὰρ ἐσθλὰ κατθανοῦσι κερτομέειν ἐπ' ἀνδράσιν – 'an adaptation, with the least possible change, of *Od.* 22, 412, οὐχ ὁσίη κταμένοισιν ἐπ' ἀνδράσιν εὐχετάασθαι' (Page, p. 155).

To take the last example, it seems unlikely that an oral poet would deliberately convert οὐχ ὁσίη into οὐ γὰρ ἐσθλά, and so on, if he were operating as a 'true' oral poet, by which I mean instinctively and with unconscious reliance on the formular arsenal of his particular tradition. On the other hand *any* poet who was steeped in the *Iliad* and the *Odyssey*, who knew the whole of them by heart in the way in which many Greeks did even in the fifth and fourth centuries B.C., might choose to reproduce an aphorism of the 'rejoicing over dead men' kind in a different verse-form; and in so doing he might naturally re-use, with some adaptation, as much of the familiar phraseology of the well-known Homeric form of the idea as was feasible. Whether he might do so with stylus continuously in hand, or just mentally, is not very important; the point is that, even if he did the latter, he would not really be acting as an oral poet in the sense in which we use that term. That Archilochus probably worked from his remembered knowledge of Homer and not from a written text; that he might have composed his poems in his head, and even recited them before ever they were set down on papyrus – these things we may concede, without thereby saying or implying that he was therefore an oral poet.

I believe that at the present stage of Homeric studies, at the present stage of theorizing about oral poetry in general, there is a serious danger of getting our categories mixed. Indeed I believe they already *are* mixed; that the contrast between 'oral' and 'literate' has already caused confusion – and I do not refer to the confusion in the minds of those who use the excesses of the comparative method as an excuse for rejecting it altogether. Even for more sophisticated minds than these, *literate composition* has come to stand as the only alternative to *oral poetry*. Yet 'oral poetry' itself is far too imprecise an expression, as we have seen; primarily it has come to refer to the mode of composition of *aoidoi* and *guslari*, but it can also be applied to elaborations by rhapsodes, for example. A truer and less confusing antithesis, I suggest, is between *natural composition in a formular tradition* (that is, 'oral poetry' in its primary sense) and *deliberate, self-conscious composition in a formular style*, whether with the aid of writing or not. The natural type of composition *depends on* a system of traditional verbal and rhythmical patterns, irrespective of whether it is significantly creative or almost completely reproductive. The self-conscious type is deliberately imitative; it *uses* but does not depend on formulas, just as it may use but does not necessarily depend on writing.

Archilochus certainly belongs to the second type, not the first. How far and at what stages he used the art of writing in the process of composition and standardization is of secondary importance, and is a matter for conjecture. Certainly his case does nothing to support the Notopoulos theory that all poetry heavily infected by the terminology of the Ionic epic was necessarily 'oral' in the full sense. On the contrary, it demonstrates that an intimate knowledge of the poems of Homer enabled people who were not true oral poets to make remarkable use of the old formular vocabulary. Let us keep it absolutely clear in our minds that the use – even the heavy use – of formular phraseology derived from true oral poetry is not a certain sign of similarly true oral procedures, unless other signs are also present; signs such as the observation of formular economy, the naturalness of formular extension and articulation, and the preservation of traditional details of rhythm and enjambment.

9

THE SEARCH FOR
THE REAL HOMER

I am not of course going to write about a very concrete person, a little bearded man who lived in Chios or Smyrna. Yet that there was someone called Homer, who was primarily responsible for the creation of the *Iliad* at least, can be taken for granted. The old jokes applied to an entirely different situation in scholarship from the one we have today, and the cause of the difference is the realization that the Homeric poems are in essence oral rather than written poetry.

Many of the narrative components, the motifs and themes, of oral heroic poems are no less formular than their language and phraseology. The singer acquires a wide range of standard incidents that can be varied in length and reference to suit the needs of a chosen situation, much as a standard phrase is selected to suit the needs of metre and immediate verbal context. Moreover for any general theme, for example a duel between two warriors, the tradition provided a variety of standard patterns: A throws a spear at B and misses, B hits A but does not pierce his armour, A kills B with a second spear-throw; or A throws at B and hits someone else, B does likewise, B throws again and misses, A throws again and kills B. The variety is not of course infinite, and in the great number of such encounters in the *Iliad* certain patterns are never used; for example it is permissible to throw a stone once, but not a second time. The range of possibilities is not arbitrary (as its recent and highly effective exponent, Bernard Fenik, tends perhaps to imply),[1] but is controlled by what is heroic and appropriate. The truly heroic weapon is the spear, with sword, stone and arrow progressively less so; and the man who has hit but failed to kill must not be allowed to succeed with a second blow – for his first failure is an indication of weakness, or that the gods are against him.

An oral tradition is likely to be enormously complex, because each singer makes his own selection from it and contributes a little to it

---

[1] B. Fenik, *Typical Battle Scenes in the Iliad*, *Hermes* Einzelschriften xxi (Wiesbaden, 1968), especially pp. 6f.; hereafter 'Fenik'.

for better or for worse. Many oral singers and audiences seem to enjoy elaboration and the accumulation of detail for their own sake, and in pre-war Yugoslavia the 'good' singer was often the one who, as well as having an extensive repertory, could stretch a typical passage (mounting a war-horse, for instance) to unusual length. We see the same sort of thing in Homer. Scenes in which a hero puts on his armour occur several times in the *Iliad* and follow the same general pattern, but some of them are more detailed and longer than others – indeed it is the rule that the more important the hero, the longer such scenes become. The oral epic singer works cumulatively, adding standard phrase to standard phrase and building up a whole scene by adding theme to typical theme. Each singer has his own favourite phrases, patterns, and methods of cumulation derived from the tradition, and every version of a poem (which means the poem as it happens to come out at any particular performance, for it varies a little each time) is a mixture of traditional elements and personal omissions or choices. One consequence is that you can only completely distinguish the qualities of an individual singer if you can hear him in action time after time, and compare his versions with those of others.

This is all highly relevant to what I have called the 'real' Homer. Homer was an individual singer who came near the end of a long tradition of heroic poetry; he presumably acquired a repertory of songs from other singers and reproduced them in his own manner. Most of the language and incident of his *Iliad* is 'typical' in one way or other, and must be the gift of the tradition; Homer took over the tradition and used it, yet he certainly made his own special contribution to it. What we wish to know, therefore, if we are interested in this 'real' Homer, is roughly what this contribution was. For his reality, to us, beyond the fact that he belonged to an oral heroic tradition, amounts to his special qualities as a poet. He has no biological or biographical substance; we know his name and approximately when and where he lived, but that tells us next to nothing. It is as a poet, and purely as a poet, that Homer concerns us, and I do not care if he wore purple shirts, hated his father or enjoyed the favours of Nausicaa. That kind of thing might tell us something about a Shelley; but Shelley, poetry and all, belongs to a tangible historical context. Homer does not. He is a shadow, or rather a voice, and the only thing we can hope to know of him, the only reality we can give him, is the unique quality of this voice. That is what we want to know – not just from meddlesome curiosity or pedantic *horror vacui*, but because his poetry can only be adequately understood when we learn how to relate its strictly creative aspect, the imagination and taste of a poetic individual, to the dense background of the inherited tradition.

One thing can be said about him without further delay: he is the singer primarily responsible for a poem of quite exceptional length. It is a fair inference that oral poems were commonly designed to be sung on a single occasion – during a single morning, afternoon or evening. Nearly all oral heroic songs collected in modern communities accord with this expectation, and most of those that do not have been responses to some special challenge or inducement. Milman Parry and his follower A. B. Lord were justifiably impressed with the length of one song they recorded in Yugoslavia, an extraordinary version of 'The Wedding of Smailagić Meho'. This version, by Avdo Međedović, has won a certain *réclame* because it contains around 16,000 verses, little fewer than the *Iliad*. But the facts are that the verses are short, the style is redundant, and the song was only spun out to such length at the special insistence of Milman Parry. Other long poems have been noted from South Russia, but again the element of experiment or bravado is often present. The conclusion that nearly all oral poems are designed to be given at a single session is not seriously damaged. It is a reasonable guess, therefore, that the Greek epic tradition on which Homer drew for the *Iliad* was primarily composed of songs of this functional length. A few somewhat longer ones might have occupied the best part of a day or filled the intervals of a protracted wedding feast; efforts used to be made to trace such larger units within the *Iliad* itself, but they were unsuccessful, and it is significant that the *Odyssey*, which gives repeated descriptions of two oral singers at work, Phemius in Ithaca and Demodocus among the Phaeacians, implies clearly enough that their songs were quite short and given on a single occasion. Obviously the *Iliad* is a highly unusual affair, and apart from the *Odyssey* itself there was probably nothing like it in the oral epic tradition. I cannot give the whole argument here; but in short it looks as though Homer invented the concept of a truly monumental epic. The circumstances in which his *Iliad* was sung remain a mystery; neither royal feast nor religious festival meets the demands; the Greeks themselves reveal nothing, at least until the time when the two great epics were recited in literate circumstances at the great festival of Athena at Athens. Yet a point I have tried to emphasize in the past is that a great singer, one who wins a prodigious reputation for his powers, can *impose* an unusual and unfunctional song on his audience, and that the ideal occasion is not in these circumstances necessary.[2]

One aspect of Homer's individuality as a poet, then, is his concept of the monumental poem. That he should have had the inspiration of massive length and the ability to fulfil it, then to impose the result on others so that it survived into the era of developed literacy, reveals something important about him. Yet it is also true that the great length and scope even of the *Iliad* are to a large extent the result of accumulation, of piling traditional theme on theme and of magnifying typical patterns of action by the multiplication of familiar details. It is theoretically conceivable that virtually every-thing in the *Iliad* is derived from the tradition – that Homer is primarily a superb blender and organizer of an exceptionally wide repertory. Personally I am convinced that he did much more than that; but in any case the whole central plan of the poem and its complex characterization, much fuller than can be expected for a short heroic song, of themselves presuppose special gifts, the nature of which we could broadly catalogue. The resulting list would still, admittedly, be a bloodless and abstract affair, containing entries like 'an unusual capacity for describing characters in depth'. We need to go beyond that if we are to catch sight of the real Homer. At the very least we need to be able to identify one or two specific passages that are peculiar to him, that reveal something of his own taste and style. Even then we should be dealing with an amalgam between individual and tradition, for we cannot in any case expect to come upon him creating freely, as a literate poet might, and without drawing heavily on typical theme and language. He was still an oral poet (as the persistently formular colouring of almost every part of the *Iliad* shows), and oral poets do not work like that.

With that reservation, one may begin the search for such special passages by disposing of some familiar suggestions. First, one cannot baldly say that all the best bits are by Homer because Homer was a great poet, and that the rest belongs to the tradition. Some of Homer's predecessors were good singers too, and the quality of even

---

[2] E.g. *The Songs of Homer* (Cambridge, 1962), pp. 280f.

the apparently oldest components of the *Iliad* is quite high. Conversely, since oral poetry tends by nature to be a little uneven, Homer himself may not have been invariably successful. Of course he is likely to have been a better poet, over all, than his predecessors, quite apart from questions of scale; I am merely pointing out that if we want a reliable test of Homer's own work then we cannot apply the criterion of quality alone, even supposing it could be measured. A second common assumption, seldom systematically discussed, is that, if the tradition deals with the standard and the typical, then anything untypical or unique is likely to be by Homer. In general, of course, every singer does tend to contribute something personal and new, and no doubt Homer did so more than most. Achilles passionately rejects the embassy in the ninth *Iliad*, and in his speech heroic formulas are distorted so as to cast doubt on the ethos they were designed to express; this belongs to a poet working in a developed oral tradition, but with a broader conception of life than the tradition had allowed for.[3] That may well mean Homer himself – but the passage is without real parallel, and certainly does not entail that other untypical passages are also Homeric. They may, for example, be later than Homer. A few parts of the *Iliad* were certainly subjected to rhapsodic elaboration; I do not go nearly so far in this respect as the old Analysts, but the night expedition in the tenth book, for instance, which results in the killing of the Trojan spy Dolon, is full of unique details of language and circumstance. It is not for that reason by Homer; on the contrary, it could be a post-Homeric accretion. Parts of the *pre*-Homeric tradition, also, may appear as untypical, often because of an unusual subject. Odysseus' building of a raft to escape from Calypso's island results in an untypical description; but no one can say that raft-building episodes had not been sung before Homer, even though they did not happen to survive in a standardized form.

Another suggestion has been that one might look for Homer's touch in obvious joining-passages, since he quite certainly had to weld together pre-existing episodes to make his monumental poem. Even if the criterion were valid, it would only tell us about Homer as a poet of joining-passages, and that is relatively uninteresting. Yet the idea, feeble as it is in practice, may be on the correct

---

[3] *Iliad* 9, 308–429; cf. Adam Parry, 'The Language of Achilles', *TAPA* 87 (1956), 5–7.

theoretical lines in trying to distinguish Homer by his special *functions* within the *Iliad*. If we are right in holding Homer responsible for the *Iliad*'s exceptional scale, then particular concomitants of that scale are likely to reveal his own poetical choice and direction. We have, therefore, to look for passages that are inextricably connected with the monumental plot as such; passages that are unlikely to belong, as they now stand, to the much shorter songs that we suppose to have been the rule in pre-Homeric poetry. That means, I suggest, three types of passage. First, those of very large scale in themselves, that are too full, leisurely, and lacking in episode or narrative content to have occurred in a song of say 500 to 1000 verses. Second, passages of special verbal complexity, such as would not be likely to arise in the ordinary tradition and, if they had arisen, would soon have lapsed because they were incompatible with the singers' normal techniques. Third, passages that belong essentially to the crucial turning-points of the monumental poem, that are likely to form part of the conception of the large-scale plot and not of any shorter song.

Even these three criteria are highly precarious. We cannot be sure that occasional longer poems in the tradition did not contain leisurely sequences, or that an unusually complex passage was not the work of one of Homer's teachers rather than himself; even the basic association of monumental conception with Homer is conjectural. But let us proceed and see what happens. I deal first with scale and complexity, but it is the third criterion, of the crucial turning-points of the monumental plot, that deserves the closest consideration.

The most obvious kind of large-scale description in either *Iliad* or *Odyssey* might seem to occur in the extended battle-narratives of the *Iliad*. Yet martial poetry was a long-standing traditional genre, and to claim all of it as specifically Homeric would be absurd. The truth is, in any case, that the battle-descriptions in the *Iliad*, with a few significant exceptions to which I shall return, are not really large in scale at all; they are composed of a succession of small-scale individual encounters cumulated one upon the other. The effect is of detailed and complex action, but the description of any particular event is cursory. What I have in mind, rather, is well represented by a scene in the *Odyssey*: the protracted passage in the fourteenth book in which the disguised Odysseus comes to the swineherd's hut, and they engage in a long conversation before turning in for the night.[4]

[4] *Od.* 14, 115–408.

Much of their talk turns on whether or not the stranger might be speaking the truth in his claim to have met the real Odysseus; then the stranger tells a rather boring tale about how he once got hold of a cloak by guile, which is a hint to Eumaeus that the night is cold and extra bedclothes are needed.[5] It is hard to conceive of an independent short song that would be substantially composed of this kind of conversation; there is just not enough episodic content. I conclude that it was specially designed for the monumental *Odyssey*. If so, then its composer was capable of operating at a level lower than the highest. Perhaps he was straining to match the length of the *Iliad*; is there any comparable scene in that poem, which would give a less ambiguous indication of the poet we call Homer? The deceit and seduction of Zeus by Hera takes up some 300 verses of books 14 and 15, and is of the right degree of leisureliness and detail; but it could have existed already in the pre-Homeric tradition, since it makes an excellent independent song.[6] The reconciliation of Achilles and Agamemnon in book 19 is more to the point, since it includes a seemingly interminable wrangle over whether Achilles should take food before re-entering the battle, whether or not it is good to fight on an empty stomach.[7] The effect (like that of the Odysseus and Eumaeus encounter) can be described not unfairly as 'rambling', and it is hard to imagine an ordinary traditional song including so little in the way of movement and climax. Post-Homeric elaboration is a possibility, but there is nothing particular to suggest it; again we are left with the impression that the monumental scheme may occasionally have encouraged Homer to develop effects that are in detail, at least, unimpressive.

Complex expression may be a more fruitful criterion; it would certainly show Homer in a better light, since two obvious instances in the *Iliad* are both quite brilliant. One is the speech of Achilles to which I have already referred, in which he questions the whole point of war in disjointed language that subtly perverts the formulas of heroic belief. The other is a scene of mass fighting in the sixteenth book. From 306 on, for almost fifty lines, the sense repeatedly spills over the natural divisions of the verse in abrupt and spasmodic statements. The effect reinforces the idea of hectic and confused fighting, and could only have been maintained by a virtuoso singer

[5] *Od.* 14, 457–506.   [6] *Il.* 14, 153–360; 15, 4–99.
[7] *Il.* 19, 154–237.

capable of re-shaping the formular language so as to achieve a spectacular variety of diaeresis and enjambment. That was not the kind of thing that ordinarily became traditional, for the simple reason that the regular techniques of oral assimilation required a steadier deployment of the whole verse as a unit of meaning. There is a good chance, then, that in the rare long sequences of this complex style we see the technical brilliance of Homer himself.

The third and most promising criterion based on monumentality involves the decisive moments of the large-scale plot. Naturally it is only if these cruces are treated with special emphasis that they can be expected to reveal any of Homer's poetical characteristics. Even then certain crucial scenes are disqualified. The theme of a warrior withdrawing from battle through injured pride is a conspicuous part of the central structure of the *Iliad*, but it was quite certainly used in pre-Homeric poetry too, and occurs in the tale of Meleagros that is given in abbreviated form in the *Iliad* itself.[8] So probably was the idea of the hero abandoning his wrath because of the need to avenge a comrade. Such themes might already have been quite highly developed in the pre-Homeric tradition, and might not in their Homeric form reveal much of the special taste and style of Homer himself. A further difficulty is that the most popular (and that often means the most eventful) parts of the *Iliad* were apt to be chosen time and again for singing or recitation in the period between the end of Homer's working life and the formation of a standard written text. Therefore they were particularly exposed to elaboration, and the opening book, which describes the beginning of Achilles' wrath, contains a surprising number of apparently post-Homeric locutions. Something similar happened with the last book, too; this also, since it describes the moral climax by which Achilles gives back Hector's body for burial, might be regarded as especially Homeric. So, in a way, it doubtless was; but its unexpected concentration of Odyssean phraseology suggests that it has been quite heavily revised, either by Homer or by a close follower. Again, the theme of ransoming a prince's corpse may have been an old one, but in this case the heightened pathos and leisurely tone of much of the book suggest that considerable development, perhaps including much by Homer himself, has taken place.

That is a subjective judgement, and it is prudent to turn to the

---

[8] *Il.* 9, 527–99.

scenes that in my belief reveal most accurately and objectively the stylistic tendencies of the real Homer. They are, in particular, those that encompass the death of Patroclus in book 16 and of Hector in book 22, two of the four or five indispensable events of the whole extended action. They imply a common poet because they have several remarkable points of motif and language in common. The general theme of one warrior killing another is admittedly so frequent that it occurs hundreds of times, and in a wide variety of forms, within the *Iliad*; yet, if we come across two scenes in which the general theme is presented in a specially elaborate way, if those two scenes represent crucial turning-points of the large-scale plot, and if they bear marked and unusual resemblances to each other, then it is reasonable to guess that they were given special attention by the creator of the monumental poem himself. Let me repeat the argument, which is critical, in a slightly different way. If it is known that a theme might be traditional, then in most cases its use in the large-scale context cannot reveal Homeric characteristics as opposed to traditional ones. But when one of the themes of heroic poetry is used in a specially elaborate form at two of the crucial turning-points of the large-scale plot, and when in addition there are independent signs of a common style, then we can reasonably expect to find the large-scale poet at work. I should add that the death-scenes of Patroclus and Hector are of quite unusual length. Scale, therefore, is an ancillary criterion (and so, in a way, might be complexity; for the two scenes are unusually complex, not so much in expression as in emotion and underlying structure).

The deaths of Patroclus and Hector cannot be completely separated from that of Sarpedon which precedes Patroclus' death in book 16. The Sarpedon death-scene is not a hinge of the monumental plot, and is less elaborate than the other two; but it is more elaborate than any apart from them, and it shows strong similarities at certain points to either the one or the other. It also contributes essential dramatic force to the crucial death of Patroclus by establishing him, for the first time, as a warrior of the first order. It looks very much, in fact, as though the monumental poet built up by stages to the climax of the death of Hector, with Sarpedon and then Patroclus providing more and more elaborate models. I begin, therefore, with a brief account of the Sarpedon death-scene and its special characteristics. Sarpedon is king of the Lycians and an important ally of the Trojans; he is also a favourite child of Zeus himself. At 16, 419ff. he determines to unmask and stop the unknown Achaean in Achilles' armour who is doing so much damage. He leaps from his chariot, so does Patroclus; they charge at one another like vultures on a rock. So far, standard battle-theme.[9] But then Zeus pities them and wants to save his son; Hera professes to be shocked at his interfering with fate, and uses three verses of reproach that occur elsewhere only in the similar scene presaging the death of Hector. Zeus agrees to compromise by letting Sleep and Death carry Sarpedon's body back to his home in Lycia, an idea unique in the *Iliad* but known to have been applied to Memnon in the lost epic *Aethiopis*. Furthermore Zeus sends drops of bloody rain to honour his son who is to die, a motif used more casually in book 11.[10] The duel begins; it is moderately detailed, with two attacks from each side, but typical in essence. Patroclus hurls his spear and kills not Sarpedon but his charioteer; Sarpedon replies but hits Patroclus' trace-horse; Sarpedon throws his second spear and misses, Patroclus throws his and wounds Sarpedon severely. He falls like a felled tree, lies raging like a bull mauled by a lion, both fairly typical similes; he calls on his friend Glaucus to save his corpse and armour from the Achaeans. 'When he had thus spoken the end of death covered him', a verse used elsewhere only of the deaths of Patroclus and Hector[11] – indeed these are the only three death-scenes in which a mortally-wounded victim speaks. Patroclus withdraws his spear, the lungs come with it, and the ψυχή or soul too. The release of the life-soul is an untypical detail that will be developed in the deaths of Patroclus and Hector.

Two hundred verses later Patroclus, encouraged by killing Sarpedon and by a mass of minor successes, pushes his luck too far.[12] Apollo himself has to thrust him back from the walls of Troy, then goes in disguise to urge Hector to attack. Patroclus dismounts and throws a stone that kills Hector's charioteer Cebriones, much as he had just killed Sarpedon's charioteer. This time, however, a long fight develops over Cebriones' body and interrupts the duel of Patroclus and Hector. Patroclus jeers over the fallen Cebriones, whose eyes have been ejected by the force of the blow and who falls

---

[9] Fenik, pp. 200f.
[10] *Il.* 16, 666–83, cf. 453–7 (Sleep and Death); 459–61, cf. 11, 53–5 (bloody rain).
[11] *Il.* 16, 502, cf. 855; 22, 361.   [12] *Il.* 16, 698ff.

from his chariot like a sea-diver; he and Hector fight over him like lions over a deer.[13] The theme of the fight over the corpse had already been elaborated in the case of Sarpedon's body; here it is carried further, and with Patroclus' corpse it will occupy a complete book. Much of the detail of the development is typical; the armies mass with the noise of woods crashing in a gale – there had been a similar image in the fight over Sarpedon. But now Cebriones is described in unusual and powerfully emotive phrases as 'lying there in a spiral of dust, huge and hugely stretched out, his horsemanship forgotten',

ὁ δ' ἐν στροφάλιγγι κονίης
κεῖτο μέγας μεγαλωστί, λελασμένος ἱπποσυνάων,   (775f.)

part of which is later applied to Achilles as he grovels in mourning for Patroclus. The strong pathos is emphasized in repeated apostrophes, or direct addresses by the poet, to Patroclus; he leaps on the Trojans and slays thrice nine of them in an access of heroic fury; 'then for you, Patroclus, appeared the end of your life; for Phoebus met you in the strong rout of battle':

ἔνθ' ἄρα τοι, Πάτροκλε, φάνη βιότοιο τελευτή·
ἤντετο γάρ τοι Φοῖβος ἐνὶ κρατερῇ ὑσμίνῃ.   (787f.)

'Terrible', δεινός, adds the poet, of Apollo, and the god was indeed especially formidable because he was invisible, concealed in a thick mist; and he stood behind Patroclus and smote him with the flat of his hand so that Patroclus' eyes whirled round. Then the god stripped his dazed victim of helmet and armour – it had belonged to Achilles, and the helmet was now unnaturally covered with blood and dirt. As Patroclus stands there helpless and naked a young fop, Euphorbus, strikes him with a running spear-cast; Patroclus retreats towards his comrades, but Hector catches him with a mortal spear-thrust, like a lion finishing off a fighting boar. Then in the heroic fashion Hector boasts over his victim, tells the expiring Patroclus that vultures will devour him, sneers at the thought of Achilles encouraging Patroclus to capture Troy. Fainting, Patroclus replies: it was Zeus, Apollo, fate, Euphorbus, and only then Hector that defeated him, and Hector himself will not live for long. Patroclus dies, and the verse used earlier of Sarpedon is expanded by the addition of a pair describing his soul flitting mournfully down to Hades. These verses,

[13] *Il.* 16, 756ff.

and the elaboration of the idea of a life-soul leaving the body, recur at the death of Hector and nowhere else.[14] Hector replies querulously, withdraws his spear, and sets off in pursuit of Patroclus' charioteer.

It is a marvellous description, typical in detail for most of the time yet built up into something distinctive. Throwing a stone, killing a charioteer, fighting over a hero's corpse, the similes as champions rush forward, the details of the duel – these are standard motifs. Even the attack on a god and its repulse had been used before; so, in a small way, had the idea of a god dazing a victim – only his total stripping of the armour is virtually unparalleled. But many of the standard elements are uniquely emphasized – the pathos, for instance, that is expressed in the repeated apostrophes to Patroclus and not, this time, by special signs from Zeus like bloody rain or weighing the contestants' fates; and the whole sense of what Fenik terms 'the gigantic and supernatural'.[15]

Hector's death comes six books later. It is the inevitable result of the killing of Patroclus, decisive for the fate of Troy and essential to the climax of the whole poem. At the end of book 21 Apollo had assumed the form of the Trojan Agenor (who had dared to face Achilles after a frantic soliloquy that anticipates Hector's), and so enticed Achilles away from the walls. The Trojans pour in confusion into the city, but Hector is 'tied down by destructive destiny' outside.[16] His parents beseech him from the walls; this whole prelude to the encounter includes much that seems special and not typical. Achilles charges at him like a hawk after a dove (this at least is typical) and he starts running. Zeus pities him, wishes to save him, but is deterred by Athena in much the same words as Hera had used over Sarpedon – indeed that passage is the fuller and more accurate, since *moira*, fate, on which the argument hinges, is specified only there.[17] The chase is enlivened by three unusual similes and particularized by realistic details unparalleled elsewhere; the two remarkable springs, one hot and one cold, past which they run, with Hector always seeking to get under the walls for protection, and Achilles always heading him off and telling the other Achaeans not to rob him of his victory. Zeus weighs the fates – a solemn and pathetic moment, not quite unique in the *Iliad*, but nowhere so

[14] *Il.* 16, 856f., 22, 362f. [15] Fenik, p. 216.
[16] *Il.* 22, 5f. [17] *Il.* 22, 179–81 = 16, 441–3; *moira*, 16, 434.

strongly developed – and Hector's sinks. Athena promises Achilles victory, then disguises herself as Hector's brother Deiphobus and so persuades Hector to stand and fight. He proposes an agreement to respect each other's corpse, which Achilles savagely rejects; Achilles throws and misses, but Athena, in a unique action, returns his spear to him. Hector does not know this, utters a confident boast and throws in turn. His spear hits Achilles' shield but does not pierce it (always a fatal sign by the Homeric conventions); he turns for Deiphobus' spear, finds no one there, and realizes in a flash that he has been divinely deluded and is doomed. He decides to die bravely, draws his sword and rushes on Achilles like an eagle; Achilles counter-charges with spear-tip gleaming like the evening star. He pierces Hector in the throat without further delay; the poet has to explain, a little awkwardly, that the dying man is still able to speak, and in reply to Achilles' ritual boasts and the threat that dogs and vultures will devour his corpse Hector intercedes for the ransom of his body. Achilles brutally refuses, Hector at last recognizes his total implacability, prophesies his death, and himself dies in terms closely matching those used of the death of Patroclus, when Hector had been victor, not victim.[18] Achilles replies angrily, much as Hector had done in that previous scene: he will die when the gods will it. He withdraws his spear, strips the corpse, and the other Achaeans gather round and jab at it; there is no fight for the body this time, for the Trojans are penned inside the city. Finally, in a unique and presumably original description that is too short to tell us much about Homer's style, Achilles pierces Hector's ankles and drives off dragging the corpse behind him: the polar antithesis of heroic behaviour, which may be brutal but is never unseemly.

Many of the elements of this remarkable scene, which in its scale (around 400 verses including preliminaries) is unparalleled in Homeric battle-poetry, are of course typical and derive from the pre-Homeric tradition. Little in it is strictly unique, but many of the constituent motifs are powerfully developed beyond their standard form; notably the debate about the victim's body, a matter which for Hector is of paramount concern; the careful localization and tactical realism; the collaboration with a god, in which Athena conspires with Achilles more in the manner of the *Odyssey* than of the *Iliad*; and the elaboration of Hector's contradictory feelings – the

---

[18] *Il.* 22, 355–66; 16, 843–61.

rapid succession of guilt, concern for his reputation, wishful fantasy, realism, optimism, blind panic, and finally acceptance of the facts and a heroic death. Much of this special development must have been determined by the general emphases of the poem's climax. Hector and Achilles are isolated outside the walls not only to stress the unique significance of the occasion, but also so that the standard fight for the corpse can be omitted and Achilles can proceed to the mutilation of the body, which in turn motivates Priam's dramatic redeeming of his son's corpse in book 24. Hector's dying exchanges are protracted even beyond their model in the death of Patroclus, to stress his sense of fate, the decisive implications of his death, and Achilles' own vulnerability; and his obsessive concern for his corpse looks forward to the scene between Priam and Achilles as well as back to the untypically humane qualities that he shared with Patroclus alone (p. 50 above).

What do the three closely-related death-scenes suggest (beyond the matter of sheer scale) about Homer's taste and style? In structure, that he was prepared to add emphasis not only in the traditional way, by extending the typical details of the event itself, but also by developing its preliminaries and conclusion – and, of course, by heightening the element of supernatural intervention. The battle over Cebriones and the chase round the walls impose a special tone on the central act of violence, as does the subsequent dying conversation that is skilfully developed in the progress from Sarpedon to Patroclus to Hector. The tone is one of melancholy and inevitability, and it accentuates the strong pathos that is already present in the apostrophes to Patroclus, in the idea of the gods calling Patroclus and Hector to their deaths (θάνατόνδε κάλεσσαν, a phrase used of each of them and otherwise unparalleled[19]), in the bloody rain and the weighing of fates, in Zeus' concern and pity. The pathetic quality of heroic death in battle was already part of the tradition; Homer emphasizes it at these key points and makes it more profound. His methods in this respect are unusually refined. In general I am cautious about tracing complex overtones and unemphatic cross-references over large intervals of oral poetry, but I am sure that the helmet-plumes that are sullied in the dust or gleam over Achilles' head, or the similes from racing that emphasize first Achilles' confident swiftness, then the special value of the stake which

[19] *Il.* 16, 693; 22, 297.

is Hector's life, are placed as they are to accentuate an underlying contrast. This careful approach to the expression of emotional nuances confirms what we might otherwise doubt, that the curious mixture of fantasy and abnormal realism that appears in each of the crucial death-scenes is no mere accident of oral cumulation. With Hector, unaccustomed topographical and tactical accuracy is immediately followed by Athena's intervention in the duel itself. In Patroclus' death the combination of the two qualities is even more striking, as the invisible and therefore mysterious Apollo dazes him with an all-too-concrete blow and strips his armour in a casual, almost mundane way. The conjunction of gods and mortals is traditional enough, but here it is intensified and made to reflect some of the ambiguities of the heroic condition, as it is too in the parts played in Hector's death by such disparate agents as Zeus, fate, Athena, Euphorbus, and Achilles.

If Homer constructed these scenes, they should also reveal something about his use of traditional language. If it were the time and place to do so, I think I could show that they display an unusually careful variation, even by Iliadic standards, of sentence-length and enjambment, and that the rhetorical mechanisms of style are uncommonly diverse without being obtrusive.[20] Less expected, perhaps, are the ways in which Homer does *not* improve on the tradition; for instance he does not attempt to sharpen or expand the generalized and rather flat formula ἂψ δ' ἑτάρων εἰς ἔθνος ἐχάζετο (16, 817), 'back into the tribe of his companions he withdrew' (nine times in the *Iliad*), when he comes to describe the wounded Patroclus struggling to reach the safety of his comrades.

Occasional looseness in the combination of phrases is endemic in oral poetry, and Homer was evidently no exception. Something analogous could happen in the combination of typical episodic material too. As Hector decides to stand and face Achilles he is like a malign snake lying in wait for its victim – but suddenly and a little incongruously he is envisaged as taking off his shield, 'just so did Hector possess unquenchable might and not retreat, leaning his bright shield against a jutting tower';[21] and he breaks into a despondent soliloquy about the chances of flight or surrender. Perhaps

---

[20] Some of the effects I have in mind are discussed in relation to the whole of book 16 on pp. 146–72 above.
[21] *Il.* 22, 93–7.

that is a small accident of post-Homeric transmission; even so there are certain things Homer does not much mind about. For instance, realism is important in the chase round the walls, but not (and this was a traditional tendency) in the details of spear-cast and armament – Hector and Achilles have a single spear each, which means that it should really be for thrusting and not throwing, yet they both throw it with apparent insouciance.

In one respect Homer is brief, almost cursory, where the tradition might be more elaborate, and that is in the use of similes to describe the appearance of Hector and then Achilles in their final charge.[22] The climax is near, and normally an exceptionally complex simile would be chosen to mark the fact. Homer is not, of course, averse to extended similes as such, and had used a complicated lion-and-boar encounter to illustrate the subduing of Patroclus by Hector. His longer images (if we judge by the three great death-scenes) are more carefully related to the actual situation than is usual elsewhere in the *Iliad*. Paradoxically they are less 'Homeric' than the typical Iliadic simile with its entrancing but not strictly relevant details strung from a single point of contact; and here, where one would expect the extreme of elaboration, Homer keeps the imagery simple, even sparse. For Hector as he rushes with drawn sword is compared briefly to a high-flying eagle swooping down through dark cloud upon sheep or crouching hare, and Achilles is distinguished (in a comparison which at first seems so standard as to be banal) by the gleam of his spear-point that resembles the evening star passing through the gloom of night. The simplicity, the vividness and pathos of these images are emphasized by the audience's awareness of the complex comparisons that Homer seems deliberately to reject. That simplicity has its own obvious force in the context; but a second hearing suggests subtler associations, for the eagle is like the hawk to which Achilles himself had been compared when Hector panicked, and the fair star of evening recalls the sinister dog-star which Achilles resembled at the beginning of the episode.[23] In both cases there is an element of contrast and reversal. Furthermore the similes have one significant detail in common; the eagle swoops through dark cloud, the evening star passes through the gloom of night, and the implication of gloom, of darkness, seems to underline the dire reality and savage consequences of Hector's destruction, which in its 'typical'

[22] *Il.* 22, 308-11, 317-21.   [23] *Il.* 22, 139-44, 25-32.

aspects might have seemed almost too close to just another heroic death.

These are only some of the ways in which, if I am right about the basic criteria, the real Homer revealed himself. Much more could be said about his particular way of combining typical motifs, which is no less important than his identifiable innovations. Fenik, whose purpose is to stress the predominantly typical constitution of the battle scenes, tends to imply that our three great encounters result from the *mere* accumulation of typical details and patterns of action; for example the complexity of the Sarpedon–Patroclus fight is claimed to be 'illusory' because it is composed 'almost entirely' of familiar elements.[24] I should be inclined to reply that, once the basic elements and patterns have been assembled, the process of arrangement and further cumulation becomes a matter of genuinely artistic choice. The author of these great death-scenes is working, after all, on a quite different plane from that of the Serbian *guslar* who simply piles together everything he can think of, or even from that of the singers responsible for most of the Iliadic arming scenes. In short, Homer can best be seen, not in isolation from the tradition on which his poetical existence depended, but against its background, in scenes in which the tradition is enriched if not entirely transcended, and in a kind of counterpoint between the typical (which can also be the quintessential) and the individual, the personal. It is in that region that this complex poetical character, the 'real' Homer, is to be sought and perhaps found.

[24] Fenik, p. 203.

INDEX

Index

Index

Index